ATRIA
BOOKS

P9-EFI-987

Dear readers,

I can state without hesitation—with fierce passion, in fact—that working on Ady Barkan's extraordinary memoir, *Eyes to the Wind*, has been one of the highlights of my entire publishing career. There are some books that truly have the potential to change the world irrevocably and for the better; this is one of them.

At thirty-two years old, Ady was already a well-respected lawyer and activist, but when he was shockingly diagnosed with ALS, he had to reexamine his place in the world and the principles that he wanted to champion for his wife and young son. In this unforgettable and powerful memoir, Ady takes us on a journey through his extensive work as a fighter for social justice, while also detailing the challenges—both physical and emotional—that his diagnosis has presented. What emerges is an engrossing, galvanizing portrait of how one man's efforts to make a more just and compassionate world have led to a seismic shift in how our society thinks of the marginalized—and how raising your voice, even and especially when it might be unpopular, is simply the right thing to do.

Ady matches the thoughtfulness of his activism with prose that is stirring and deeply moving. His is the rare book that identifies a turning point in our culture at large and meets it with all the intelligence, subtlety, and warmth you could ask for. We at Atria could not be prouder to be publishing this vital book, and we hope that you will share it with your family, friends, and anyone who needs an extra spark of hope in this tumultuous time.

All best,

Rakesh Satyal
Senior Editor

Atria Books | 1230 Avenue of the Americas | New York, NY 10020

EYES TO THE WIND

EYES TO THE WIND

A MEMOIR OF LOVE AND DEATH, HOPE AND RESISTANCE

◆

ADY BARKAN

ATRIA BOOKS

NEW YORK   LONDON   TORONTO   SYDNEY   NEW DELHI

ATRIA BOOKS

An Imprint of Simon & Schuster, Inc.
1230 Avenue of the Americas
New York, NY 10020

First Atria Books hardcover edition September 2019

ATRIA BOOKS and colophon are registered trademarks of Simon & Schuster, Inc.

For information about special discounts for bulk purchases, please contact Simon & Schuster Special Sales at 1-866-506-1949 or business@simonandschuster.com.

The Simon & Schuster Speakers Bureau can bring authors to your live event. For more information or to book an event, contact the Simon & Schuster Speakers Bureau at 1-866-248-3049 or visit our website at www.simonspeakers.com.

Interior design by Alexis Minieri

Manufactured in the United States of America

1   3   5   7   9   10   8   6   4   2

Library of Congress Cataloging-in-Publication Data TK

ISBN 978-1-9821-1154-0
ISBN 978-1-9821-1156-4 (ebook)

[[dedication TK]]

I'll set my eyes to the wind
But it won't be easy
To leave it all again

—THE WAR ON DRUGS,
"EYES TO THE WIND"

CONTENTS

CONTENTS

FOREWORD

[[TK]]

EYES TO THE WIND

CHAPTER ONE

DIAGNOSIS

On September 30, 2016, Rachael and I celebrated one year of marriage and eleven years together by dropping Carl off with my mother and checking into a boutique hotel in West Hollywood. After four months of bliss with our new son, we were ready for our first night away from him—and for a full night's sleep. We arrived at the hotel around five p.m. and decided to have sex immediately, in large part so that we could go to sleep right after dinner. It was hot, just like in the olden days, but I'll spare you the details.

Later, we got gussied up and went out to dinner at a chic Asian fusion restaurant in Santa Monica, where we indulged in delicious, overpriced cocktails and chili lamb and cold noodles that set my mouth on fire. This was the life. Not only could we each enjoy our intellectually stimulating, meaningful work from the comfort of our Santa Barbara home—Rachael as a newly minted assistant professor of English at University of California, Santa Barbara, me as an activist/lawyer at the Center for Popular Democracy—not only could we raise a wonderfully chubby and friendly baby boy, but with help from Grandma we could even have the occasional evening to ourselves, featuring adult conversations, adult food and drinks, and adult . . . you know . . . full nights of sleep.

What more could we ask for? We were the happiest and luckiest people we knew.

After a lazy Sunday morning we met up with my oldest friend, Katy, for brunch. Ever since kindergarten Katy had always been the best athlete and the best student in class. She was eventually recruited to play soccer in the Ivy League, barely missed turning pro, and had spent recent years studying the brain. She was now a first-year medical resident in neurology at UCLA and had just completed her PhD in neuroscience to boot.

"By the way," I told her nonchalantly after she had finished recounting her experiences treating veterans at the local VA, "I'm going in to see a doctor on Tuesday to look at my left hand. It stopped working properly. I think I have carpal tunnel syndrome from holding Carl in my left arm so much over the past four months."

After our plates were cleared, Katy took a look at it, asking me to spread my fingers against her resistance, to hold them pinched together tight while she pulled them apart, and to touch my nose and her moving finger in rapid succession. Yes, she said, there was clearly more weakness in my left hand than my right.

"Well, I *am* right-handed," I said.

"Yeah, Ady," she snorted with some exasperation. "I'm not stupid."

After we paid the bill, Katy made me pace toe-to-heel down the Los Angeles sidewalk. That seemed fine. And then she sat me in the back of her car and tested the reflexes under my foot and on my knee. She wasn't happy with what she found. They were exaggerated, jumping excessively at a tickle or a well-placed pluck.

"Well, it ain't carpal tunnel," she said. "You should see a neurologist."

"What are you worried about? Should I still go to the primary care doctor on Tuesday?"

"Yeah, you should go. Just tell him that your hand is weak and see what he says. Tell him to test your reflexes, too."

We said goodbye and Rachael and I drove back to Santa Barbara. The bliss from the previous night was now tinged with worry. Was there something wrong with my brain? But we laughed it off; Katy had seemed so nonchalant. Surely there was nothing seriously wrong.

From nine a.m. to three p.m. the next day, I had my typical Monday conference calls and supervision meetings for the two projects I was leading, Local Progress and Fed Up. My colleagues and I were coordinating our work to promote progressive local policy in cities around the country and developing a strategy to work with the new president of the Federal Reserve of Minneapolis, who appeared interested in trying to promote racial equity. I finished early and took Carl out so that Rachael, who was still on maternity leave, could do a couple of hours of work.

I had succeeded in ignoring the previous day's discussion about my hand, but while walking with Carl on the beautiful cliffs overlooking the Pacific I had more time to think and worry about my situation, so I started sending increasingly concerned text messages to Katy, asking her for more information about what she had found in her brunch-time examination. She refused to say. She told me I had "hyperreflexia" and muscle weakness. I looked up these terms and found results for cancer and thyroid disease. I texted her again: my dad had had thyroid disease when he was young; was it that? "Stop googling!!" she responded. "It has nothing to do with your thyroid!"

Finally, later that night, I got her to say that she was worried because I was showing signs of both upper and lower motor neuron damage. Rachael and I sat in bed and googled those words. We learned that upper motor neurons were nerve cells that originated in the motor cortex of the brain and ended within the medulla or spinal cord; damage to these cells could result in exaggerated reflexes. Lower motor neurons originated in the spinal cord and ended in a muscle; damage to these cells could lead to weakness and loss of muscle mass. Exhibiting both of these types of neuron damage, as I had during Katy's informal exam, was a bad sign.

As we scanned the results from Wikipedia and the Mayo Clinic, it didn't take us long to land on this:

ALS, commonly known as Lou Gehrig's disease, is a [gobbledygook gobbledygook gobbledygook gobbledygook] leading to complete paralysis [gobbledygook gobbledygook gobbledygook] death by respiratory failure . . . 6,000 new patients in the United States per year, with an average age of 50 to 70 . . . 20% of patients live more than 5 years . . . 5% of patients live more than 10 years . . . The only available treatment extends life by 2 to 3 months.

Holy shit.
I texted Katy immediately. "ALS? You're worried about ALS??"
"I don't know. That's why you need to see a neurologist."
Holy shit. Holy shit. Fuck. Fuck. Seriously? Seriously? Holy shit.
I spent the night pacing and muttering to myself. *Yeah, that's a great idea: Just develop an incurable illness at age thirty-two. Fantastic. Fuck. Impossible. Fuck. Things were going so well. I don't believe it. This is impossible. No way.* I paced and paced, repeating the same thoughts over and over and over in my head.

I ended up on the sofa, finally dozing off as the sun came up.

Mid-morning on Tuesday, I got a phone call from my primary care doctor's office notifying me that the doctor was out sick. They would have to cancel my afternoon appointment.

"When is the soonest I can get another appointment?" I asked.

"Two weeks," the cheerful office assistant said.

Hell, no. I wasn't about to wait two weeks to find out if I had a terminal illness.

As I took a short walk around my peaceful, sunny neighborhood, I called my best friend from college, Simeon, who had recently finished his residency in internal medicine. A calm and level-headed guy with great emotional intelligence, Sim always offered thoughtful guidance. When I updated him on everything, he seemed relatively unconcerned, because, hey, I was thirty-two years old and ALS was super-rare, even among older people. I was glad to hear that he thought I probably didn't have ALS, but he hadn't examined my hands, and Katy was not a worrywart—and she was, unlike him, a neurologist. If she was concerned, something had to be wrong.

"Should I go to the emergency room?" I asked Sim.

"No, they don't diagnose ALS in the emergency room; they'll just refer you to a neurologist and charge you hundreds of dollars."

"How about urgent care?"

"Same thing," he said, "except it might be a little cheaper. Just wait for the primary care appointment and then get a referral to a neurologist if necessary."

I hung up and tried to focus on work, but my mind was racing. There was no point in sitting there, letting the hours tick by. Then, against Sim's advice, I hopped into an Uber and went to urgent care.

"How are you doing today?" the driver asked me.

"Fine," I said, lying.

Minutes later, as I sat in a sunlit and nearly empty waiting room at urgent care, two men walked in. "We think he might be having a heart attack," the fiftyish man told the receptionist, pointing to another man in his seventies. *Yeah,* I thought to myself, *that's when you're supposed to get terminal illnesses, not at age thirty-two. Fuck. Fuck. Fuck.*

"How are you doing today?" the medical assistant asked as she took my blood pressure and weighed me.

"I'm a little worried about the weakness in my left hand," I said, deciding to share my stress instead of hiding it.

Ten minutes later I described my symptoms to the primary care doctor on call and told her that I was worried I might have ALS. "Boy, I sure hope you don't have ALS," she said, rubbing her hands together and exhaling deeply. I saw her wracking her brain to remember the symptoms and diagnostic technique for this disease. She ran through the same battery of simple tests Katy had performed over brunch. She banged on my knees a few times. Then she went to talk to the neurologist on call, Dr. Karen DaSilva.

When the primary care doctor came back, she told me that Dr. DaSilva wanted her to order a couple of MRIs for my spine and brain to see if there was something obstructing my nerves. Sure, I said, let's do the MRIs. The assistant told me that they couldn't be scheduled until the following week, plus she needed to get preauthorization from the insurance company. But I pushed, and she found some time for me on Wednesday. I would have to do the two of them separately, instead of back-to-back, but I was fine with that.

That night Rachael and I tried to watch *Silver Streak*, a Gene Wilder comedy about murder on a train, but I couldn't focus or sit still.

The next day, when my name was called in the radiology department, I stood up and walked past the elderly patients and down a long hallway. I entered the MRI room and lay down on a board. The radiology technician, a quiet man in his thirties, secured my head with some foam blocks, stuck plugs in my ears, conveyed me into a tiny cylinder, and told me to lie absolutely still for twenty minutes.

As the machine whirred to life, I once again cycled through my disbelief and outrage: *ALS. I can't believe I might have ALS. Holy shit.* After some loud buzzing, a jackhammer started to reverberate against the cylinder. *Okay, focus on something else,* I told myself. *Lakers, Clippers, Blazers, Kings.* I started to name each of the NBA teams and their divisions, keeping track on my fingers, trying to count all thirty. I lost track a couple times. Did Charlotte have a team again? The buzzing stopped. The lab tech told me I had held incredibly still and the picture was very clear. Good job. It was the first of innumerable times in the coming years that kindhearted medical professionals would congratulate me for performing simple tasks effectively. Oh, goodie. I had held very still for the MRI, but I still probably had goddamn ALS.

That afternoon Rachael was moderating a discussion in the English department on pedagogy. I went with her and rocked Carl back and forth in his stroller during the first half of the meeting, trying to focus on what people were saying instead of the fact that I might be dead by the time the fall quarter started. Then I handed off stroller duties to a friend sitting next to me and drove off to do the second MRI, this one of my spine. I could name all thirty NBA teams this time, so I opted for naming all twelve Federal Reserve presidents, then tried to name each U.S. president—but struggled in the 1840s, '50s, and '80s. Who was president in between the two Grover Cleveland administrations? The machine's pounding stopped, and again I was told I had done a good job: the spinal picture was crystal clear. Yippee ki-yay, as Bruce Willis would say.

I went back to pick Rachael and Carl up from the English department. Then I got a text message from my father in New York complaining that he hadn't received any pictures of his grandson lately. In the parking lot Rachael took a picture of me holding Carl and smiling. It was the first of hundreds of photographs that I would take while trying to put a good face on a very difficult situation.

At ten a.m. on Thursday, I logged into the clinic's patient portal to see what the MRIs had shown. There were no test results yet. My hope, at this point, was that there was some sort of an obstruction impacting the nerves leading to the muscles in my left hand (the lower motor neurons). But the hope was thin, because the obstruction would also need to impact the nerves that were causing hyperreflexia in my feet (the upper motor neurons). Still, Katy said there was reason to be optimistic. ALS was super-rare, we kept telling ourselves, especially at my age. But the foreboding was intense.

At midday we got a call from a junior staffer in the clinic. I sat down on our living room sofa. "Good news!" the voice said. "Your MRIs were negative."

"No. That's not good news," I said, my heart dropping into my stomach. "That's terrible." A negative result meant there was no physical obstruction of my nerves causing these symptoms. The nerves just weren't working. ALS was the most likely explanation.

Rachael walked over to hold my head against her body. We started to cry.

After about half an hour I decided I couldn't wait any longer: I needed to get a more official answer immediately. I got in the car and drove over to the neurologist's office. I told the receptionist I had to see the doctor. He said that was impossible, as Dr. DaSilva had a fully booked schedule. I told him the details of my situation and that I had to see the doctor right away. He said that was impossible, that I needed to make an appointment. "I understand that there are rules," I said, "but those rules need to be broken right now. Please go talk to her."

After a wait, the neurology nurse called me into her office and we talked through the situation. She had a friendly smile and long, curly hair. She sat behind a desk and asked me to tell her my story.

Through my tears I told her that I had a beautiful four-month-old baby at home and an amazing life and what a shame it would be if I had ALS. She handed me a box of tissues and said I shouldn't despair yet, shouldn't lose hope, and that she would adjust the doctor's schedule so that I could see her in the morning.

Rachael and I took Carl for a walk along the shoreline just south of Santa Barbara. I got a text from Sim. "How would you guys feel about a visit this weekend?" It was a grand gesture: he and his wife worked ridiculous hours as residents and had a baby girl at home; flying out from Boston for the weekend was certainly unusual. "That would be amazing," I texted back.

After one of the longest nights of my life, Rachael and I put Carl in the car and drove to the neurologist's. As we walked into the office, Rachael holding Carl in a carrier, all the staff oohed and aahed; thankfully, they didn't see many infants in the neurology department. Although Rachael and I were both skinny, four-month-old Carl had the shape of the Michelin man. The staff loved the huge rolls of fat on his dangling legs. And, as usual, he was all smiles.

In the examination room I sat on the bed, my feet dangling over the side. Dr. DaSilva, who looked just a few years older than we were and who had classic Santa Barbara sun-stroked sandy hair, was warm and welcoming. She listened to my story and ran the battery of muscle and reflex tests with which I had become familiar.

And then she tried to let us down easy, using tentative language. "I do see concerning signs of upper and lower motor neuron loss, which are indicative of ALS."

I stared at the ground, then put my head in my hands.

"Are you all right?" she asked me.

"Well, you've just given me a death sentence."

Rachael started to shake, tears coming down her cheeks. She held

Carl. Then I held them both. The doctor moved toward the door and asked if she should give us some space. I said no. I wanted her there, sharing our sorrow. I didn't want to be just one more patient she saw in her busy day. I wanted her recognition that my case was tragic and shocking and unreasonable.

"This is so outrageous," I told her. "I'm thirty-two, with a four-month-old baby." Had she ever had an ALS patient as young as me? "No," she said: I was the youngest she had seen. I wanted her to cry, too. "We had our whole lives ahead of us," I told her, "and now it's all disappearing." Would I not be able to see Carl grow up into a boy and a man and a father himself? Would I not be able to sit with Rachael in our old age and look back on a joyful life filled with meaningful work and rewarding friendships? Our lives had been so different just the day before.

The doctor's tears came.

As we gathered ourselves, Dr. DaSilva said that we should go to Cedars-Sinai Medical Center in Los Angeles to get a second opinion. I asked her what the odds were that her diagnosis was incorrect. Five percent? One percent? "You should get a second opinion. But I would never give anyone this diagnosis if I weren't certain," she said. Zero percent was what I heard.

As Rachael and I walked out through the waiting room, I looked at the receptionist who had insisted just yesterday that I needed an appointment to see the doctor. "See," I wanted to tell him, "I'm not some lunatic hypochondriac. I really did need to see the doctor yesterday, and today my life is ruined." But I just smiled and said thank you as we filled out some forms and scheduled a follow-up visit.

That afternoon, not knowing what on earth to do with ourselves, Rachael and I took Carl to the park, where a group of new mothers was doing some light yoga while their infants rolled around on a pic-nic blanket. I stretched and breathed and looked at sunlight beaming down through the trees; I cried silently through downward dog and then laughed as the babies cooed at one another.

In the evening, before putting Carl to bed, we Skyped with my father and stepmother in New York. Rachael and I sat on the sofa next to each other and pointed the camera toward Carl, who was playing on his floor mat with toys hanging above him. He could hold them in two hands now and was becoming a master at tummy-time push-ups. Watching him, my father laughed and exclaimed with joy. And, seeing him laugh, I thought to myself, *These are the last minutes of unadulterated joy that you will ever have. After today, you will be sad every day and your happiness will always be tentative and constrained and inhibited. These are the words you think to yourself before you break your father's heart.*

Finally, we mustered the courage to turn the camera away from Carl to ourselves. Never in my wildest nightmares did I anticipate having to deliver news like this, but here we were. Like ripping off a Band-Aid, we told them about my diagnosis, that my life expectancy was two to five years, and that there was no good treatment or cure. They were predictably shocked.

"Oh, no!" my stepmother gasped repeatedly, unsure of what else to say.

"I just wish it could be me instead of you," my father said through his tears.

In that moment and in many moments after, I thought of my father's cousin Udi, after whom I was named. Udi and my father had grown up in the 1950s and '60s in the suburbs of Tel Aviv, Israel. They were best friends. Their parents had fought in the 1948 Arab-Israeli War and they had been the first generation of children born in the new state of Israel. Udi had been killed at age eighteen while serving in the Israeli army: a friend's gun went off accidentally while they were in the barracks. Udi's parents, who had no other children, were utterly destroyed by their son's death. I remember them as always reserved and sad, even in moments of laughter and joy. I always wondered if my cousins and I were constant reminders of what they lacked, what they had lost.

"There is nothing harder than burying your child," I remember my grandmother, Udi's aunt, telling me once. "Nothing." On Skype, through my tears, I recounted her sentiment to my father. "I am so sorry that you have to go through this," I told him.

It wasn't supposed to be like this. *I* was supposed to lose *him*— and at some distant point in the future, a fact that had overwhelmed me whenever I had thought about it. Sigmund Freud wrote that a father's death was "the most important event, the most poignant loss, in a man's life," and I had been sure that the same would be true for me. But now the roles were reversed: it was me telling him that my years were coming to an end and that he would have to live on without me.

My father and stepmother booked plane tickets to come out on Monday. First, however, we would have a visit from Sim and his wife, Davida. I was desperate for their company.

We met Sim and Davida at the LAX In-N-Out Burger for a classic California arrival lunch. They had just flown in from Boston, and I had already shared the news by phone the day before, as soon as we had left the neurologist's office. As Sim walked in the door, we embraced, cried, and tried not to make too big a scene. Sim had been my first really close friend at college, and he and Davida had been together even longer than Rachael and I had, hooking up on some crunchy lefty Jewish spring break trip to Central America during our sophomore year of college. The four of us had been close for over a decade. This was their first time meeting Baby Carl, who sat in a high chair playing with the wrapping paper from my Double-Double, unconcerned with the adult conversation going on around him.

"I'm going to be doing three things," I told them, recapitulating the thoughts that I had worked through with Rachael and in my head the night before, lying on our bed, crying. "I'll have to spend time on medical shit, with doctors and physical therapists and experimental medicine. And we'll spend time mourning what I've lost, and what Carl and Rachael have lost—decades together learning and laughing and loving. But we will also need to have fun and enjoy whatever time we have left together. Hopefully we spend as little time as possible on the first two and as much time as possible on the third."

Sim was amazed that, twenty-four hours after receiving my diagnosis, I already had a working theory of how to handle my decline and death. I took that as a compliment but didn't see any alternative. The clock was ticking and there wasn't much I could do about it except push forward.

That, at least, was how my ego wanted to approach it. My id had other ideas. At In-N-Out, I looked at the older children and teenagers with sadness, jealous that I would never see Carl grow to their age; on the freeway home I looked at the senior citizens in other cars with fury, jealous that I would never get to enjoy a drive along the coast with my wife during retirement.

Over the course of the next day, we talked about my feelings and their feelings and the disease. We tried to talk about other things, but my mind always returned back to a loop of outrage and disbelief. It was October, and we went to buy a pumpkin. We drove to a neighboring beach town that was also hosting an avocado festival. As we walked through the masses of people, I thought to myself, *Your lives are all proceeding normally, just as they were yesterday, but my world has been turned upside down, and you have no idea.* But of course I also had no idea what was happening in their lives.

We gave Carl his first bites of solid food, a somewhat underripe avocado that he spat out. Since my father was from Israel, where avocados were a special treat in the middle of the twentieth century, they were a big deal in my family. As my father told it, when he was a boy, he always spread the avocado thinly on his toast in order to save the precious commodity, while his cousin Udi would slather it on in heaps, provoking outrage in my father. When we moved to California in 1989 when I was five years old, my father planted an avocado sapling in our backyard and tried to grow another from a pit suspended in water. Rachael and I now had our own small tree growing in our backyard. *Will I live to eat its fruits?* I wondered.

As we sat at the picnic tables watching kids play volleyball and the sunset over the Pacific, I hoped that Carl would change his mind about avocados. Sim and Davida promised me that he would come to love food just as much as I did, and they've already been proven right: by the time he turned one, Carl was eating four square meals a day.

In the morning I insisted that Sim and I go for a run. I didn't know how many more opportunities I would have to do so. We drove to a beautiful path in nearby Montecito that rose up on the cliffs above the beach. There wasn't a cloud in the sky. The run was short, less than a mile each way—much easier than my usual runs. But this time I began to feel that my left leg's stride was slightly off; it didn't quite plant properly or turn over with the smoothness that I was used to. When we got to the turnaround point, next to a cemetery and surrounded by gorgeous wildflowers and enormous blue agave cacti, I told Sim that I had often imagined scattering my ashes at this point, overlooking the vast Pacific. And then I made a joke about *The Big Lebowski*, the Dude and Walter weeping as they wiped Donny's ashes off of their clothes. We soaked up the moment in all of its intensity and ran back down the hill.

Later, exhausted from the run and from a week of near sleeplessness, I took a long nap—and woke up daydreaming of Janet Yellen and Hillary Clinton. That sounds odd, but these two women were central to the future of my career, and our country—and focusing on my work allowed me a much-needed moment of clarity and purpose. Through the Fed Up campaign that I directed, I hoped to help reshape the Federal Reserve into a fully public entity representing the interests of all the American people, not just those on Wall Street. This, I knew, was the path to a fair economy and full employment.

As I lay in bed, I plotted out the broad strokes of our strategy. The major banks, I knew, would fight us each step of the way. But the logic of our position was unassailable: there was no good reason that portions of the Fed should be literally owned by Wall Street banks, unlike every other institution of government. We would mobilize community-based organizations and labor unions around the country and enlist the support of consumer groups and student activists, and maybe even some family farmers. With well-organized allies like John Conyers, Elizabeth Warren, Bernie Sanders, Maxine Waters, and Sherrod Brown on our side, and with the momentum from a Democratic victory in the upcoming presidential election, we might actually be successful.

I pictured myself lying in a hospital bed, wheeled into the West Wing for the ceremony where President Hillary Clinton would sign the Federal Reserve Reform Act, then hand me one of the pens she had used. Lying in that hospital bed, I would throw my fist up in the air, and I would be happy.

Energized for the first time in a week, I jumped out of bed and joined Sim, Davida, and Rachael in the kitchen. Sim had rolled out some fresh pizza dough; Davida had prepared an exquisite plate of cheese, salami, and olives, and was now shaving asparagus onto the pizza. I devoured the appetizers and told them in breathless excitement about my plan to transform the Fed. The pizzas came out of the barbecue crispy and aromatic, with cheese melting over the side, and the sheer deliciousness broke through my dead appetite. I ate enough to make up for a week of starvation. All of a sudden, fueled by sleep and food and hope for the future, vitality had returned to my body and mind.

"You saved my life," I told Sim and Davida as they departed for the airport, and I meant it.

They told me how incredibly moving the weekend had been. And they surely appreciated my sentiment. But they were doctors. They knew that saving my life was not in their power.

"Brace yourself," I said. "It's the worst thing you can imagine."

"I can imagine some pretty terrible things," my stepfather said, his face ashen and his eyes wide.

"It's worse than that," I said.

Rachael and I had driven down to my mother and stepfather's house outside Los Angeles in order to break the news in person. My mom already knew something awful had happened: we had called them on the drive down and said they should leave work and meet us at home. A few minutes later she texted to ask for assurances that whatever news we were coming to share did not involve the health of Rachael, Carl, or myself. We didn't respond, so she had her answer.

After we arrived, we took Carl inside and put him on a play mat. Mom went to the kitchen and brought out a tray of warm *bourekas*. (She was, after all, a Jewish mother.) I asked her to sit, took a bite of one of the savory, flaky pastries and spat out the news. Jed, my stepfather, was in a state of disbelief. My mother was calm and composed. She had experience dealing with bad news. Her mother had died relatively young, she had nursed her father through his death, and she had lost a number of friends prematurely.

It was from my mother that I had gotten my copious self-confidence. As an ambitious young woman in Communist Romania, she had studied hard, tested well, and then bribed and squeezed her way past the Iron Curtain into Israel, where she went to graduate school and met my father. "You can go to any college you want," I remembered her telling me when I was young, just one of the countless times she had instilled in me the audacious notion that I could be the author of my own narrative, that my hustle and skill would steer me past the cragged rocks of error and misfortune. For three decades she had been proven largely correct. But now I was bringing her an obstacle considerably larger than either of us had seen before. Not even master sailors had much experience navigating waters this rough.

Jed called his son, Zach, a resident in radiation oncology. I got on the phone with Zach for a few minutes and he told me about a patient of his who had ALS *and* cancer and whose ALS seemed to respond very positively to stem cell interventions. My mother went outside and called one of her closest friends, a psychoanalyst. I understood the impulse to reach out for support, guidance, and perspective. These were things I craved, too.

But I also craved distraction from my thoughts. ALS was already taking over my life, even though, physically, little had changed so far.

Later that week, propelled by both the need to do something to occupy my mind and a newfound appreciation for how quickly my life's clock was ticking, I drove with my father and Rachael to her office at UCSB and finally performed a task I had been meaning to do for nearly two years: washing the outside of her windows, which were caked with dirt from the live oak tree that stood above them and had become neglected due to budget cuts. Sitting on the frame of the window with my back hanging out over the ledge, reaching to scrub the glass clean, I felt for the first time in nearly a week the satisfaction of simple purpose and a mental focus on something other than ALS. For thirty, maybe even sixty seconds in a row, my mind didn't ruminate or rage about the fact that I was dying. I just felt normal, alive, again doing everyday tasks.

Over the coming day and weeks, I would spend an enormous

amount of mental energy seeking to re-create and expand upon that feeling. The diagnosis would not go away if I became more enraged at it, I told myself, and time was short. It was no good being angry and sad every hour of the day. Better to focus on good things.

But turning that apparently simple goal into reality was nearly impossible, particularly since every interaction and observation held reminders of what I was losing: How many more times would I get to see this ocean view? To eat this delicious pad see ew?

At first, I could hardly bear to spend time with Carl. He was so happy and beautiful and innocent. My illness and death transformed each bit of joy into sadness—because that joy had suddenly become fleeting and limited. The more pleasure Carl gave me now, the more I had to lose. Every time he laughed or cooed or craned his neck during tummy time like *Jurassic Park*'s baby velociraptors emerging from their shells, all I could think of was the tragedy of what he and I were losing: years and decades of games and conversations and kisses, of silly jokes and delicious meals, of camping trips in California's majestic parks and adventures on unfamiliar streets across the globe. Who would teach him how to box out or use a drop step on the low post? Who would talk to him about the triumphs and the tragedies of LBJ? Or show him how to turn a few unlucky opening rolls in backgammon into a miraculous backgame that would bewilder and infuriate his opponents?

More importantly, who would be there to listen when he'd had a tough day in seventh grade? Or to hold him when his grandmother died? Or to counsel him when he landed his first job interview and had no idea what to do?

The answer to these questions, I told myself, was that he might not even like basketball and that there were many better coaches than me—that many historians and gamers and tour guides could teach these and other lessons in my stead. And his mother and family members and friends would give him all of the support and love that he deserved. But I knew that although this answer was entirely correct, it was also entirely unsatisfactory. Because nobody could replace a boy's absent father.

There was, therefore, no way to ask these questions without becoming overwhelmed. And yet there seemed to be no way to interact with my baby and keep such questions out of my head.

Even performing discrete and constrained tasks was emotionally wrenching. Reading innocent books to Carl at bedtime became an exercise in self-abuse. " 'Little Guy runs away so fast Little Guy's daddy has to run like anything just to catch that baby up,' " I heard my voice saying. But my mind was focused on tragic questions: *Will I ever get to run after my little guy? Will I even live to see him run?*

Within a year I would learn the answer to those questions: No. And yes.

Cedars-Sinai Medical Center in Los Angeles is one of the leading institutions for ALS research in the country, and so it was there I went, five days after my initial diagnosis—along with a small entourage including Rachael, my father (who had arrived the previous day from New York), my mother, and Katy—to get a second opinion and discuss treatment options. I would be seeing Dr. Bob Baloh, whom I had been told was Southern California's leading ALS doctor. Coincidentally, Katy had studied under Baloh for a few weeks during medical school.

Cedars-Sinai, like other top ALS institutions, coordinated a comprehensive once-a-week clinic during which patients could see the full battery of experts in one visit: neurologist, pulmonologist, physical and occupational therapists, nutritionist, psychologist, and others. The model was intended both to provide people with comprehensive care and to facilitate research into therapies and treatments. Because ALS is a fast-moving disease with few treatment options, researchers had a hard time convincing patients to rigorously monitor their symptoms and rate of decline; the lack of good data on the course of the disease made it even more difficult to develop and evaluate effective therapies. Therefore the clinics tried to build ongoing relationships with patients in the hope that they would stick with the monitoring and evaluation.

In the clinic, they took my weight and height: 165 pounds, five feet ten inches. I once again had my muscles and reflexes tested. My mother was holding out hope that perhaps the hinterland Santa Barbara doctor had gotten my diagnosis wrong; I refused to indulge such a fantasy. When the resident subtly pointed out the hyperreflexia in my foot to a medical student, I tried to embrace my newfound role as a guinea pig and educational resource. Dr. Baloh confirmed the diagnosis, and my mother couldn't stop the tears from rolling down her cheeks. As with Dr. DaSilva, I asked whether he had ever had a patient a young as I was; yes, he said, he'd even seen teenagers with the disease. I asked him how long people my age and in my condition could expect to live. Unlike most doctors, Baloh was willing to reveal the ugly statistics: three to four years. Anything more was possible but unlikely.

He spent an hour with us, explaining the disease, discussing the lack of meaningful treatment options, and answering my father's queries about clinical trials. The nutritionist told me to eat a lot. The psychologist and fellow talked with Rachael and me about coping and depression and hope. The physical therapist didn't have much to offer: I was still in pretty good shape, able to walk on my heels down the hallway, and balance on one foot without any difficulty.

By the time we made it back to Santa Barbara that evening, I was preoccupied with a new question: How fast would my disease progress? Some patients live many years: Stephen Hawking, the most celebrated and exceptional example, lived for more than fifty years after the onset of his disease. Others die within months. Where would I fall on that spectrum?

I began a constant series of silent and informal tests and assessments. Was it harder for me to carry a coffee mug in my left hand this morning than it had been yesterday or last week? Did my left foot feel more awkward when jogging? Suddenly every twitch and fumble was a sign of decline.

As I lay in bed the next afternoon, I realized that the twitching that had started in my left arm had spread not just to my right arm but also to my belly. This was a disaster. Twitching, I had learned, was a sign that muscles were not receiving regular and sufficient communication from the central nervous system. They were essentially requests for instruction and information. ALS killed by destroying the diaphragm's ability to expand and make the lungs breathe; if the motor neurons leading to my torso were starting to die off already, I didn't have long.

I called Dr. Baloh's office in a panic, asking what this meant for my future. Through an aide he conveyed to me that the twitching did not necessarily mean muscle loss would follow. We couldn't draw any conclusions from this development. Although I took some solace in his message, it was limited: the twitching was *obviously* related to the spread of the disease, even if the correlation between twitching and muscle loss was less than one. Fuck.

I called my father into my bedroom and told him about this new symptom. He looked at my belly. It didn't look like it was twitching to him—just like I was breathing and my belly was jiggling a little bit when I did. What was actually happening to my body? And what did that mean about what would happen to my body in the future? We didn't know the answers to anything, yet my fear was settling upon answers whether they were true or not.

What we did know, however, was that we had to take our lives one day at a time. We couldn't see much farther than that anymore. While we had previously made our plans in years and decades, Rachael and I were now limited to thinking in terms of weeks and months. We decided that we would finally—and immediately—take that trip to the majestic national parks of Utah that we had been discussing for years. We invited people over for a big election night party in early November. And we chose to keep our plans to travel east for Thanksgiving to introduce Carl to the extended family. But that was as far as we could plan.

My diagnosis hit Rachael hard, as it would any wife. Her entire future was upended, her fulfilled life shattered. Like me, she had her bouts of despair and grief. But, unlike me, she now knew that she had to be the rock for our family. Sitting in the living room, watching Carl play, I became overwhelmed and infuriated. Rachael comforted me and reminded me of our mantras: "We haven't lost each other yet. Let's focus on how cute Carl is and on what we have left." Breathe, she would tell me time and time again. Stay active. Stay in this moment.

In those early weeks I often checked out of the room. Disappeared into my own head. Walked away from conversations. But Rachael was steady. She made sure that Carl's routine remained undisturbed. That we had dinner to eat. That life went on.

When you're diagnosed with a terminal illness, you spend a lot of time reflecting on your life and the choices you've made and the unfathomable predicament you find yourself in. As a white man who had been the beneficiary of a racist and classist society—and who had devoted himself to eliminating the very systems of oppression he had benefited from—this meant grappling with the paradox of my privilege and my misfortune.

Ten days earlier, when Rachael and I had celebrated our eleven years together, I felt like we had reached the mountaintop: we literally knew nobody who seemed happier or luckier. But now, so soon after that, we had fallen from grace. Nobody I knew was facing an untreatable terminal illness in their thirties. Did I know anybody who had died this young? There was one kindhearted giant on my high school track and field team who had been killed in Iraq, but that was it.

I thought of Rachael's colleague who lived across the country from his wife and children and commuted every couple weeks. I thought of my friends who were unlucky in love, unhappy at work, or depressed. I used to pity them all and sometimes even wondered how they got up in the morning. Now I wished my problems could be as easy as theirs.

But I also knew that my field of vision was severely limited. I didn't know people who had died young simply because upper-middle-class white folks in the United States didn't die very often of opioid overdoses or gun violence or foreign combat. Poor people did. Black and brown people did.

And we lived in a country that was segregated by race and class. Most of the people I interacted with were relatively well-off, highly educated, and white. And that was true even though I worked at a diverse nonprofit organization advocating for marginalized people.

And, of course, if I widened my vision more broadly, my story ceased to become such a tragic outlier. In other parts of the world, people died young every day as a matter of course. They died from malaria, from malnutrition, from war; they died from domestic abuse and car accidents, from earthquakes and tsunamis and fires.

It was this recognition—of my privilege and my place in the world—that I tried to remember in those difficult first days and months, taking pains to put my suffering in context. A few days after my diagnosis, I sent seven close friends this email:

My dear dear friends,

I was really excited to see some of you this week in Berkeley at the Universities Allied for Essential Medicines meeting. But I have some absolutely devastating personal news.

On Friday I was diagnosed with ALS.

It is outrageous, incomprehensible, devastating, and depressing. I was so looking forward to the next 50 years living my perfect life with Rachael, Carl, our friends and family, and my amazing job in paradisiacal Santa Barbara. There was so much beautiful life to live.

I'm going to Cedars-Sinai tomorrow to meet with the top-notch clinicians there; we'll see what is possible in terms of treatment and research. Maybe there is some hope for prolonging life, and maybe a miracle will come over the horizon very soon. But it's a devastating and very negative diagnosis. One in 50,000 people in the US gets this disease, and our average age is 55. So I definitely drew an unlucky hand this round.

But the truth is I've had an amazing hand so far in life. Compared to the billions in abject poverty, the tens of millions killed in war, the untold number who aren't happy, I've been very lucky. So rather than bemoan "Why me?"—which I certainly have the urge to do almost every moment—I want to be happy and energized and squeeze every last drop out of what I've got left.

So I am now moving full steam ahead, trying to seize these last few months/years and live them to the fullest—including being with Rachael and Carl and friends and family, doing some beautiful things, and trying to see a big victory in the Fed Up campaign.

I would love to see you soon, if you can come down for a day or two or three. Also, we're gonna host an election night party, since it's looking like it'll be a great night for our country and the world. And then I wanna have a big-bash celebration for everyone whom I love in NYC on the weekend of December 3/4. I would love to have you all there.

I will need to depend on you and others to support me through this. And then, most important of all, I need to be here for Rachael and Carl, now and for a long long time in the future. She loves you all so, so much.

I am so deeply grateful to each of you for what you have given me, how you have taught and inspired me and made me laugh and love.

Ady

Two weeks after my diagnosis, Rachael and I tried to make good on that desire to carpe the diem. We packed up all of Carl's many essentials and flew to Salt Lake City so that we could finally take that long-discussed trip to Utah's famed national parks. My college buddy Jeremy put down his dissertation in progress, flew in from Philly, and was waiting for us near our gate. Rachael's younger sister, Lucy, a graduate student in psychology at Stanford, met us outside of baggage claim. Then Ciel, a Utah native and Rachael's best friend from college, rolled up in an enormous black GMC Yukon. She would be our chaperone for the week.

Jeremy and I held hands as we walked in Capitol Reef National Park; every fifty yards, the gentle path turned to reveal a sublime new vista, with soaring cliffs and playful shadows in the late-afternoon sun. The ratio of incredible views to physical effort was better than any other hike I had been on in my life. But never before had I cried so much on vacation.

Rachael urged me to be like Carl. Stay in the moment. Look at the rocks and the colors. They have been here for so long. Millennia worth of humans have been born and died here, admiring these formations. Eons worth of reptiles and dinosaurs. We are made of stars and we return to dust in the blink of an eye. Our civilizations will fall. But these rocks will remain.

Afterward, as we drove across the vast expanse, the day and our vacation coming to an end, the gray-blue sky opened up and the rain pattered down on our civilian tank. I plugged in my iPhone and turned on my new favorite album, *Lost in the Dream*, an immersive, lyrical, layered, and iterative meditation on disappointment and loneliness by the Philadelphia band the War on Drugs. We looked. We listened. We felt ourselves looking and listening.

A cold wind blowing. Lost inside our heads. We didn't know what lay ahead. But home we would go. And set our eyes to the wind.

CHAPTER TWO

AWAKENING

In the spring of my senior year at Columbia University, having been accepted into law school and bored with my studies, I began following my friend Simeon to the evening meetings of a radical student group called Students for Environmental and Economic Justice. For a couple of years they had been unsuccessfully trying to convince the administration of our wealthy, liberal university to ensure that the workers who made the university-branded apparel (in the sweatshops of Southeast Asia) were paid a living wage and had safe working conditions. The university had already adopted policies requiring reasonable labor standards, but those standards were being ignored. So, in coordination with activists at other schools, we were trying to establish effective enforcement mechanisms.

The students of SEEJ had made polite requests of the administration, written op-eds in the school paper, and tried various other gentle pressure tactics. But the university had a well-developed playbook for dealing with such annoyances: Make sympathetic noises in private, promise to consider the issue, stall and delay, and wait until the handful of committed student leaders graduate or get distracted with other pursuits. Graduation was indeed approaching and we weren't quite sure what to do.

After I recounted our predicament to my father one evening, he nonchalantly suggested that we occupy the administration building to get our point across. I took the recommendation back to the group. Over the course of a middle-of-the-night strategy session, we debated the merits of the idea. Some of the other students, particularly the women, were worried about the consequences of occupying the Low Memorial Library, the administration's headquarters, which had been the site of the famous 1968 uprising, when students occupied buildings to protest the university's connection to the Vietnam War and its relationship with the black community in Harlem. So, budding law student that I was, I walked the group through a reading of the university's disciplinary policies. They had good reason to be worried: our planned infraction seemed to subject us to suspension or perhaps expulsion. But I cavalierly dismissed their concerns and assured them—baselessly—that the administration would never impose such a harsh penalty.

"I think we need to break up into gender caucuses," Davida said. She was a fierce and principled activist, and Simeon's girlfriend of eighteen months. I had no idea what she was talking about, but I suddenly found myself in the hallway with Sim and a couple other dudes.

"Why did we get kicked out?" I asked him aggressively.

"I think they just wanted some time to consider these issues calmly," he said.

I was flabbergasted by the notion that I had prevented such calm consideration, and when Davida came out a few minutes later to invite us back in, one of the other alpha males and I petulantly told her that we needed a few more minutes to ourselves. I was still processing the novel idea that gender could play a role in the dynamics of group decision-making and that maybe I shouldn't treat the conversation like a debate tournament. Sim and Davida calmly walked our group through more discussion, and by about midnight we had a critical mass of women and men who were ready to take action.

A day or two later about fifteen of us gathered on the sunny steps leading up to Low Library and marched into the lobby with our hand-painted banners and a few hundred flyers. In two hours the university was going to host one of its highest-profile events of the year, a panel discussion featuring Paul Krugman, Joseph Stiglitz, and a couple other famous economists about globalization and inequality. It was the perfect place to highlight the ways in which Columbia was profiting off of exploitation in poor countries. We expected a confrontation with campus security upon arrival. But after we plopped down on the floor, nothing happened. It took about half an hour before a security guard calmly walked over and asked us how we were doing. About thirty minutes before the event began, an administrator told us we were welcome to stay there and hand out our flyers to all of the event attendees, but he asked that we clear a path so people could enter safely. We counted this as a win. Two hours later, with the event over and the building ready to shut down, the university provost came by and asked us to go home. "The president and I will meet with you tomorrow," he said, "but only if you leave now. You can always come back again if you're not happy." We hadn't planned properly and had no food on hand. Rather than spend an unpleasant night on the floor, we decided to go back to our dorm rooms and prepare for the negotiations.

The next day, we returned to Low Library and were escorted to a conference room on the second floor where the university president and provost sat with twenty of us around a big table. President Bollinger recapitulated our argument to us, appearing to be rehearsing the lines he would use with his trustees and other stakeholders: Columbia had made a commitment to ensure that its apparel was not manufactured in sweatshops, but that policy was being ignored by the university's licensees; therefore Columbia needed to join the enforcement program for which we students were campaigning. I was eager to declare victory and accept the draft statement that Bollinger handed out. Sim, more careful than I was, insisted that a few more details be included. We left the meeting beaming, surprised that our activism had been so successful.

It was in this brief springtime campaign that I had my first real confrontation with power and saw how fragile it could sometimes be—how tigers are sometimes made of paper and jaws are sometimes made of glass. I also started to learn something about myself: that I had a knack for creative campaign tactics and for moving people into direct action. It would be years before I learned how to be a good listener—to other people's words *and* to their sentiments—but I never forgot Davida's intervention.

That senior year was also witness to a second, more consequential moment in my life. The first week of fall semester, I sat in the back of a small seminar room with two of my best friends, Carlo and Jeremy. We were taking the last of our required "core curriculum" courses: Western music appreciation. As we waited for the class to begin, in walked Rachael Scarborough King, a friendly acquaintance of mine from the student newspaper. She had a calm confidence and beautiful long red hair. Although there were many empty seats in the classroom, Rachael came over and sat in the seat to my left. I glanced at Carlo, in the seat to my right. He raised his eyebrow and cocked his head an inch to the side. Oh, yeah, he said telepathically. *Oh yeah*.

For our first date, Rachael and I watched the Red Sox take on the Yankees in the American League Championship Series from her dorm room. Then I took her to my favorite restaurant: a hole-in-the-wall taqueria where the final bill for a party of two was always under $20, *including* Negra Modelos. Jeremy, Carlo, and Simeon had been skeptical of the plan. Rachael was a classy girl, they said. But I arrogantly told them that if she was too good for our favorite joint, then I was probably too good for her. It turned out we were perfect for each other.

Rachael and I first met back in 2004, at the end of sophomore year, at the *Columbia Daily Spectator*, where I was an op-ed columnist and she had recently been appointed editor of the opinion page. She came in with a mandate to reinvigorate the page by expanding the diversity of voices and topics that it covered, and also by eliminating some of its repetitive and banal writers. In particular, that meant reducing the number of Jewish men opining self-confidently about Israel and the Middle East. She fired half of the columnists but kept me on because I had proposed to use my column to cover political developments on campus, not merely across the world. We developed a cordial and mellow working relationship, interacting briefly every two weeks when she edited my column.

I spent that summer interning on the editorial board of the *Miami Herald*. It was my first time earning a steady paycheck and paying rent—for a furnished Miami Beach studio with a view of the Atlantic from my bed, no less. I spent the days selecting which letters to the editor would be published and writing two-hundred-word editorials about state and national politics. I spent the lonely evenings frying pork chops, wandering past the nightclubs, and wondering if I had made a mistake by breaking up with my high school girlfriend. When a friend from work invited me back to the apartment she shared with her husband, I was grateful for their company—and their marijuana. The neon lights and Art Deco hotels had never been so beautiful.

Back on campus in September, with the presidential election imminent, Carlo, Simeon, Jeremy, and I joined a group of politically active artists and took a road trip to Ohio to register voters. Standing on the Columbus sidewalks, trying to stop the young students passing by and ask them if they were registered, I was clearly in my element: I regularly collected about twice as many voter registration cards as the others. Carlo and I returned to Ohio for Election Day weekend, when we tried desperately to get out enough voters to unseat George W. Bush. On election night we went to sleep without a final result, but were staring down what looked like an imposing vote deficit. In the morning, sitting in the back of a van headed for New York City, we listened dejectedly as John Kerry gave his concession speech. We were facing another terrible four years.

That spring, after just barely failing to get an internship with the *Washington Post* editorial board, I began to think that perhaps I would rather participate in the nation's politics than comment on them. Writing op-eds was fun but insufficiently impactful. America wasn't lacking in Ivy League–educated liberals spouting off critiques of Bush; it was lacking the institutions and individuals who would build the power we needed to defeat him. I came back for my senior year ready to apply for law school, eager to build a career of doing, not just talking.

Within a few weeks of our first date, I already felt like Rachael and I had settled into a long-term relationship. Senior year was a vivid, consequential season of transition. My law school acceptances rolled in before Christmas, including in the form of a flattering phone call from Harvard dean Elena Kagan. When Rachael applied for a Fulbright fellowship to study literature in the Dominican Republic, I told her I would defer law school and come with her for the year; she was dejected when her application was denied, but my gesture had made my intentions clear.

She then applied for forty journalism jobs around the country and ended up with a three-month gig in Anniston, Alabama, a town best known as the site where a Freedom Rider bus had been burned by segregationists. I was also ready to begin my career: antsy after sixteen straight years of school, enraged by the Bush administration and the Iraq War, which was killing one hundred Americans and thousands of Iraqis every month, and feeling secure with my acceptance to Yale Law School in my back pocket, I decided to go work on an election campaign to help Democrats take back the House of Representatives.

On the day of our graduation, the New York skies opened up and drenched us in warm rain. Alongside Rachael, Simeon, Carlo, Jeremy, and a couple dozen of our fellow lefties, I turned my back on our war-mongering graduation speaker—who was giving an I-haven't-yet-declared-my-candidacy-for-president campaign speech—and proudly sported my bright orange umbrella and lapel button that read "McCain does not speak for me."

Rachael and I packed up her station wagon and drove down the Blue Ridge Mountains toward Alabama. We were starting a new phase of our lives—together.

But first we had to be apart. After dropping Rachael off in Anniston, I headed north for Cincinnati, where I had landed a job as the communications director for a long-shot congressional race. My boss was a hippie doctor named Victoria Wells Wulsin, running in one of Ohio's reddest districts against a Cruella de Vil incumbent, known in D.C. as "Mean" Jean Schmidt. We started the general election campaign with almost no staff and even less experience, but by the fall we had a sizable budget and a trivial army of outraged volunteers. I loved the fast pace and the adrenaline highs, but I also had little perspective and zero equanimity. "Shoot me in the fucking head," I regularly exclaimed to my office mates, in response to challenges both large and small.

I had a naive misconception about the importance of policy proposals in congressional races, so I spent an inordinate amount of time writing up detailed papers and press releases about what Vic would do when she got to Congress. But I got other things right, including writing and producing some top-notch television and radio ads that we blasted throughout the suburban and exurban counties east of Cincinnati. None of the pundits had given us a snowball's chance of winning, but as Election Day approached, all the polls showed us tied. We ended up losing by less than 0.5 percent; the national Republican Party had poured hundreds of thousands of dollars into a race that should have been easy for them, so I felt we had done our part to help Democrats win back the House.

In January, I joined Rachael in the town of Bend, Oregon, nestled in the high desert, surrounded by majestic mountains and infused with the aroma of sagebrush. Our cozy, recently renovated one-bedroom apartment sat forty feet from the sparkling, powerful Deschutes River. And it cost $650 a month. She had gotten a job at the local paper, and I was along for the ride, biding my time until law school started in the fall. Most days I slept until noon and then got high with my neighbor, who gigged as a ski instructor and parks department groundskeeper. Eventually I found work as a short-order cook at a local bar and grill; I lasted two weeks before I was fired for incompetence. (That shit is hard.)

I was much better-suited for my next job, as a waiter at a big new corporate steak house that opened in the redevelopment district. The middle-aged ladies loved me, and I regularly came home with a hundred dollars in my pocket after a short shift. (In Oregon, unlike in most states, tips came on top of a full minimum wage, rather than replacing it.) One late night, over drinks with the other servers, I said that the job made me feel icky: although I was never sexually harassed like most waitresses were, I was still always pretending to be nice just for the tips. A bespectacled sommelier named Ron told me I should shift my perspective: I was there to help my guests have an enjoyable evening, and there didn't need to be anything fake or icky about it. It was a lesson for me not only about taking pride in my work and finding meaning in the moment but also, more importantly, about seeing the full humanity of everyone who I interacted with. Beginning at first contact, Ron was saying, I could work to form genuine relationships, no matter how brief.

As fall and my first semester at law school approached, Rachael began looking for work on the East Coast. We were excited when she found a job listing from the *New Haven Register*. I still remember vividly the bright morning when she ran into the bedroom, jumped onto the bed, and woke me up with an ecstatic kiss. She had gotten the job, and we could move to Connecticut together.

After a lazy summer of mountain hikes and river floats, and an impressive appearance by Rachael on *Jeopardy!*, we resold our furniture on Craigslist, jammed every inch of her station wagon with our belongings, and drove back east.

Although the students at Yale Law School had all excelled in college and arrived with impressive résumés, and although perhaps 80 percent considered themselves Democrats, we were at the school for an array of different reasons. The majority of students intended to build careers as highly paid attorneys in the country's fanciest law firms. A significant minority hoped to become academics. And then another small minority, myself included, hoped to use our law degrees in pursuit of social justice.

This last group of students congregated in the basement of the building in what was called "clinic." The law school offered a series of different small, hands-on seminars in which we were able to practice law under the supervision of clinical professors. We represented real clients with real problems and gained practical experience in the work of lawyering, and we also built relationships and community with like-minded lefty students.

One clinic had a reputation for being more exciting, more impactful, and dramatically more demanding than all the others. It was called the called the Worker and Immigrant Rights Advocacy Clinic (WIRAC). It took on a variety of impressive cases, from defending immigrants from deportation to helping low-wage restaurant workers recover unpaid wages. It also had a series of legislative advocacy cases representing organizations that were trying to change government policies, including, for example, helping the National Domestic Workers Alliance pass a law in New York State guaranteeing minimum wage and working conditions for the overwhelmingly black and brown nannies, housekeepers, and health aides who had been excluded from labor protections for nearly a century.

Even though I was vying for a spot in clinic rather than a prestigious summer internship at a fancy law firm, I still thought I needed the best. I applied to join WIRAC my first year, fairly confident I would impress the professor, but I ended up ninth on the waiting list and never got in. I settled for joining the landlord-tenant clinic, where I had the opportunity to represent a resident of public housing who was being evicted. Under the supervision of a kind, meticulous, and brilliant professor who had been teaching in the law school's clinic since the 1970s, I learned to use creative and technical legal arguments to keep my client in her apartment. She had a very difficult life and I was glad to help her. But I also saw the ways in which her self-interest, and my work, may not have been in the public interest: she was living in a three-bedroom apartment by herself, and the public housing agency wanted to move her to a smaller place to allow a different family to have her apartment. She was waiting to regain custody of her children and argued that she would need the big apartment when they returned. But neither my professor nor I had any confidence that she would be getting her kids back anytime soon, so we were ambivalent about the situation. Nevertheless, we were her lawyers, and she wanted to stay in her apartment. So we made it happen.

The next year I applied for the elite WIRAC clinic again, optimistic that my experience in the landlord-tenant clinic and my new acquaintance with WIRAC's professor—who had encouraged me to apply this year—would gain me admission. So, when I logged into the class schedule website and saw that I was first on the waiting list rather than admitted, my heart sank into my belly with disappointment. Surrounded by excellent classmates, I was no longer able to excel; in fact, I wasn't even able to pursue the career opportunities that I wanted to. I picked up the phone and called Simeon. For the first time in years, I told him, I felt like I was failing.

Then I jogged the one mile from my apartment to the law school to confront the WIRAC professor. Mike Wishnie was a legend among lefty law students. As a clinic student himself years earlier, he had sued the Clinton administration all the way up to the Supreme Court and won a ruling protecting the rights of Haitian refugees to settle in Florida. He had gone on to clerk at the Supreme Court. And he was now building the most interesting clinical practice in the country, defending the rights of Muslims persecuted by the Bush White House, among many other cutting-edge cases.

"I am sorry," he said. "I didn't mean to promise that you would be admitted to the clinic, only that I was excited for you to apply." He told me that he and the other professors had had to make some very difficult decisions about which students to admit. He told me he was unable to increase the class size by even one more student. But there was still a chance I could get in if just one student decided not to take the class. I left, dejected and sure that no one would pass up such an opportunity.

But, to my great joy, one student did indeed decide to drop out, deciding that thirty hours a week was just too much to devote to a single class.

I threw myself into the work with gusto. Within a few weeks I was negotiating a settlement agreement with an assistant U.S. attorney regarding a Freedom of Information Act lawsuit that the clinic had filed a couple of years earlier against the Department of Homeland Security. All there was left for us to do was agree on how much the U.S. government should pay us in attorneys' fees. It was the perfect assignment for me: I could combine my stereotypically Israeli love of *souk* negotiating with my hatred of the U.S. immigrant-incarceration system to try to extract as much money as possible to help fund the law school's clinic. What could be more fun? I proposed to Mike that our opening bid be about $100,000, but he said that was extravagant; we opened around $60,000, settled at $46,000, and moved on to other work.

For the next year and a half I focused my clinic work on a wage-and-hour case representing ten Chinese immigrant cooks who had been mistreated by their employer in central Connecticut. Like tens of thousands of other immigrant restaurant workers on the East Coast, they were paid less than minimum wage (and no overtime) for long, grueling hours. We were suing the restaurant in an attempt to get the workers back some of the money they were owed. Representing these workers was a crash course in civil litigation. I learned much more in a week about discovery and motion practice and many other elements of the American federal litigation system than I had all semester in my course on civil procedure. Working with my two clinic partners, under the supervision of a gentle and methodical activist professor named Muneer Ahmad, I deposed the restaurant's owner. We drafted hundreds of interrogatories, demanding information on how much our clients had been paid and whether the restaurant had kept any records of the hours they had worked. Most challenging of all, we spent late nights in the clinic working to answer the interrogatories that the restaurant's lawyer had sent to our clients.

Since leaving the Connecticut restaurant, our clients had scattered around the eastern seaboard, so we had to communicate with them by telephone. They spoke no English. We spoke no Mandarin.

This made things difficult. So we hired a brilliant sophomore from Yale College to translate on our behalf. Our clients were working at their new restaurants until eleven or twelve at night, and we could speak to them only once they got home. Late into the night we would ask them again and again for their recollections about their time working at the restaurant: What month had they started to work? How much were they paid? What were their hours? Did the restaurant use MSG in the food? What were the conditions like in their basement apartment?

The most shocking part of this case was, in fact, our workers' living conditions. The employees at Chinese restaurants in New York City live in cramped shared apartments and pay rent. But at Chinese restaurants in the hinterlands, where there was neither a robust rental market nor a vibrant Chinese community, there was often a different arrangement: the restaurant owner provided housing as part of the employees' compensation. Our clients had been housed in their boss's cold, dark, poorly ventilated basement apartment—about seven of them in three small rooms, none of which was a lawful habitation. And they weren't being paid what they were owed.

Our clients understood why we were keeping them up until the middle of the night, asking them for these details over and over again. But they still thought it was crazy—that the lawsuit would never make a real difference in their lives. We shared this sentiment, but at least we were learning how to be good lawyers. When discovery was over, sometime in the fall of my third year, we filed a motion for summary judgment, seeking to win the case without a trial. Although we didn't prevail on every claim, the judge agreed that the restaurant had clearly violated the minimum wage and hour laws. The restaurant owner could not afford to go to trial, and our clients were eager for some cash and some closure after years of litigation. So, once again, I went into settlement negotiations. But this time I had little of the joy from my experience battling with the U.S. government the previous year. This time, my opponent was a struggling small businessman who would never be able to pay the many hundreds of thousands of dollars that he owed our clients. He, too, was a Chinese immigrant who spoke little English; he, too, had worked horrendous hours as a cook before cobbling together enough money to open his own restaurant. Yes, he had exploited his employees. But, like them, he was still a pawn in a system of global capitalism that was built to benefit others at his expense. He had just made it a couple of rungs higher up the ladder.

We couldn't reach a settlement agreement; our clients had waited too long to accept pennies on the dollar that they were owed. The restaurant owner, with only about $100,000 in his bank account, simply could not pay them what he owed them. (We tried to look for hidden assets but found nothing.) Graduation arrived for me and my two clinic partners. We handed the case off to two younger students. Finishing these negotiations would become their job. (The case eventually settled for $136,000. Like so many victims of wage theft, our clients were never paid what they deserved.)

That spring I also had the opportunity to do a different kind of lawyering. A local union approached the WIRAC clinic and asked for help promoting a new living-wage law for the city of New Haven. The current law featured a low wage and no benefits, and it covered too few workers. The union wanted to raise the labor standards and extend the law's protection to all of the contractors and grant recipients who did business with the city. Over the course of a couple of months, I got advice from the country's leading living-wage lawyers about how to craft a better policy and then sat down to share my recommendations with the union and its two young progressive allies on the city's board of aldermen. This kind of lawyering lacked the personal connections that I had made in the landlord-tenant clinic or when representing the Chinese cooks. But, to me, it felt less tedious and more systemic. I began to get a sense for the type of lawyer I would like to become: one who partnered with community organizations to identify creative solutions to serious problems and then turn those ideas into laws.

That sentiment was reinforced when I decided to add an additional clinic to my coursework for my third year. In the legislative advocacy clinic I represented a local nonprofit organization that was part of a coalition of groups that was trying to pass a millionaire's tax through the state legislature in order to avoid cuts to crucial services. It was the kind of coalition advocacy work that would become my bread and butter in the years following graduation.

And I also got to advocate for a new law directly related to my earlier representation of the public housing tenant. In her eviction case, which had taken place in front of a housing department bureaucrat (as opposed to a judge), there was no recording of the proceeding. If we had lost the case, it would have been very hard to successfully appeal by arguing that the bureaucrat had made an unreasonable mistake. There was an easy fix to this. The department should tape record each of these hearings, we argued. We drafted a law to mandate this, convinced a legislator to sponsor it, testified at a sleepy hearing, and were pleasantly surprised when it became law that spring.

It was a victory, but it felt like the epitome of incrementalism. Mandating that the public housing authority record the proceedings in which it evicts its tenants is a pretty sad way to try to realize the fundamental notion that all people deserve access to safe and affordable housing. Like litigation, I realized, legislative advocacy could be tedious and underwhelming, too.

As if my clinical work didn't provide enough opportunities for rabble-rousing, I also joined a student group fighting to improve access to essential medicines in poor countries around the world. Like many other major research universities, Yale spent many millions of dollars each year conducting basic research that had the potential to lead to the discovery of new medicines. The scientists who worked in the university labs did so primarily in order to advance human knowledge and welfare. But for Yale University, which is a multibillion-dollar enterprise, this scientific research was also a tantalizing opportunity to generate enormous new revenues. It had a well-funded office—the technology transfer office—whose sole responsibility was to try to sell the basic research from Yale's laboratories to pharmaceutical and biotechnology companies for as much money as possible.

The problem was that when those companies sold their new medicine based on Yale's research, they charged exorbitant prices that were out of reach for many millions of patients in low- and middle-income countries. In the 1990s, when the HIV/AIDS epidemic was spreading rapidly through sub-Saharan Africa, the pharmaceutical companies refused to sell lifesaving drugs at prices affordable to the people who needed them. That horrific reality began to change in 2001 when a small group of Yale law students, led by Amy Kapczynski, realized that the patent for a key AIDS drug called d4T, sold by the multinational Bristol-Myers Squibb, was owned by the university. Amy and the other students joined with the international organization Doctors Without Borders to launch a campaign to force Yale and BMS to agree not to enforce their patent in South Africa. It led to a monumental victory. By allowing generic companies to manufacture d4T and other crucial therapies, it lead to a 95 percent reduction in the price of AIDS medicine in Africa.

Although Yale had eventually acted correctly in that one case, it still had no good policies in place to ensure affordability of all medicines developed on the basis of Yale research. The students who had led the 2001 fight established a permanent student group at Yale and a number of other major research institutions. They called it Universities Allied for Essential Medicines (UAEM). I joined the group when I arrived on campus in 2007.

As the Columbia University administration had done a few years earlier in response to our demands for better workers' rights policies, the Yale administration was operating off of a tried-and-true playbook: Delay, ignore, and obfuscate until students graduated or got distracted. The leader of the technology transfer office, in particular, saw us as a threat to his authority and his business practices. He told his bosses that our demands were unreasonable and uninformed. We—a collection of medical, public health, and law students advised by expert professors in our fields—had other opinions. In the fall of 2008, as I was beginning my second year in law school, Yale appointed a new provost who had the reputation for being responsive and open to student voices. I had recently agreed to be one of the leaders of our student chapter of UAEM. Frustrated and sensing a new opportunity, an older mentor and I marched over to the new provost's office and told his secretary that we needed to see him urgently. We sat and waited for an hour. We were told that his deputy and the technology transfer officer would be happy to meet with us in a few days. We accepted this minor victory and went back to our classmates to plan a strategy for the meeting. To our pleasant surprise, the political dynamics in that meeting were new and different: the deputy provost was expressing an openness to our demands, and the technology transfer office, which reported to her, was frustrated and on the defensive. That meeting was the first of a series of fruitful negotiations.

That October also witnessed another important breakthrough. Former president Bill Clinton came to the law school for his thirty-fifth reunion. He had spent the past eight years working on issues of access to medicine through the Clinton Foundation, and we saw this a valuable opportunity to put additional pressure on the university. We enlisted the support of the law school's dean, Harold Koh, who had served in the Clinton administration and shared our progressive politics and concern with global health. Harold arranged for me and two other students to meet with President Clinton just before he gave his speech to thousands of alumni and the Yale community. Sara was an MD-PhD student with an expertise in infectious diseases, and Robynn was a law student with experience in global development who had worked with the Clinton HIV/AIDS initiative; together, the three of us would try to convince Clinton to join our lobbying efforts. In the days before the meeting, we met repeatedly with the other students activists to come up with the right request for Clinton and narrow down our pitch to a few punchy sentences: we were only going to have a moment with him and needed to get straight to the point.

It was a sunny fall day when Clinton's motorcade pulled up. Harold introduced us to him; he towered over us and with his friendly charisma seemed in no rush to get into the speaking engagement. We jumped into our pitch, explaining why we thought Yale needed to do a better job to make its scientific research accessible. We asked him for a meeting back at his offices in Harlem to discuss the issue further. He told us he agreed with our general goals and shared some story about his work on the issue. We pushed again: Would he be willing to meet with us for a longer conversation? All of a sudden, his friendly warmth disappeared. "Look, I don't control my schedule," he barked at us. "I don't know if that is possible." We tried to mutter some pleasantries, but the conversation was clearly over. He stormed off, with Harold trailing behind.

The Yale administrators ushered Robynn, Sara, and me to the front row of the enormous auditorium. Our fellow activist students and the in-the-know professors, who were all in their seats already, watched us with anticipation. "How did it go?" they whispered to us. We were too flabbergasted to have a coherent answer.

Clinton's speech began with pleasantries about the university

and meandered through amusing insights about the presidential primary that his wife had just lost to Barack Obama and about his
prescriptions for the American economy, which was in the throes of
the financial collapse. Then he began to talk about his work on the
international access to medicine. My pulse quickened. Would Clinton talk about our issues? Would he push Yale to do better?

He told the audience that he had just met with three Yale students outside the auditorium. He said that we were worried that Yale
had become part of the problem, rather than the solution. The students, he said, were "working on the idea that the universities, which
are big engines of biomedical research, should be able to take a lead
in changing America's policy so that the patent process does not prevent lifesaving drugs in new areas from getting to people who need
them." He expressed his support for this mission, saying, "I like that,
because that's turning good intentions into positive change."

Our stress and uncertainty disappeared. He had given us what
we needed. In front of Yale's entire leadership, he had validated our
critique and called on his alma mater to do better—even if he had
used more polite and nuanced language than I would have liked.

Combined with the arrival of the new provost, the pressure that
we were able to put on the university with that boost from Clinton
was enough to generate a series of productive negotiations. We presented the administrators with a comprehensive policy proposal. They
seemed willing to accept much of it. And then one spring morning,
as we appeared close to our final agreement, I was surprised to wake
up to a Bloomberg headline: six major research institutions announcing a new shared commitment on access to medicine. We were blind-
sided but also hopeful. Our advocacy at Yale, combined with student
efforts at other universities, had led to a major breakthrough for our
organization. But the language of the universities' commitment was
not as strong as what we had thought we would be getting out of
Yale, and certainly not as strong as our proposed language.

Was this a victory? A setback? Would Yale and the other universities actually implement the new policy commitments—or would they just continue with business as usual and wave the document at the next generation of students who complained to them? The only way that this announcement would actually lead to better access to medicine in poor countries was if students remained vigilant, insisting that Yale prioritize the public interest over the pharmaceutical companies' profit margins. That meant that our UAEM chapter needed to develop new generations of educated activist students—students who could organize broad support from across the campus, identify strategic campaign opportunities, make use of connections and resources (as we had done with Harold Koh and Bill Clinton), hold their own in negotiations with university administrators, and use the media to put pressure on Yale to do the right thing.

It required, in essence, building a strong institution that could survive beyond any one student leader. Political change, I began to learn, was achievable only through sustained struggle, which required sustainable and powerful institutions that could continue pursuing their objectives for many years.

When the time came for me to start thinking about finding work after law school, I asked for advice from Amanda Shanor and Shayna Strom, two older students in UAEM. They told me about a special organization in New York City whose offices were filled with Spanish-speaking immigrants taking classes, singing songs, registering voters, cooking chicken and rice, designing campaign plans, filing lawsuits, phone banking, and making art. I knew I had to see it for myself, so I traveled into the city and then took the 7 train out to Queens, watching through the window as we rattled over vibrant immigrant neighborhoods. I descended onto Roosevelt Avenue in Jackson Heights and walked into a storefront office; the walls were covered in revolutionary art, the air filled with purpose and dignity. I fell quickly in love.

The fellowship that I received to work at Make the Road New York lasted only twelve months, but it was the best political education I ever got. As the lawyer for the organization's Queens workers' committee, my job was to help our members win justice after they were deprived of minimum wage, overtime, or other workplace rights. But along the way I got to see what it means to do community organizing in pursuit of collective liberation: to meet people where they are, bring them into a shared space, and move them together toward a common goal. In the decade since then, I have seen organizing succeed and I have seen it fail. But I have never seen it practiced like at Make the Road New York. The organizing done there was more profound and more powerful because it embraced the full humanity of its members. The members of Make the Road New York were residents of the local communities, but they were also so much more. When they walked into the offices, they were recognized as workers and immigrants, as mothers and sisters, teachers and artists, students and musicians, readers and writers, dreamers and leaders. They were treated as full human beings—human beings facing tremendous obstacles but also bringing incredible resources to bear, bringing incredible power and creativity to their fights for dignity and justice.

The organizing done at Make the Road New York begins with a one-on-one conversation, and over the years, through tens and hundreds of thousands of such conversations, the political power built within those colorful walls has delivered to New Yorkers more livable apartments, better schools, larger paychecks, safer medicine, more affordable university, a less oppressive police force, and a less intrusive deportation machine. When my year there ended, and I left for a job in the federal courthouse downtown, I didn't yet know exactly what kind of a lawyer I wanted to become. But I had seen what kind of power I wanted to help build and what kind of movement I wanted to join.

CHAPTER THREE

APPRENTICESHIP

"All rise!" said Jim, the flamboyant, clever, socially awkward court-room deputy. Fifteen reporters sitting in the jury box rose, along with about one hundred members of the public. Two tall, handsome pros-ecutors stood with confidence, one sporting a Sikh turban, the other a mop of sandy-blond hair. A few feet away stood a Russian immi-grant defense attorney in a fancy suit with his hair gelled straight back. Beside him, his client's quiet demeanor and simple appearance belied his ferocious reputation: this man was Viktor Bout, the infa-mous "Merchant of Death," known throughout the criminal under-world, portrayed by Nicolas Cage in *Lord of War*, and now in federal custody after two decades on the most-wanted list.

Judge Shira Scheindlin, razor-thin and toned at age sixty-five, marched in quickly, cradling a foam Koozie with a Diet Coke in her right hand, and climbed the three steps to her bench overlooking her large packed courtroom. I sat below her to the right, with my back to her, soaking up these new and fascinating proceedings.

It was my first of fifty-two weeks as a law clerk in the federal trial court in downtown Manhattan. The commute from our bright two-bedroom apartment in Astoria was now twice as long and, due to the business dress code, much sweatier. But I was incredibly lucky: I was starting my clerkship with a front-row seat and backstage pass to the most anticipated criminal trial in years.

After jury selection was complete, the two assistant U.S. attorneys began methodically laying out their case: Bout was a world-class international arms smuggler who had for years sold weapons to African despots in violation of UN sanctions. Although he claimed to be in "retirement," he agreed to sell antiaircraft missiles to men who said they were Colombian FARC rebels for use against American planes. Unfortunately for him, these buyers turned out to be undercover DEA agents.

The prosecution had emails, text messages, and secret audio recordings with which to prove its case. Bout's lawyer responded with shifting, confusing, and ultimately ineffective counter-narratives. At sentencing, Bout broke his long silence. He stood, thanked the judge for conducting a fair trial, and then, finger pointing accusingly, began loudly berating the prosecutors for dishonestly pursuing a political agenda.

Judge Scheindlin handed down the lightest sentence that she could under federal law: twenty-five years. She was uncomfortable with the fact that the entire prosecution was based on a sting operation. Because there were no real FARC rebels looking to buy arms, without the DEA's artifice there would not have been a crime. Sure, Bout sold arms to dictators. But so did Lockheed Martin, with the full blessing of the American government. Sure, Bout knew that his weapons would end up being used by criminals to kill innocent people. But so did thousands of gun shop owners across America. Even in a case against a notorious arms dealer, the judge was teaching me, justice is not as simple as good guys and bad guys.

When I was two weeks into my clerkship, the judge handed me back a draft opinion that I had written for her. "This needs a lot of work," she said brusquely and with no sugar to coat her words. I can't remember if she said it with her lips or her eyes, or if I simply projected my own insecurities onto her, but the message I took from her first evaluation of my performance was clear: I would need to improve dramatically if this clerkship was going to work out.

I had a lot to prove. Judge Scheindlin knew and I knew that I had gotten the position with the help of family connections. My great-aunt had worked with the judge when they were young prosecutors, and they had stayed friends for years. When Judge Scheindlin had originally called me in for an interview, she made clear that she wouldn't have selected me out of the hundreds of applicants if it hadn't been for my aunt's effusive recommendation. Now, I feared, she was regretting her choice, worried that she would be stuck for a full year with an underperforming clerk.

I looked through the document. Large portions were crossed out. The language was pared back. A trial court opinion was, I realized, no place for intellectual musings or abstract theorizing about the law and the role of a judge in society. Those were pastimes for Ivy League law professors and their acolyte students. Courts had to speak with a different voice.

I stayed late, after the other clerks, law students, and Jim had gone home. I needed to improve, particularly because of what was coming up soon. That first month had been an entertaining, educational, and relatively easy introduction to my job; Jim and my co-clerk Mark had handled most of the work, while I simply got to watch and learn. But we were about to receive in chambers the reply brief from the plaintiffs in *Floyd v. City of New York*, then the most watched civil rights lawsuit in America, and I would be tasked with helping the judge issue a historic ruling.

Beginning in the 1990s, under Mayor Rudy Giuliani, New York City adopted a more aggressive strategy known as "broken windows" policing, bolstered by pseudoscience theories about the criminal mind and the environment. The NYPD's new approach was to let no infraction—no matter how minor—go unpunished in order to prevent more serious crimes before they happened. The key to stopping violent crime, went this theory, was to eliminate the minor nuisances of graffiti, turnstile jumping, public urination, and broken windows. A disorderly world led to an attitude of lawlessness—an attitude that could be "reformed" if police officers gave young perps no breathing space in which to make New York City disorderly.

"Broken windows" policing was also driven by a resurgent belief in the power of metrics. Embracing wholeheartedly the wisdom of CompStat, the department's elaborate software for tracking crime in real time, the leadership of the NYPD began to set higher quotas for "proactive" police activity. If petty crime rose in a particular precinct, the department would respond by assigning more officers to that zone and instructing them to bear down upon the people who they believed were responsible for the misdeeds.

By the middle of the next decade, this system of aggressive and proactive policing had swelled dramatically, resulting in constitutional violations against New York City residents on an almost unimaginable scale. More than 500,000 times each year, NYPD officers would stop pedestrians, demand to know what they were up to, and often conduct invasive pat-downs and searches of their bodies. The targets of this police action were, of course, not residents of the Upper East Side or employees of the Wall Street megabanks. Indeed, they were rarely white: they were nearly all black and brown men from neighborhoods like Crown Heights, Harlem, and the South Bronx.

David Floyd, a medical student, was one of them. On February 27, 2008, he ran into the tenant of the basement apartment in the small building owned by his grandmother in the Bronx. The tenant had been locked out, so Floyd brought down a handful of keys to try to unlock the door. As he struggled to find the right one, two police officers accosted him from behind. Their stop, question, and frisk of Floyd was standard operating procedure, emblematic of the way in which young black men in New York were under surveillance for behavior that is considered perfectly acceptable when done by white people.

In 2008 the Center for Constitutional Rights, with the support of a fancy law firm, filed a class action lawsuit against the city, naming Floyd as their lead plaintiff. The department's actions inflicted grave physical and emotional harm on the civilians whom they targeted, according to the complaint. And these actions violated two fundamental constitutional rights: the Fourth Amendment right to be free from unlawful searches, and the Fourteenth Amendment right to be treated equally under law, regardless of race.

By the time I arrived in Judge Scheindlin's chambers in the fall of 2012, the parties had been engaged in four years' worth of grueling litigation. Eventually the city turned over millions of pages of documents, including the notecards that police officers were required to complete after each stop. Depositions were taken from civilians, police officers, and department officials. NYPD policy memos were submitted to plaintiffs' lawyers. Expert statisticians were enlisted to analyze the enormous data collected by the NYPD. Finally, legal briefs were filed, replete with highly charged debates over when it was appropriate for a police officer to stop a civilian.

American courts have been grappling with this question for decades. Although the liberal Supreme Court of the 1960s had attempted to find an appropriate balance between the right of individuals to autonomy and dignity and the need of law enforcement to ensure law and order, the more conservative jurists appointed by Republican presidents from Richard Nixon through George W. Bush had consistently granted police widespread latitude to stop people for allegedly suspicious behavior.

The city filed a motion to dismiss Floyd's claim, arguing that even under his version of the facts, the officers had reasonable suspicion to believe that he was engaged in criminal activity: not only was he trying multiple keys and rifling through his bag (potentially in search of tools for breaking in), and not only had he looked suspiciously over his shoulder, but he was also in a high-crime neighborhood that had recently witnessed a spate of burglaries. Although any of that conduct in isolation might not have provided a basis for a stop, argued the city, the totality of the circumstances meant that the officers were legally authorized to detain Floyd and investigate. My job was to help the judge evaluate the city's argument for dismissing the case.

I spent a solid week combing through previous cases, learning all about reasonable suspicion, "furtive movements," and high-crime areas. The plaintiffs submitted evidence to show that in fact there had not been a spate of recent burglaries in the area and that, according to the police department's own definition of the term, most of New York qualified as a "high-crime area." If the "high-crime area" and the "recent burglaries" were eliminated as a basis for the stop, the only potentially incriminating details left to the city's argument was that Floyd had been looking through his backpack and over his shoulder. Under these circumstances, the judge decided that it would be unreasonable to suspect Floyd of committing a crime and denied the city's motion to toss the case. Floyd's claims survived, and the parties would soon move on to a major moment in pretrial litigation: the plaintiffs' motion for class certification.

Five months later, after handling numerous other cases and watching the seasons pass, I turned my attention to the enormous stack of briefs that had been filed in *Floyd v. City of New York*. Plaintiffs were moving to be certified as representatives of a class of hundreds of thousands of black and brown New Yorkers who had been stopped unlawfully in recent years. This would allow them to more persuasively argue that major injunctive relief—requiring the city to stop wrongfully detaining people—was the only appropriate remedy. The city opposed the plaintiffs' motion precisely because winning class status would be a legal and political victory for the plaintiffs that would be difficult to overcome later in the litigation.

The rules governing class action lawsuits are found in Rule 23 of the Federal Rules of Civil Procedure. They are appropriate if and only if the plaintiffs seek to represent a large group of people for whom there are common questions of fact or law, and if their particular situation is typical of the situation for other class members. The plaintiffs in *Floyd* were bringing claims that, to my eyes, were precisely the type for which the class action rules were developed: civil rights claims seeking to reform government practices that impacted enormous numbers of people.

But the United States Supreme Court had recently issued a major decision limiting the use of Rule 23 class action lawsuits, and we would have to grapple with it. In *Dukes v. Wal-Mart Stores, Inc.*, store greeter Betty Dukes alleged that Wal-Mart had discriminated against her for many years, paying her less than her male counterparts. In its decision, the Supreme Court issued two important rulings.

First, the Supreme Court explained that trial courts handling class certification requests must conduct a "rigorous analysis," examining the facts of the dispute (not merely the plaintiffs' allegations) in order to decide whether the prerequisites for class status have been met. The court recognized that this analysis would often overlap with the ultimate judgment of the merits of the lawsuit—which meant that the class certification decision was a practice run for the final ruling.

Second, the Supreme Court ruled that Ms. Dukes could not lawfully represent a class of over 1 million women employees of

Wal-Mart, holding that the employment practices and managerial decisions within Wal-Mart were made at the store level, not at corporate headquarters, and therefore the plaintiffs across different stores did not have "common" questions of law and fact that could be adjudicated in one lawsuit. It was a deeply flawed anti-worker decision, like so many decisions issued by the court in recent decades, which favored the interests of corporations over those of working people. But the countersuit, *Wal-Mart Stores, Inc. v. Dukes* was the law of the land. And my judge was a trial-level judge, with no authority to question or ignore the rulings of the Supreme Court, no matter how wrongheaded she believed they were. Therefore, we needed to conduct the "rigorous analysis" of all the facts of the *Floyd* case and determine whether or not the Rule 23 prerequisites for class status had been met. And, importantly, in order to certify a class in *Floyd*, we would need to distinguish our facts from those in *Wal-Mart v. Dukes*.

The mountains of evidence submitted by the parties led to two powerful conclusions: first, unlike in the *Wal-Mart* case, the New York Police Department was a centralized, hierarchical institution and its policies were set at headquarters and distributed to all of the precincts. The rules, forms, procedures, and guidelines governing the use of stop-and-frisk were department-wide. Headquarters collected and analyzed stop-and-frisk data for the whole city. It was, as the judge's final opinion would explain, "a single stop-and-frisk program" that was "far more centralized and hierarchical" than the employment practices at Wal-Mart.

Second, the evidence made clear that the NYPD had conducted hundreds of thousands, or likely millions, of unlawful stops in recent years. The evidence was dramatic. It showed that police officers were systematically making stops without even giving sufficient legal justification and that the justifications they were listing were often undermined by the evidence. The evidence also showed that the police targeted black and brown people for stops even when controlling for crime and geography, and treated black and brown people more harshly during stops. Here's a taste of the court's findings, based on a database containing written records for all 2.4 million stops at issue in the case and the statistical analysis conducted by the plaintiffs' expert witness and reviewed in detail by the court in a previous opinion.

- In more than 170,000 cases, police officers wrote down reasons for making the stop that were legally insufficient to justify that action. For example, officers noted that suspects had made a "furtive movement" or were in a "high crime" area, neither of which, alone, was enough to merit a stop.
- In one precinct, a whistle-blower police officer named Adrian Schoolcraft recorded supervisors repeatedly telling officers to conduct unlawful stops and describing the pressure from NYPD headquarters for such "proactive" policing. The data show that that precinct was no outlier bad apple: the percentage of stops that were facially unlawful in that precinct was below the city-wide average.
- The percentage of stops for which police officers failed to list an interpretable "suspected crime" grew dramatically, from 1.1 percent in 2004 to 35.9 percent in 2009. Overall, in more than 500,000 documented stops—18.4 percent of the total—officers listed no coherent suspected crime, even though a police officer must suspect a person of committing a crime in order to lawfully stop that person.
- Only 12 percent of stops resulted in a summons or an arrest. In the remaining 88 percent of cases, police officers ultimately concluded that there was no probable cause to believe that a crime was being committed. That is to say,

according to their own records and judgment, officers' "suspicion" was wrong nearly nine times out of ten.

- Guns were seized in only 0.15 percent of all stops, despite the fact that "suspicious bulge" was cited as a reason for 10.4 percent of all stops. Thus, for every sixty-nine stops that police officers justified specifically on the basis of a suspicious bulge, they found only one gun.

With regards to discrimination based on race, the court concluded that:

- "NYPD stops-and-frisks are significantly more frequent for Black and Hispanic residents than they are for White residents, even after adjusting for local crime rates, racial composition of the local population, police patrol strength, and other social and economic factors predictive of police enforcement activity."
- "Black and Hispanic individuals are treated more harshly during stop-and-frisk encounters with NYPD officers than Whites who are stopped on suspicion of the same or similar crimes."
- Police officers are more likely to list no suspected crime category (or an incoherent one) when stopping blacks and Latinos than when stopping whites.
- Police officers are more likely to list as the stop justification "furtive movement," which is highly nebulous and not particularly probative of crime, when stopping blacks and Latinos than when stopping whites.

It was April of 2012 when the parties' briefing materials arrived in our chambers. I had been clerking for seven months and was now fully comfortable with my role and intimately familiar with the facts of the case and the law governing these issues. As I opened our word-processing software and began to write a draft of the opinion, I could feel the profound importance of the moment—for New York City and for me personally.

The dispute over the NYPD's stop-and-frisk program had become one of the most divisive and important public policy debates in the city. The *Floyd* case was four years old, and the class certification decision would be the most significant one to date—and the final one before the case went to trial the following year. Because we needed to conduct a "rigorous analysis" of the facts of the case, it was also a preview of the final judgment. The ruling therefore would have tremendous impact on the NYPD and on the lives of millions of black and brown New Yorkers.

The power of the decision came not only from the legal authority of Judge Scheindlin to order the NYPD to do or not do certain things; as with most landmark civil rights cases, the importance of *Floyd* was due to its place in the broader political context. While top-notch civil rights lawyers from the Center for Constitutional Rights were filing motions in court, organizers and activists from across the city were engaged in a multi-year effort to build popular political opposition to the police department's practices.

Communities United for Police Reform (CPR) was a broad coalition of dozens of organizations in the city opposed to stop-and-frisk and the mass incarceration that it facilitated. CPR's campaign was groundbreaking in its sophistication and rigor. Through its coalition members, CPR built a base of thousands of engaged grassroots leaders and supporters with first-and experience of police misconduct. Some of the most important multiracial organizing work was done by an activist named Linda Sarsour, a Brooklyn-born Palestinian who brought together Muslim New Yorkers, who had been subjected to extensive surveillance and abuse since 9/11, with non-Muslim black and Latinx residents targeted under different justifications. The coalition built and used political relationships in City Hall and the state legislature to put pressure on the NYPD and pursue an affirmative agenda—for example, collaborating with city council member Jumaane Williams, a former tenant organizer with long dreadlocks and a sharp critique of the NYPD, to introduce a package of major reforms in the New York City Council that would significantly reduce the frequency and harmfulness of stops-and-frisks by the police department. The lawsuit, therefore, was only one (powerful) tool among many in the effort to reform the NYPD.

These policy and legal disputes were happening in the shadow of an upcoming mayoral race. With Mayor Michael Bloomberg finally termed out of office, the September 2013 Democratic primary for mayor would be a major moment in the political life of the city. Would New Yorkers select Christine Quinn, the Speaker of the New York City Council, who had allied herself with Bloomberg in support of the NYPD and who was preventing the CPR reform agenda from passing? Or would they choose a critic of stop-and-frisk, perhaps the progressive public advocate from Brooklyn, Bill de Blasio?

The class-action decision that I was drafting would likely impact both the legislative fight inside City Hall and the race for mayor. It would be the most high-profile, rigorous, and detailed review of the NYPD's actions to date. It would have the authority and force of the federal courts—which had, since the famous civil rights lawsuits of the mid-twentieth century, often forced local and state governments to respect the constitutional rights of their residents.

I also suspected that the decision would reverberate well beyond the borders of our city. This case was the most important and highest-profile dispute in a burgeoning national debate over the role of the police and the constitutional rights of black Americans. That spring, both Judge Scheindlin and I had studied the powerful new book by Michelle Alexander, *The New Jim Crow*, which laid out in potent detail the scope of the destruction resulting from mass incarceration in America.

Sitting behind my large wooden desk, I contemplated the mounds of evidence that were literally piled up all around me. They provided a graphic, detailed image of how the new Jim Crow operated—how the police imposed the threat of deadly force onto hundreds of thousands of black and brown New Yorkers every year, how it pushed tens of thousands of those people into jail and criminal justice proceedings, and how this reign of terror unlawfully and unfairly disrupted the lives not only of the victims but of so many of their wives and husbands, daughters and sons, parents, siblings, and friends.

All across the country, people who shared my values and vision for America were watching this case. After the opinion was published and the newspapers summarized its findings in dramatic headlines, I hoped it would become an important touchstone in the movement to reverse mass incarceration: civil rights lawyers would cite it in their court filings, law students might read about it in their courses, activists and community organizers would draw inspiration from their New York City counterparts' success, judges would cite it as precedent, and elected officials might even change the way they legislated and oversaw their local police departments.

But beyond the city and its potential impact on the civil rights movement, this opinion had significance for me individually. It would be, I assumed, the most important decision of my clerkship year and the most important document I had ever helped to author—probably the most important I ever would. I had landed in this clerkship at an opportune moment, when my judge was responsible for adjudicating major political questions of national importance, and had been tasked with helping her issue the most rigorous and wisest decision possible. I knew I would remember my work on this case for the rest of my life.

This opinion was also an opportunity for me to prove myself worthy of the clerkship and to help me assuage my white guilt: if I was going to benefit from my privilege and the family connections that had helped me land the job, I hoped to do both what was right under the law and at the same time make a lasting change for the better in the lives of so many New Yorkers.

My clerkship was the envy of many of my classmates. I believe it was, with the exception of the elite Supreme Court clerkships, the most interesting and influential clerkship in America that year: no case heard by a trial court was as important as the stop-and-frisk case. And I had the privilege of working with a judge who was willing to protect civil liberties and pursue racial justice, regardless of what Rupert Murdoch's minions said about her on Fox News and in the *New York Post*.

So I cherished every day working in her quiet, comfortable chambers high above New York City's Chinatown and Financial District. On my walk from the bustling subway to the towering United States Courthouse in the morning, I passed beautiful blossoming trees and groups of old Chinese immigrants calmly practicing their tai chi or their synchronized dance routines set to blaring pop music. As I flashed my badge and passed the lawyers, jurors, and litigants who were waiting to go through security, I felt smug in my anonymity: *You may not know who I am*, I thought to myself, *but you will soon read about my work.*

On the morning of Wednesday, May 16, 2012, I got to the office early and printed out a copy of the final draft of the decision, which the judge had finalized the night before. I took it into her room for her signature. We were both proud of the work we had done in what we knew would become a landmark ruling. She had been adjudicating stop-and-frisk cases since 2003, when the predecessor to *Floyd* arrived in her courtroom. She knew that her name and photo would be plastered throughout the New York media and that although many commentators and colleagues whom she respected would think highly of her for issuing this decision, many other powerful voices would disparage her. The *New York Post* and *New York Daily*

News would echo the rhetoric of the police union and accuse her of putting New Yorkers' lives in danger by handcuffing the police and empowering the criminals. The mayor and the top brass at the NYPD would question her intelligence and her impartiality. And although she didn't know it at the time, a white supremacist running an insurgent law-and-order campaign for president a few years later would attack her for being a "very-against-police judge."

But she was filled with the steely confidence that comes from doing justice in the face of power. The confidence that comes from stepping back and seeing how your life's work fits into a longer arc of history. From knowing that you are giving voice to the people who are too often silenced, defending the rights of people who are too often oppressed, standing in solidarity with the people whose struggles are too often lonely. "What good is the life tenure of a Federal judge if you're not willing to do what you think is right?"

I took the opinion into the front room, marked it with a satisfying whomp of the handheld date stamp, scanned it, and uploaded it into the court's official filing system.

Within the hour the *New York Times* had a bold headline at the top of its website: "Judge Grants Class-Action Status to Stop-and-Frisk Suit." In his opening line, the reporter zeroed in on some of the most powerful language from the opinion, highlighting the judge's conclusion that she was "disturbed by the city's 'deeply troubling apathy towards New Yorkers' most fundamental constitutional rights.'"

A year later Communities United for Police Reform scored a major victory, passing through the city council its legislation establishing an inspector general to oversee the NYPD and strengthening the prohibition on bias-based policing. Mayor Michael Bloomberg was fiercely opposed to the reforms, and so it was momentous indeed when, at three a.m., the council passed the bills with precisely the number of votes needed to override his veto. It was a historic achievement for Council Member Jumaane Williams, who gave a memorable speech from the floor of the council; his lead co-sponsor, Brad Lander, regularly highlighted the effort as a model of how "inside/outside" collaboration between elected officials and movement allies can yield transformative change.

Over the ensuing years, the *Floyd* case took various turns, and the battles in City Hall remained intense, but eventually the reformers won and were vindicated: constrained by new municipal law and supervised by the federal court, the NYPD was forced to curtail the number of stops-and-frisks by over 90 percent. And crime in the city continued to drop, refuting the fearmongering from the likes of Donald Trump and Michael Bloomberg.

As the late summer humidity of New York City turned commuters and playgrounds sticky with sweat, I was happy to take refuge in our cool, pristine chambers high above the streets—particularly since the pace of work had slowed. I had time to read the newspaper and enjoy a delicious lunch from a Chinatown dumpling shop before turning to work. One afternoon the judge called me into her office and handed me a draft opinion.

"Take a look at this," she said, "and let me know if you think it's right."

It was short decision granting the government's motion to dismiss the complaint of a man who was imprisoned upstate. Leroy Peoples had filed a thirty-page handwritten lawsuit pro se, meaning that he had no lawyer, alleging that New York was violating his constitutional rights by imprisoning him in solitary confinement.

Judges in federal court receive many pro se complaints from prisoners, and most of them are thrown out quite quickly. It's not always easy to read the handwriting, the arguments often aren't well structured, the evidence isn't laid out clearly, and the government lawyers opposing them have lots of practice explaining why such filings are frivolous. And, of course, there's also the law: in 1996 the Republican Congress and President Bill Clinton agreed to enact procedural reforms making it much harder for prisoners to receive a fair hearing in federal court. Clerks and judges are busy, so the odds are stacked heavily against any prisoner hoping to challenge the conditions of his or her confinement.

But Judge Scheindlin sensed something special in the complaint of Leroy Peoples. For twenty years she had seen up close how the criminal justice system ignored or dismissed the rights of defendants—how excessive sentences and harsh punishments could dehumanize a person. The draft opinion dismissing Peoples' complaint that she had handed me had been written by one of the junior law clerks. She asked me to review the decision because she knew that I shared her objections to America's system of mass incarceration.

Leroy Peoples had been sentenced to three years in solitary confinement for filing liens against property belonging to prison officials—an action that the officials viewed as illegal and menacing. They had retaliated by seizing his legal papers and other belongings, taking away his prison privileges, and sending him into the euphemistically named "special housing unit," more commonly known as solitary confinement. His lawsuit alleged a wide array of constitutional violations, but one claim in particular stood out: the notion that his incarceration in solitary might violate the Eighth Amendment to the Constitution, which prohibited the use of cruel and unusual punishment. Could solitary confinement ever be considered unconstitutional? In what circumstances? As I searched for a precedent that might help us evaluate his claim, I was dismayed to discover that few courts had even addressed the question. One or two federal trial courts. A state court here or there. But there were no significant opinions to suggest that solitary confinement was anything other than one more tool at the disposal of American jailers.

So I turned my attention to the social science literature. What was solitary confinement? Why was it used? And what impact did it have on the prisoners, on people like Mr. Peoples? The answers that I found were voluminous, disturbing, and unambiguous: solitary confinement was torture.

The opening battle in a civil lawsuit often takes place at the motion-to-dismiss stage. It is at that point, after a plaintiff has filed the lawsuit, that the defendants try to get it thrown out. They argue that even if all of the plaintiff's factual allegations are true, she still has no legal right to be in court or receive the remedies she seeks. That is to say, at this stage in the proceedings, the judge's job was to accept all of Leroy Peoples's allegations as true and then ask the question: Does the Eighth Amendment prohibit this kind of treatment?

Judge Scheindlin, marshaling all of the powerful social science evidence, found that it could. After she issued her ruling, the state filed a motion asking her to reconsider her decision—a polite way of saying that they thought she had made a serious mistake and were giving her a chance to correct it before appealing. At the same time, the decision attracted the attention of the lawyers at the New York Civil Liberties Union, who were involved in a long-term project to reduce mass incarceration in the state. One of their attorneys reached out to the court and requested permission to see whether Leroy Peoples would like them to represent him (for free). If Peoples was going to successfully challenge New York State's system of solitary confinement, he would need first-class attorneys. So the judge put the case on hold while the NYCLU began discussions with Peoples.

That was the last I heard of the case until I read the news headlines in 2014: Leroy Peoples and his lawyers had turned his case into a class action. The parties then reached a settlement in which New York State agreed to overhaul its solitary confinement system. The state agreed to dramatically reduce the number of prisoners sent to solitary confinement and to narrow the list of eligible reasons for that punishment. Specifically, nonviolent offenses would be far less likely to end with the punishment of solitary. What had begun as a hand-written pro se complaint had turned into one of the biggest victories in the fight against mass incarceration.

One warm evening in September, after twelve hours of reading briefs and case law, I was finally ready to call it quits. I flipped off the lights, restocked the mini-fridge with Diet Coke for Her Honor's morning refreshment, and headed down past the security guards and into Manhattan's fall air. I crossed Foley Square, surrounded by towering courthouses and federal office buildings, turned left past City Hall sitting at the foot of the massive Brooklyn Bridge, and walked south on Broadway for eight blocks.

There, in a tree-lined, concrete plaza a few hundred feet from Wall Street, tents and camping stoves and displays of revolutionary art stood jarringly out of place. Dozens of people mingled about, talking in small groups. "Mic check!" a solitary voice rang out. "Mic check!" many voices called back. In one corner of the park, fifty or seventy-five people stood listening to a speaker and echoing her every word. The mic was checked two or three more times and then the speaker began her remarks. Every few words she stopped and let the crowd repeat back what she had just said so that even people across the plaza could hear. This "people's mic" had arisen in response to the fact that artificial amplification was banned on the plaza.

Two weeks earlier a group of protesters had retreated, under police pursuit, to Zuccotti Park. They still had not left, and their encampment, which they called Occupy Wall Street, had grown by the day. It was now attracting international attention and that highest form of flattery, imitation by other activists and protesters, in cities across America. This nascent occupation of Wall Street felt novel, provocative, and confusing. What was its aim? Who was in charge? What could it accomplish? I stood and listened as speaker after speaker decried American capitalism, which left millions of people homeless, hungry, and indebted in the richest country in the history of the world. Wall Street banks and the corporations they controlled had co-opted American democracy, the speakers alleged, depriving us of a political voice, economic security, and even our humanity. Three years had passed since Wall Street had brought down the global economy by leveraging risky bet upon risky bet, and the widespread human suffering that the collapse had caused was engendering a new, radical politics. The problems with America's political economy were fundamental; moderate policy reforms could not deconstruct the deep structures that allowed the Wall Street bankers to enrich themselves at the country's expense and get away scot-free while millions of families lost their jobs, homes, and life savings.

I had grown up in a mainstream Democratic household. My parents and step-parents were all professors of history. They were very well-informed but not politically active; liberal, not radical. They had confidence in rationality, the rule of law, and technocratic expertise. America had real problems, but those would be best addressed by smart elected officials enacting smart reforms. I became fluent in that language, winning local and California-wide speech and debate championships in high school on the basis of well-reasoned, impassioned defenses of liberal public policy.

But as I left Zuccotti Park, taking the subway up the East Side and over the river to our apartment in Astoria, Queens, the protesters' revolutionary message forced me to reconsider the mainstream left political world that I inhabited.

In the ensuing days, my co-clerks and I had wide-ranging debates about Occupy Wall Street: about whether the city should evict the protesters or whether their First Amendment rights should permit them to stay in the park; about whether Wall Street's banks should have been nationalized in 2008 rather than bailed out at taxpayer expense; about whether a random assortment of unwashed protesters without a platform or any organization could really light the way forward for the nation.

I was also having important debates with myself about what kind of a career I wanted to craft. In law school, at the Worker and Immigrant Rights Advocacy Clinic, I had been able to do it all: litigate, engage in legislative advocacy at the Connecticut statehouse and New Haven City Hall, and partner with local community-based organizations to help them build their memberships and power. But there weren't many jobs that permit that kind of jack-of-all-trades diversity; organizations wanted specialists who could excel at their craft. So it was time for me to choose what kind of a lawyer I wanted to be.

Throughout my clerkship year I was witness to top-notch litigating, both by $1,000-an-hour corporate partners and by civil rights attorneys dedicating themselves to the movement. These lawyers, from organizations like the New York Civil Liberties Union, designed wide-ranging impact litigation that sought to push back against some of our government's most egregious injustices. They did impeccable research, marshaled drawers full of evidence, wrote succinct and powerful briefs, and displayed tremendous skill in the courtroom. But I knew that they were also toiling away in tedious obscurity for much of their year: buried in document review, having exhausting and endless disputes over interrogatories and requests for admission, waiting months and even years for courts to issue opinions that might let their litigation continue. And, as in the Chinese restaurant case, they might wait for many years before ever delivering a modicum of justice to their clients.

The alternative? To become a full-time activist, wearing jeans to work and spending my time in the streets outside of City Hall and the hallways of Congress, rather than in the courtroom. Progressive organizations and coalitions are always in need of lawyers with a good head for public policy and the ability to identify politically viable solutions.

Legal research and writing were intellectually stimulating: sitting with the evidence and the law and crafting a powerful argument was like fitting together the pieces of a vibrant, multifaceted puzzle. I could lose myself for hours in the work, and each new case or law review article could provoke and stimulate my mind. But my heart was elsewhere. Arguing about public policy, organizing protests, convincing a reporter that my cause was worthy of front-page coverage—these were the activities that got my blood pumping. This was not the usual work for Yale-trained lawyers who had clerked in the Southern District of New York. But it was the work that called to me.

So, as my clerkship came to an end and I told Judge Scheindlin that I was turning down an offer to go work at a civil rights law firm across the street in favor of a position with a new organization called the Center for Popular Democracy, whose offices were located in some hard-to-reach corner of Brooklyn, she was skeptical and perplexed. But she wished me well and insisted that I stay in touch. I promised her that I would

In the evenings that fall, I often found myself walking back to Zuccotti Park, sometimes bringing along a friend or visitor who had heard about the would-be revolutionaries and wanted to witness them for herself. One late evening comfortably back home, I received an emergency text message. The Bloomberg administration was planning to clear the park and destroy the encampment. The only way to stop them was by filling the adjacent streets with thousands of protesters, making it logistically and politically impossible for the police to invade.

I got back on the subway and headed downtown. When I arrived at Zuccotti Park, there were a couple thousand people milling about. I found Joe Dinkin, a friend from college who had spent every day since graduation at the Working Families Party, trying to move

New York politics to the left. It was Joe's mass text message that had brought me to the park that night. We traded gossip and rumors and reflected on the unexpected revival of radical political action in the city.

The Working Families Party, founded at the turn of the century, aspired to organize progressive labor unions and community groups into a potent force by supporting left-wing candidates in Democratic primaries and pushing an ambitious city and state policy agenda. Through hard work and creativity, it had become the organizational home for left-wing politics in New York State, electing real champions to office and winning important policy victories like the repeal of the Rockefeller Drug Laws and an increase in the state minimum wage.

But Occupy Wall Street was a different beast. Its ideology was fiercely anti-organization. Its rhetoric fiercely anti-compromise. It was a movement with no clear leaders, no IRS employer identification number, and certainly no five-year strategic plan.

Joe and I talked big-picture strategy about what the Working Families Party should have been doing in that moment. We wanted more than anything to help the Occupy Wall Street movement translate raw energy into immediate impact and lasting political power, but we were worried that the party's help would not be welcomed by the activists in the park—or, conversely, that too much organizational interference might squelch the energy of the movement.

Nelini Stamp was the Working Families Party staffer assigned to Zuccotti during those weeks, and she knew that the party had to try to thread the needle properly. Popular political energy sparked too rarely. And the arrival of those sparks—when mass numbers of people were suddenly alerted to the injustices around them and inspired by a vision for an alternate future—was a precious, fleeting opportunity. If those sparks were to transform the world around them, if they were to grow into a roaring blaze that swept away even some of

the structural forces or ideological detritus that constrained our freedom to thrive, then they had to be nourished by kindling and fuel
sufficient to overcome the establishment's fire hoses and helicopter
drops. Strong organizations with resources, relationships, and capacity, Nelini and Joe and I believed, needed to provide that kindling
and that fuel to ensure that a bright moment of energy would not
dissipate upon contact with the first firefighter.

Suddenly a wave of enthusiasm spread through the crowd. The
NYPD had announced that it would not be clearing the park that
night: the prospect of violently arresting thousands of energetic protesters was too frightening even for bellicose Mayor Michael Bloomberg and Police Commissioner Ray Kelly. We hooted and hollered,
delirious with the momentary sense that our popular revolt could
defeat the money of Wall Street and the guns of America's milita-
rized-policing industrial complex.

Within two months those police officers returned, dismantling
the Occupy Wall Street encampment with the ferocity of victori-
ous counterrevolutionaries. What remained was a newfound political
awareness—both in my mind and in the mind of the nation. New
concepts became entrenched truths of American political discourse:
that the 1 percent have too much wealth, corporations too much
political power, and elected officials too little accountability to the
public.

That newfound political awareness became a potent force in
American politics—potent enough to bring a democratic socialist
within striking distance of the presidency—yet too impotent to prevent the ruling class from reasserting its dominance over national
politics and enacting a legislative agenda that exacerbates economic
inequality and political disenfranchisement. Our kindling proved
too meager, their fire hoses too overwhelming.

Six years later, my body wrecked by ALS and my political optimism shattered by Donald Trump's victory, I sat in a wheelchair in the halls of Congress and tried to bring back the spark of Occupy Wall Street, tried to once again light a fire under the political imagination of our nation. After a whirlwind day of meetings with senators and interviews with reporters, a few dozen protesters and I rolled into the majestic rotunda of the Russell Senate Office Building. Accompanied by a solitary guitarist, we sang along to that most radical piece of Americana, Woody Guthrie's "This Land Is Your Land."

When we were done, I called out for a mic check: "Mic check Mic check." The Capitol police encircled us and began closing in. "Can I get a mic check?

Mic check?
Mic check?
The mic check comes to us
From Zuccotti Park.
From a movement called
Occupy Wall Street.
And from a belief
That a better world is possible.
That greed is not good.
That corporations are not people.
That democracy is not
A spectator sport.

We are using a mic check today
Because we believe that it is time
For the voices of the American people
To be heard by the leaders
Of the American government.

We are using a mic check today
Because we believe that it is time
For the needs of the American people
To be addressed by the laws
Of the American state.

We are using a mic check today
Because we believe that it is time
For the American people
To take back our government
To preserve our democracy
To rebuild our economy
To save our planet.

The obstacles in our way
Are enormous.
Our opponents are so powerful.
They have the money.
They control the White House
And the courts
And the Congress.

But I believe
That we are more powerful.
Because on our side
Are the people.

Speaking alone,
My voice is weak.
But when we come together,
Our voices echo so loud.

Echo through the halls of Congress.
Echo out to those nine justices.
Echo up Pennsylvania Ave.
Echo all the way to Wall Street
And echo out
To every corner of this land.
Can you hear us America?
We are here to fight
For this country
That we love.

That is why
We use a mic check.

And that is also why
We come together.
In the streets
In our houses of worship
In our community organizations
In our unions
On our campuses
In the halls of Congress
And at the voting booth.

We come together
Because we are stronger together
We are braver together
We are louder together.
We come together
Because when we do
Their money

Is no match
For our people power.
People power.
People power.
Power to the people.

CHAPTER FOUR

IN SEARCH OF PEACE

Rachael and I had moved to Santa Barbara in the summer of 2014. It was our very own slice of paradise. I loved working from home, pacing around the backyard and sitting on the deck, talking on the phone with coworkers for hours every day. She was proud to be teaching at a public university, where many students were the first in their families to go to college, and found fulfillment and pleasure in her research. My days started early, because of the time zone, which often left the late afternoons and evenings free for walks through the neighborhood or by the shoreline, delicious home-cooked dinners, and movies on our projector screen. We went to bed happy almost every night; we were living a great life, and we knew it. When Carl was born in the summer of 2016, we had everything we could ask for. Our world was complete.

Being diagnosed with ALS removed the ground from under our feet. It destroyed the stable life that Rachael and I had built. It washed away with one enormous and unexpected wave, the decades of a future that we thought we would have together. Now I had only three to four years left to live. And most of those would be spent struggling with increasing levels of disability. My clock was ticking very quickly: I had only months or even weeks of solid physical health left. I therefore felt enormous pressure to enjoy the limited time that remained to me, to seize the days that I had rather than bemoan the days that I had lost.

But how could I enjoy life in the shadow of my shocking new tragedy? In the days and weeks after my diagnosis, an endless loop of outrage, anger, and disbelief ran through my mind. I had a visceral urge to rage against the disease—to be so angry that it would go away. But I quickly learned that the more time I spent thinking about ALS, the more miserable I was. If I could focus on something else just for a few minutes, the knot in my stomach began to dissipate. But directing my attention elsewhere was incredibly difficult. How could I train to my mind to focus on something other than the disease?

I recognized that my predicament was not unique, only extreme: most people feel like there aren't enough hours in the day; many also struggle with depression or a general proclivity to focus on bad or troubling facets of their lives. But I wanted a way out. So I looked for answers in meditation and Buddhist philosophy. A couple of weeks after my diagnosis I was cycling through a series of panic attacks, my mind swirling down rabbit holes of anger and distress. I picked up my phone and called a friend, Dash, for advice. I had been introduced to him by my college buddy Carlo; they had been in medical school together. At Carlo's wedding on the pristine beaches of the Turks and Caicos Islands the previous year, Dash had told me about his dissertation on the use of meditation in the West and how he hoped to integrate it into his psychiatry practice. And then I tried to keep up with him as we led the wedding party on a boisterous run down the beach. Caribbean waters had a way of soothing the soul.

Dash picked up the phone immediately. Carlo had broken the

news to him so I wouldn't have to, and he was expecting my call. I paced around the room maniacally. I bemoaned my fate. I told him I didn't know what to do. Suddenly I heard a loud bump. I turned around to see Baby Carl on the floor next to the sofa, screaming uncontrollably. Apparently he had learned to roll over and had tumbled off. I hung up with Dash immediately and threw myself into comforting Carl. The necessity of being a father had pulled me out of my mental spiral.

After Carl calmed down, Rachael and I decided to walk over to a friend's house for some Halloween pumpkin carving. I scarfed down the cured meat and cheeses that they laid out in front of me, but I couldn't focus on the festivities. I walked out into the parking lot and called Dash back.

"I don't know what's wrong with me," I told him. "I can't focus on anything besides ALS."

Dash told me not to be self-critical: "I know exactly what's wrong with you," he said. "You've just been given a horrible diagnosis."

Okay, so I wasn't to blame for my distress. But how could I escape it?

Dash asked me what, specifically, was upsetting me the most. I told him that I was overwhelmed thinking about the years and decades of wonderful moments with Carl that I was losing. This loss felt too enormous and overpowering to fathom. He asked me if I had lost those moments yet or if I was only distressed by the prospect of losing them in the future. I had lost nothing yet, I acknowledged. Nor was the future hurting me right now, we agreed. What was painful was *thinking* about the future. The pain went away when I redirected my attention from the future to the present. I needed to not guilt myself over the fact that I was distressed about the future; instead, he advised, I should acknowledge my distress and then let it pass.

"Think about your emotions like clouds in the sky," he said.

"Watch as they arrive, acknowledge them, and then let them pass." The goal was not to repress my emotions or scold myself for having them; it was simply to see them, accept them, and then redirect my attention to the present. Because the present was filled with Cambozola and salami and pumpkins. The present was still good.

"Okay," I told Dash, "I'll go home and I'll try to focus on something other than ALS for the rest of the evening." He told me to pare back my ambitions. "Shoot for ten minutes instead," he said. That would be accomplishment enough.

Dash also gave me a reading recommendation: Pema Chödrön's *When Things Fall Apart: Heart Advice for Difficult Times.* The secret to dealing with pain and tragedy, Chödrön says, is not to escape or ignore these difficulties. Rather, it is to be become comfortable and accepting of them. When the ground is pulled out from under your feet, she writes—when you find yourself plummeting down—it is a mistake to flail wildly in search of a handhold; instead, you can find peace by accepting your velocity and the fundamental instability, unpredictability, and impermanence of our world. Everything falls apart. That is the nature of things. Enlightenment requires us to accept this *anicca*—this impermanence—rather than rage against it.

A couple weeks later a former coworker, Nisha Agarwal, reached out to tell me that she, too, had fallen on hard times. She had an incurable brain cancer. She told me that she was finding solace in her daily routine: in washing the dishes, walking in the park, staying in this moment. She recommended that I practice my mind control with the help of Jon Kabat-Zinn and sent me a link to his body scan meditation on YouTube. I lay on my bed with my phone on my chest, his soothing voice methodically guiding my awareness from my left foot up to my torso and head. In breath. Out breath. Holding my whole body in my awareness.

Meditation, Kabat-Zinn explained, was an opportunity to move out of the mode of doing and into the mode of being—to move away from our incessant desire to make things better and toward an acceptance of things just the way they are. Accepting the pain rather than running away from it. "As long as you are breathing," his voice intoned, "there is more right with you than wrong." I tried not to dwell on the fact that I would soon lose the strength to breathe.

Dash's clouds, Pema's weightlessness, and Jon's mode of being became touchstones for me, helping me get through difficult hours and days. I wanted the techniques to solve my problems, make the sadness and the tragedy go away. But of course that was exactly the authors' point: the problems wouldn't go away, my tragedy of ALS was not a joke and not a bad dream, and sadness was inevitable. The key to enjoying the time that I had left would be to accept life's impermanence, accept the tragedy, and find comfort even when there was no ground under my feet.

The contradiction I had to reconcile, however, was that my career, my daily work at the Center for Popular Democracy, and my entire self-identity were built around what Kabat-Zinn described as the "mode of doing," of molding the world to our wishes. Activism and politics were precisely about *not accepting* the tragedies of the world, about insisting that we could reduce pain and prolong life. Social justice meant creating a stable floor beneath our feet and then putting a safety net under that, to catch us if it suddenly vanished: universal health insurance, affordable housing, unemployment benefits (or, even better, a guaranteed good job) . . . Being part of a progressive political movement was precisely about fighting back and building toward a better future. Accepting was not part of our vocabulary.

The theologian Reinhold Niebuhr—whose most famous disciple, Dr. Martin Luther King Jr., would become the patron saint of American organizers—sought to resolve this tension in his Serenity Prayer: asking for the serenity to accept what cannot be changed, the courage to change what can be, and the wisdom to know the difference. I tried to embrace this philosophy by living in two different mental worlds. When the Federal Reserve issued a bad decision, I embraced my outrage and worked with my comrades to craft a response to try to prevent it from happening again. But when ALS imposed on me a new symptom, I tried to be comfortable in my new reality, to accept my body as it was, not as I wanted it to be. My challenge—like that of everyone who has ever faced adversity or tried to create change—was in knowing what to resist and what to accept. Was it worth trying to slow down my ALS? Which experimental interventions were worthwhile and which would only cause more heartache? I didn't know where to turn for the wisdom these questions required.

Rachael was grappling with these questions and others. When I looked years in the future, I saw Rachael and Carl living a beautiful life that I would not get to share. But when she looked in the same direction, she saw uncertainty. Would she and Carl be lonely? Would they be able to craft a happy life? Sitting on the sofa together one evening watching TV, I let out a robust plume of gas. "For my next husband, I'm definitely going to insist on no farts," she said with smile in her voice. I laughed but then started crying.

How quickly would my ALS progress? How many intense medical interventions would I want to keep me alive, and for how long, and what kinds of burdens would that impose on her? How miserable would life have to become before we decided to pull the plug? How old would she be when she was finally widowed, and what would her options be at that point? We talked about some of these questions but commiserated about others telepathically instead.

A month after my diagnosis, we invited all of our Santa Barbara friends over for an election night party. It was going to be a joyous occasion. A Hillary Clinton presidency would solidify the gains made under President Obama, finally establish a progressive majority on the Supreme Court, and repudiate the racism and misogyny of Donald Trump. Republicans would soon be cannibalizing themselves for their failure to nominate a more reasonable candidate and bemoaning their third straight presidential loss.

Crucially, a Clinton presidency would also help me find purpose in my final years. Over the course of the campaign I had built strong relationships with her policy team and pushed them to come out with a strong position on the Federal Reserve. In May my efforts paid off when the campaign released a statement saying that Clinton believed it was high time for reforms that would make the Fed more accountable to the public and less beholden to Wall Street. I was eager to build off of that statement and work with allies in Congress and the new administration to craft a comprehensive reform bill in the new year.

My father had flown in from New York, as had Shawn Sebastian, my deputy on the Fed Up campaign. Local friends started arriving in the early evening. One brought a Donald Trump piñata, which we hung from a tree on the back deck. Everyone who came had heard about my diagnosis, and it was my first time seeing some of them. Most people didn't mention ALS, opting instead to give me a meaningful hug and talk about the election instead.

Folks spread out through the house, enjoying drinks and finger food. I was disappointed when the early results came in from Florida and North Carolina: there would be no landslide victory. Panic set in about an hour later when it became clear that the Midwest was favoring Trump as well. I bumped into my father in the hallway. We held each other's arms and looked at one another, silent and bewildered.

I texted my contact in the Clinton campaign. I asked him whether there was a huge swath of votes yet to come in from Wayne County, Michigan, where Detroit should have delivered Clinton a major cushion. He had no inside knowledge and was refreshing the *New York Times* web page along with everyone else. By eight thirty p.m. in California, our hope had run out. "World turned upside down, first for me, then for everybody," I texted him. "Not sure how to survive this . . . So many lives will be destroyed. I dunno. Maybe we move to India and find solace in a different universe. . .

"I'm gonna die under President Trump?" I asked him.

"I think you're gonna beat the odds for a long time to come. We'll fight again together another day yet," he replied. I tried to believe him.

By then, all but a few people had trickled home. The Trump piñata hung undisturbed. Somebody opened a bottle of champagne and poured out glasses. We mumbled some words about fighting back, about resistance. It was good to be with close friends. But my world had already fallen apart, and I wasn't sure how I would tolerate this second blow. With Donald Trump as president, neither change nor acceptance seemed possible

A few days later Rachael and I packed up and took Carl on his first trip to the East Coast. She was scheduled to attend a weeklong workshop at the University of Virginia, and we figured there was no point in canceling just to stay home and sulk. It would also be a good opportunity to stay with two old friends from Yale Law School who now lived in Charlottesville. After we had put all the children to sleep, the four of us sat down for a calm dinner. Somebody mentioned the future, when the boys would all be older. I broke down instantaneously, weeping uncontrollably. Rachael came over to hug me, and Dan and Geri could do nothing but look on with pity. Later, sitting in the den, Dan told me that his sister had died of cancer in her early twenties. He had somehow managed to remain boisterous and playful. He and Geri opened up their songbooks, and we sang tunes by Dylan and the Grateful Dead. I reached for his guitar hopefully. But it was no use. My left fingers simply could not stretch or apply enough force to the strings. They were already noticeably weaker than when Dr. DaSilva had given me my diagnosis just five weeks earlier.

Ten days later we were up in Boston for Thanksgiving with the extended family. Everybody cooed over Baby Carl, and during dessert eleven people surrounded him and watched intently as he was fed pecan and cherry pie. When Rachael and I bundled him up to leave, the whole family stood in line to give us hugs and express their love.

Throughout the early weeks and months, most friends and family struggled to know what to say or ask. They were afraid to say the wrong thing. They didn't want to bring up ALS if I preferred to talk about something else. At one particularly excruciating playdate with Rachael's colleague and her family just after my diagnosis, we sat and made small talk for two hours without referencing the elephant in the room. I left feeling exhausted and infuriated. The pit in my stomach was the size of a watermelon, and nobody had offered to share its weight. Much more helpful was the approach taken by Henrietta and Anne, friends of my mother who were visiting from Holland. Five minutes after sitting down in our living room, they told us that they were terribly sorry about my disease and asked how we were holding up. "We don't have to talk about it if you don't want to," Henrietta said, "but I don't want to just pretend like nothing is wrong." She said that her sister had died in her thirties after a long battle with illness, so she had some sense of what we were going through.

My aunt Deb was also familiar with this terrain. Over the years, she had treated hundreds of patients with pancreatic and colon cancer and had counseled their families through their shock and grief. On the phone with me in the early days, she had given me hope—not hope for a cure, or even the promise of a return to happiness, but the optimism that I would "make meaning" from my journey. Brad Lander, the New York city council member with whom I had built Local Progress, shared with me a similar sentiment: that if I spent my remaining days purposefully, I would "find peace." These thoughts buoyed me in my darkest hours. They acknowledged the enormity of my personal tragedy while reminding me that I still had good reasons to live, important goals to pursue. "I know that you will guide us through this," my stepmother had said in an early-morning phone call the day after my diagnosis. "Just like you always do." I appreciated the vote of confidence, and I wanted to make it true.

A few days after Thanksgiving, Rachael and I went to Massachusetts General Hospital to meet with Dr. Merit Cudkowicz, one of the leading ALS doctors in the country. Her last name is pronounced nothing like it looks, so everyone just calls her Dr. Merit. My aunt Deb had gotten the appointment for me. The neurology department waiting room was jam-packed with patients, most of whom were much older than me. Merit met us in a small examination room but didn't do any examination. She had my records from Santa Barbara and Cedars-Sinai in Los Angeles, and felt no need to revisit the diagnosis. Instead she jumped right into a discussion of treatment options.

First was riluzole, which was the only drug approved by the FDA to treat ALS. That approval was based on studies that had shown that riluzole slowed down the progression of the disease slightly, extending life expectancy by a few months. Back in Santa Barbara, Dr. DaSilva had put me on a standard two-pill-a-day regimen; Merit suggested that I double my dose. Should I also take vitamin E, vitamin D, the coenzyme Q10, and alpha-lipoic acid, as a family member had recommended to me? Sure, she said. None of that would hurt and might even help.

Next she suggested that I inject myself with an enormous quantity of vitamin B12. There was some evidence that this, too, slowed the progression of the disease. It wasn't an FDA-approved treatment, so my insurance would not cover it. But for $300 a month I could get a compounding pharmacy in New Jersey to ship me refrigerated boxes of shots, which I could inject relatively painlessly into my butt. Merit failed to tell me that the most immediate and noticeable impact of the B12 shots would be to turn my urine bright red.

Merit continued to lay out a dizzying array of different potential treatment options, jotting them down on a blank sheet of paper. None of these had been proven to help, but there was reason to be optimistic about each of them. Masitinib was currently being sold in Europe to treat dog cancer; preliminary studies showed that it might also be effective against ALS. NP001 was being tested in a new clinical trial; I was welcome to enroll in it, either at Mass General or closer to home, at UC Irvine. Merit had recently completed a phase 2 trial of tirasemtiv, which had actually led to an increase in muscle strength among the patients who had been able to persevere through the intense nausea that the drug produced. One particularly exciting option was edaravone, a powerful antioxidant that was administered intravenously ten to fifteen days a month. It had been approved for ALS in Japan a couple years ago, and the company that manufactured it was waiting on approval from the FDA as well. But Merit knew a doctor in Tokyo who treated international patients, and she could put me in touch if I was interested. Finally, there was the promise of stem cell treatment. Taken either from the patient's own bone marrow or a fetal line, the hope was that stem cells would either replace my dying motor neurons or help clean their environment so they could live longer. Merit had recently collaborated on a phase 2 trial with an Israeli company called BrainStorm Cell Therapeutics, and she hoped to soon begin a phase 3 trial as well.

I was bewildered by the scope of different options that she had described, and I didn't even try to follow her simplified explanation of the mechanisms by which these drugs might treat my ALS. Rachael did a better job of keeping everything straight. Mainly I was surprised by how hopeful and proactive Merit seemed. Back in Los Angeles, Dr. Baloh had told me that there were no good treatment options; not even riluzole, which the FDA had approved, would do much to help me. By contrast, Merit told me to double my dose of riluzole and offered five to eight other possibilities that were worth exploring. Her assistant took a blood sample from me to see if I would qualify for the NP001 trial, and I headed out into the cold Boston rain with a new bounce in my step. That night, driving down I-95 to New York City with Rachael and Carl and my cousin, I turned up the volume on Mumford & Sons and drummed on the steering wheel as their banjo tap-danced off the walls. If each of these interventions slowed down the pace of my decline by 10 or 20 percent and those benefits were cumulative, then I could buy real time—maybe even enough time to live to see a cure.

A couple nights later the excitement of our visit with Dr. Merit had worn off, but the permanence of ALS remained. I sat, nearly comatose with depression, in the living room of my father's Upper West Side apartment with Rachael, my college buddy Carlo, and his wife, Dorothy, who was a child psychiatrist. Six weeks earlier, in a late night FaceTime consult, Dorothy had urged me to be gentle with myself, to permit myself to be distraught, infuriated, and dysfunctional. But now she took a different approach. It was time for me to get back to living. I needed to exercise the mind control that Pema Chödrön and Dash and Jon Kabat-Zinn had taught me. And I could start by focusing on concrete, physical tasks. I shouldn't leave all the housework to Rachael, thinking I need not spend my remaining time doing dishes; instead I should see that work as an opportunity to focus on something other than myself, other than ALS.

Dorothy's tough-love pep talk was a landmark for me. For seven weeks I had cycled through bouts of despair, insight, and meta-despair: despair at my diagnosis, insight about the need for mindful redirection, and meta-despair at my inability to fill that prescription. Dorothy told me it was time to end that cycle. Time to do what I knew needed to be done.

Halfway through dinner, Carlo noted that I suddenly seemed like my old healthy self: cracking vulgar jokes, asking insightful questions, and rudely telling people why their political opinions were wrong. I told him that his wife was a good doctor.

The following afternoon I jogged into Central Park with my stepmother, Pamela, and headed for the reservoir. There were many brown leaves on the ground and a few remaining in the trees; the paths were filled with righteous New Yorkers burning off their turkey and stuffing. My left foot was misbehaving, and I had to work hard to keep up even a moderate jog. After rounding the reservoir, we stopped on the north side to catch our breath and stretch. We looked down at the crisp skyline on Central Park South. We walked west. Squirrels scampered up and down the trees. The smell of roasted nuts wafted through the air.

"Thanks for the good run," I said.

"Thank *you*," Pamela replied.

Neither of us knew it would be my last one, ever.

In the weeks after my diagnosis, I asked myself a question that everyone struck by misfortune asks: Why me? My world had been overturned while all around me life proceeded apace. Among the various texts I turned to to help me process my new reality was *When Breath Becomes Air*, Paul Kalanithi's beautiful meditation about dying from cancer at age thirty-six. In it, Paul wrote that the correct answer to the question "Why me?" is "Why *not* me?" And that certainly was a compelling and succinct response. But to me it was incomplete.

Many of my undergraduate classmates from Columbia went to work on Wall Street, executing schemes like the packaging and selling of fraudulent mortgage-backed securities that brought down the economy, costing millions of people their jobs and homes. Others became consultants to the oil and gas industry, which is destroying our planet and displacing millions of farmers and city dwellers from Brazil to Mali to Bangladesh. And they have been paid handsomely for their labor.

Likewise, most of my law school classmates—even at a place like Yale, which prides itself on its students' commitment to public service—have gone on to work for fancy corporate law firms, where they help multinational companies lower their tax burdens (cue Paul Ryan saying we can't afford to expand Medicaid for poor children because of the budget deficit) or eliminate the competition via mergers (watch as your cable company jacks up its rates for monopoly-sized profits) or advise major employers on how to develop "union avoidance strategies" (watch as Latino immigrants get fired for speaking up about health and safety conditions on the job, and American inequality skyrockets as unions lose their power to raise wages for working people). For their labors, my classmates have been earning hundreds of thousands of dollars a year; as they start making partner, in their mid-thirties, it will be closer to a million.

(Of course, many of my classmates have used their first training for incredible ends: They are suing to improve conditions in the most horrendous prisons of the Deep South and protect civilians from police misconduct; they work every day to prevent the deportation of children and parents back to countries where they will be impoverished and persecuted; they rushed to John F. Kennedy International Airport and then into federal court to stop the Trump administration's "Muslim ban"; they helped Florida farmworkers win historic wage increases that have transformed their lives . . . The list goes on and on.)

I was no saint. No martyr. I was compensated generously for my work and derived psychological satisfaction from it. But I also dedicated my entire career to the public interest—to promoting justice and equity for people who deserved it and did not have it. In the past decade, I've helped improve the lives of millions of people by coauthoring the law that guaranteed paid sick days to all workers in New York City; by helping end the abuse of stop-and-frisk against millions of black and Latinx New Yorkers; and by moving the Federal Reserve to adopt policies that prioritize job creation and wage growth for the American public. And I thought I had forty more years ahead of me to try to do it again and again. I realize I might come across as a self-important blowhard for saying this, but I honestly think that my work is more valuable than that of many of the privileged elite with whom I studied. Is it offensive to say, therefore, that my life is more valuable, too? Offensive but, perhaps, accurate.

So when I asked "Why me?" I was also asking the rather mean-spirited question "Why not them?" Why is ALS destroying *my* life, which has so often been focused on improving the lives of others? Why not destroy the life of somebody who has enriched himself at the expense of others? As Rachael said to me, lying in bed a mere month after my diagnosis, "You get ALS and fucking Donald Trump gets to be president."

And so, for me, a more complete and satisfactory answer to the question "Why me?" is "Because the world is unjust."

People with less privilege than I know this and live this reality every day. When an immigrant nail salon worker in Queens is told by her boss that she's not going to be paid this week, she's outraged but not surprised: the world has never treated her fairly or justly. When a black man sees a promotion go to his incompetent white coworker, or feels the aggressive hands of a police officer on his body during an unjustified stop-and-frisk, his dignity is under assault in a familiar way: for black people in America, racial discrimination is a fact of daily life.

And, of course, I, too, knew that the world is unjust: I had read about and witnessed and fought against the injustices of poverty and oppression and hatred. But until my diagnosis, the world had not visited its injustice upon my shoulders; I had seen its effects but had not yet felt them myself. As it has for other middle- and upper-class people of my race, global capitalism and America's commitment to white supremacy have redounded to my benefit. And, indeed, I have built a successful career and a proud self-identity upon confronting those injustices. In that strange way, I have benefited from them doubly.

The injustice of ALS was, of course, different. It hurt worse than wage theft and job discrimination. But it was also not the fault of greedy employers or racist politicians. Scientists may eventually discover some of the environmental factors that contributed to my ALS. Perhaps polluting multinationals are to blame. But we don't know, and that level of culpability is surely less direct.

Unlike the victims of lung cancer or heart disease, I probably couldn't blame deceptive cigarette and fast food companies for my illness. And unlike the victims of the HIV epidemic, I couldn't blame the religious fundamentalists who outlawed sex education and needle exchanges and who for decades forced queer Americans into the closet, or even the rapacious pharmaceutical companies who charged such exorbitant prices for medicine that people in most of the world couldn't afford them. Who was the villain in my story?

Perhaps I could blame the politicians and the weapons manufacturers who connived to spend our public dollars on bombs instead of on scientific and medical research. Perhaps I could blame the billionaires who used their power in pursuit of a lower tax rate, or the ideologues who tried to shrink the American government to such a small size that it could be "drowned in a bathtub." Maybe I could even blame the religious fundamentalists' opposition to fetal stem cell research, which delayed new therapies by years or decades. But these were generic villains; their liability for my ALS attenuated at best.

My villain, I came to realize, was older than they were, as old as humanity itself: for thirty-two years, Lady Luck was on my side; she bestowed upon me nearly everything that I wanted. And then she changed her mind.

By early January, Rachael and I had decided that it was worth trying to push back on Lady Luck and demand that she repair some of the destruction she had wrought. We decided, that is, to explore the experimental medicines that Dr. Merit had told us about. In the middle of the night I logged into Skype and started calling Japan in search of Dr. Hiide Yoshino. After a few tries, I reached his clinic and was told to call back the next day when he would be available to speak with me. By the end of the week Rachael and I had plane tickets and an Airbnb reservation on the east side of the sprawling Tokyo metropolis. Neither the medicine nor Yoshino's services would be very expensive. Best-case scenario, we slowed down my ALS; worst-case scenario, we had a fun trip to an amazing new place.

We left Carl with my mother and drove to LAX. One flight, two trains, a bus, and a short walk later brought us to the Yoshino Neurology Clinic. The waiting room was filled with frail elderly folks; we immediately made eye contact and smiled at a middle-aged black couple who stood out just as much as we did. They were from Wyoming. Roscoe had been diagnosed two years earlier; his arm was totally useless and his torso was weak, but he still spoke and walked easily. He was the first person living with ALS I had ever met.

Dr. Yoshino performed a standard examination on me to get a baseline. A nurse took some blood; then I was hooked up to an IV bag from which transparent saline and mystical edaravone dripped into my arm for forty-five minutes. Dr. Yoshino had authored two of the earliest studies on the use of edaravone to treat ALS and had more clinical experience with the drug than anyone else in the world. He told me that he had seen it slow the progression of many of his patients. One young patient from the United States had witnessed the twitching in his arm disappear only hours after his first infusion. Yoshino was giving me real reason for hope.

For five days that week, Rachael and I settled into a wonderful routine: we woke up around seven a.m. and took the crowded commuter train east; we disembarked and then enjoyed a pastry and coffee at the Francophile bakery in the train station; then we took a bus fifteen minutes to Dr. Yoshino's clinic, where I received an infusion and we compared ALS notes with Roscoe and his wife. By eleven Rachael and I were free to gallivant around the city. Rachael took responsibility for all the planning, but I can't blame that traditional, gendered distribution of labor on my ALS, since it had been going on for a decade. The endless urban vistas from the Tokyo Skytree lattice tower; the controlled mayhem of the Shibuya crossing, where gazillions of pedestrians converged and then dissipated with each new "walk" light; the ostentatious materialism of the Harajuku shopping district, nearly indistinguishable from Rodeo Drive or Fifth Avenue, except for the orderly line of two hundred young people waiting on the sidewalk to go into a nondescript building; the surprisingly deserted and tranquil paths lined with towering oak and camphor trees, leading up to the Meiji Shrine, where one of the hundreds of wooden *ema* plaques jumped out at me, praying as it did to "END ALS."

There was so much to see and even more to eat. Vegetable tempura washed down with easy-to-drink Japanese lager; *toro*, the fatty part of tuna, at a bustling shop on the outskirts of the famed, gargantuan Tsukiji fish market; a two-inch-thick pork chop, breaded and deep-fried rare, just the way I love it, at the smooth oak bar of a dimly lit, silent tavern; a giant bowl of umami-rich pork broth ramen overflowing with wide, chewy hand-pulled noodles, worth every painful second of the hour-long wait in the freezing cold that the hip Japanese youth had charged us for the privilege of sharing their favorite spot. We had never eaten so well in our lives. There's something deeply discordant about fatal-disease tourism, like a cruel and compressed version of *1,000 Places to See Before You Die*. But I was working hard to savor every bite and every moment.

On Friday, Dr. Yoshino and his staff gave us a six-month supply of edaravone, which we stuffed into an oversized suitcase, and a prescription letter to wave in self-defense in case we got stopped by U.S. Customs and Border Protection. We gave him a box of chocolates in appreciation for his care, and we wished Roscoe good luck. Then we boarded a train out of town, heading for the healing hot springs of Hakone, in Kanagawa Prefecture.

With each passing hour, I felt more and more like Hans Castorp, the chronically ill protagonist of Thomas Mann's *The Magic Mountain*, whose search for health took him to the alpine air and water. We transferred from our modern train to a much smaller and older variety, which slowly winded its way up steep mountain slopes and deposited us at the foot of an even steeper funicular, which we rode ever higher. At the top, we rolled our suitcases down a quiet snowy road—my steps deliberate and cautious, like an old man who is no longer sure of his balance—and turned left into our *onsen* (hot spring) hotel.

We immediately traded our shoes for slippers and were shown upstairs to our room, where mattresses were unrolled on the floor. In the evening Rachael helped me maneuver my legs under the low table and propped me up with some pillows; the staff then delivered a string of courses, each more elaborate and colorful than the one before, with countless small bowls of fish and vegetables, steamed and smoked, pickled and braised. I delighted over the presentation, even though the flavors could not compete with Tokyo's offerings.

After dinner we each headed for the indoor hot springs on the floor above, separated by gender. Mine was deserted, dimly lit, and warm. The sulfuric, opaque, steaming water was piped up from the natural springs below. I disrobed, rinsed off, and climbed in. In breath. Out breath. The condensation on the glass. The sound of trickling water. The minerals on my wrinkled fingertips. I stepped outside, where two white bathtubs sat overflowing with water piped into them by bamboo tubes; snowflakes danced their way out of the sky and past my balcony. In breath. Out breath. *This moment,* I told myself. *Right here. Right now.*

I turned the pampering knob up to 11 and called for a masseuse to come to our room. She pounded and pulled on my limbs and left me a gelatinous pile on the floor, sleeping peacefully.

The next day we joined the stream of tourists traipsing through the sights of Hakone, aided by the multimodal transportation network: an antique cruise ship across the lake, a bus up the mountain for a close-up view of Mount Fuji, a ropeway gondola soaring above the winter landscape. And then back to the train station, where we headed for the final destination on our trip.

Kamakura was the twelfth-century feudal capital of Japan, and it has the shrines to prove it. We started at the Daibutsu, a forty-foot bronze Buddha that had been sitting for eight hundred years. He had survived so many wars and earthquakes and fires. My life was a blink of his eye. The next shrine had incredible flora, even though we were too early for the famed cherry blossoms. But after the third one, nestled in a towering bamboo forest, my left leg revolted. Walking was suddenly painful. My body was decaying. No amount of denial or mindfulness could change that reality. And if a week of treatment was any indication, edaravone couldn't, either. My twitching, unlike that of Dr. Yoshino's earlier American patient, was still going strong.

When we got back to Santa Barbara, I turned my attention to the task of designing a system for administering my new drug. No licensed medical professional in the U.S. would be comfortable giving me the drug on a regular basis, since it wasn't approved by the FDA. Rachael was up to the challenge, but she needed training, equipment, and a plan. Nurses at Yoshino's clinic had connected the IV to a vein in my arm, pricking me each day anew. I worried that this wouldn't work for me and Rachael: it would be tricky, painful, and damaging to my veins over the medium term. Instead, my aunt Deb found me a local oncologist—much closer to the end of his career than the beginning—who was willing to order the placement of a PICC line in my arm and teach Rachael how to access it. From then on I walked around with a thin plastic tube hanging out of my biceps, secured with a short white fishnet stocking. To shower or swim, I slipped on a rubber sleeve and suctioned out the air with a small rubber pump. And fifteen evenings per month, after a day of teaching and research and an evening of cooking, cleaning, and child care, Rachael became my infusion nurse and went through a elaborate, regimented recipe: Put on gloves, break the ampule, fill the syringe, inject into the saline, hook up the secondary IV line, clean the PICC line, attach the two tubes, open the line. . . and then pray that the dripping begins. I was responsible for sourcing our contraband paraphernalia, including the saline, the price of which was being artificially inflated by the duopoly that controlled its manufacture in the United States.

Having a PICC line led to plenty of curious glances and dispiriting conversations, so I was glad to eventually trade it in for a port—shaped like a Ping-Pong ball cut in half—implanted just under the skin in my right peck. The kind oncologist gave us a prescription for Huber needles, and Rachael learned to stab confidently until the tip of the needle met the small metal plate in the back of the port. Things got simpler in the fall of 2017, after the FDA approved edaravone and a visiting-nurse agency provided us with all the equipment and medicine we needed. Our costs went down, but the costs to the American public skyrocketed, because the brand-name price was fifty times more than I had been paying to my generic distributor in India.

For a few precious months in the spring of 2017, we managed to settle into a rhythm that approximated our pre-diagnosis life. I returned to working on both Fed Up and Local Progress, albeit at a less ambitious pace. I dedicated real time to my health, swimming at the local YMCA, going to physical and occupational therapy for stretching and light exercise, seeing a kind and thoughtful psychotherapist each week to help me work through the difficulties, and doing my calf exercises during conference calls. I also returned to a basic role as a father and husband, picking Carl up from school, cooking dinner, bathing him and putting him to sleep, and doing the dishes—deliberately, with as much focus and calm as I could muster. We had not returned to parity—Rachael was still doing much more of the housework and child care—but I was no longer depressed, and we had a real partnership again.

But it could not last.

CHAPTER FIVE

LOCAL PROGRESS

I kissed Rachael and gave a goodbye head rub to each of our beloved gray-and-white cats, Francesca and her litter-mate big brother, Dante. Then I left our Astoria apartment and joined the stream of commuters heading down into the subway. On the humid platform I was happy that the dress code at my new job encouraged jeans and a T-shirt. After three stops on the M train, I followed the underground signs pointing me toward a mythical creature about which I had only ever heard urban legends. The G train was subject to frequent derision and mockery. "Does it really exist?" Manhattanites asked with a grin. "Nobody has ever actually seen it," came the condescending reply. I stood on the platform at its northern Queens terminus, peering down the dark track, looking for evidence of its potential arrival. The other dozen people waiting with me seemed unconcerned, so I, too, scrolled through my phone.

Eventually two white lights emerged from the darkness and ushered the short, four-car train into the station. We shuffled on and spread out in the cool, air-conditioned car, each occupying a different segment, keenly aware that our compatriots around the city were jammed together like sardines. The train reversed directions, slowly chugging its way south toward Brooklyn.

I exited six stops later onto Flushing Avenue. I pulled out my phone, which told me to walk twelve minutes west. I passed rows of dreary beige-brick apartment buildings with bars on the windows and trash cans parked out front. There were no trees on the narrow sidewalks, which were littered with detritus. On the south side of the street, a few black men were playing basketball on a court inside the Marcy Houses projects; across the street, Hasidic women with long black skirts and headscarves pushed strollers and ushered along large posses of children. I passed kosher groceries and a small factory where workers were manufacturing doors, then turned left up the hill onto Kent Avenue.

Casa Kent, as we would soon christen the building, was a three-story brown-brick house, with beautiful hardwood floors and a wide spiral staircase. The furnishings were still sparse, but my comrades had already begun to adorn the walls with colorful revolutionary posters. I was greeted by my boss, Amy Carroll—a tall, charismatic thirty-seven-year-old whose one-two approach to banter was to disarm you with genuine warmth and then smack you across the face with her vulgar sarcasm. "Welcome to our wonderful new home," she said, "right here in the filthy armpit of Brooklyn."

It was the second time in my short career that she had hired me. She had been the legal director at Make the Road New York when I got a fellowship to work there the year after law school, and she had then left to found the Center for Popular Democracy with her boss Andrew Friedman, who was a bit older, a lot balder, and only a little less vulgar than she was. They had asked me to join them in their new venture because I was, to use Amy's favorite word, scrappy.

Over the preceding fifteen years, Make the Road New York had become an institution in the city by providing crucial services to its

Latinx membership and organizing them into a potent political force. By 2012, Andrew and Amy were ready for a new challenge, and the mission of the Center for Popular Democracy would be to help community-based organizations learn from one another and build power through the provision of services, leadership development, and political mobilization. As we explained in our promotional material and grant applications, we would help our partner organizations build their muscle and flex it in pursuit of a pro-worker, pro-immigrant, racial justice agenda.

Most community organizations that engage in politics focus on the local. The city council is where you go to get more funding for your neighborhood after-school program, to strengthen protections for tenants facing eviction, to win paid sick days or fair schedules for workers, or to demand accountability in the aftermath of a police shooting. Local governments make many of the quotidian decisions that impact residents' lives. And, of course, it's also where you focus your energy if you have limited political power. It is much easier to influence the vote of a council member than a member of Congress.

This was particularly true in the fall of 2012. With Republicans controlling the House and the Senate, there was no hope of progressive change coming from Washington, D.C. With Republicans also in charge of most state legislatures, progressives' primary opportunity for enacting an affirmative agenda was at the local level. I had been hired at CPD to try to improve the ability of community-based organizations to win progressive victories at the local level by building a network of progressive legislators. While many city council members around the country shared strong social justice values and confronted many of the same challenges, there was no place for them to come together to build solidarity and share their experiences and best practices. Hence my job, building what we called at first the National Municipal Policy Network.

Our first conference was scheduled for early December, so I had ten weeks to prepare. I wrote up a dozen policy briefs highlighting the best practices from cities around the country on issues like protecting worker rights, empowering immigrant communities, and building affordable housing. I worked to line up a series of policy panels, and I cold-called council members from around the country, inviting them to attend.

In a small windowless room in a Washington, D.C., hotel, our embryonic board of directors met the morning before our conference began. A dozen of us sat around the table; although I didn't know it at the time, our group included three of the most accomplished local legislators in the country: Wilson Goode of Philadelphia, Brad Lander of New York, and Nick Licata of Seattle. In the years before and after that meeting, the three of them would author and shepherd to passage dozens of major laws on nearly every conceivable topic. Also at the table were council members from smaller jurisdiction, like Faith Winter of Westminster, Colorado—an organizer who went on to train hundreds of aspiring candidates for office—and Karundi Williams, representing the Service Employees International Union, which was investing in our nascent effort as part of its long-term agenda to build progressive power in America. There was plenty of kibitzing and a bit of grandstanding in that first meeting, but we did accomplish one important task: coming up with a better name for our network. We settled on Local Progress, which conveyed the two central ideas behind our project.

As we wrapped up our day-and-a-half-long conference, it became clear that we had already begun to achieve two of our stated goals: helping elected officials learn about best practices from one another and from the policy experts whom we had assembled in the room, and giving them a space to build relationships and solidarity with one another, which was a precious opportunity for progressive elected officials, who are often surrounded by colleagues more interested in self-aggrandizement, machine politics, or neo-liberal policy than in pursuing social justice. And because Local Progress would be housed at the Center for Popular Democracy, we were confident we could help deepen relationships between progressive elected officials and members of grassroots community-based organizations, in order to strengthen the practice of "outside/inside" organizing that can be critical not only to winning specific campaigns but to building relationships and power for the longer term. But we hadn't yet developed a theory of how we might accomplish our broader goal: getting elected officials from cities around the country to move forward on a shared agenda in a coordinated way that would enhance local policy, and simultaneously help advance the national political discourse.

As with many start-up projects, our challenge with Local Progress was to build the plane while we were flying it. We needed to convince elected officials that we had something valuable to offer them. But it was hard to offer them much of value with only a few part-time staffers working on the project. So we simultaneously had to persuade some nonprofit and labor funders that it was worth investing in our network of elected officials even as the network was tiny and weak. Whenever I fretted that our promotional material was overstating the extent of our work, Amy would flash her big grin and remind me to put my head down, work hard, and "fake it till we make it."

The first opportunity to make it came in early 2014, when our board chairman, Nick Licata, called my cell phone with an idea. The city of Seattle was considering establishing a minimum wage of $15 an hour for all workers and he thought that Local Progress could be helpful. Opponents of the measure were arguing that Seattle would be venturing into dangerous, uncharted territory with such a high minimum wage, so Nick thought that it would be a good idea show them that many other cities were also moving forward on a bold workers' rights agenda and that if Seattle paved the way, others would follow. We got to work planning a symposium—cum—pep rally that would showcase the rising municipal workers' rights agenda in America.

The new mayor of Seattle had recently set up an advisory committee of community, labor, and business leaders, along with a few elected officials, including Nick. He hoped that the committee would reach consensus on the important, controversial details: how high to set the minimum wage, over what time frame to raise it, and whether or not to include any carve-outs for workers like waiters who receive tips. The event that Nick had asked me to help produce was meant to offer answers those questions, and it featured an array of voices ranging from skeptical business leaders on the center-right to Kshama Sawant on the left. Kshama had recently been elected to the city council, running as a member of the Socialist Alternative, and her unapologetic commitment to equity and justice had excited a large portion of the Seattle public, which has for many decades included a significant radical contingent. To my dismay, she was even too much of a purist to join the membership of Local Progress: we weren't left enough for her and her base. (This prefigured by five years some of the tension on display today, with activists from the Democratic Socialists of America and other movements pushing progressives to be bolder and move faster—a dynamic that I generally think is good.)

Nick's theory was that the symposium could highlight the smart policy reasons for raising the minimum wage significantly and also permit Kshama and her allies to showcase the public enthusiasm behind the idea. Together, he hoped, the strong evidence and the political energy would force the mayor and the committee's business leaders to support the reform. In the end, it worked like a charm.

In a large auditorium on a local college campus, about five hundred people gathered for the one-day event. The panels featured smart, progressive economists laying out the rationale for raising the wage and dispelling the notion that it might lead to significant job losses or business closures; a dozen Local Progress members from Philadelphia, New York, Chicago, and various California cities explaining how their local governments were also moving forward with plans to raise wages; and inspiring speeches from workers and their allies, met with boisterous support from the audience, which included a large contingent of red-shirted Socialist Alternative members.

As the day came to a close, Nick and I huddled in the lobby. He seemed very pleased. No new decisions had been made, and he had yet to receive any new commitments from the mayor or the business leaders, but he felt like the event had meaningfully strengthened his bargaining position. He promised to keep me updated on the internal deliberations. We hugged, and I headed for the airport with a new bounce in my step. Our political project was finally paying some real dividends.

Within a few months, Seattle had passed a $15 minimum wage, although the phase-in period was significantly longer than Kshama and Nick had hoped it would be. Nevertheless, it was a watershed moment in American politics. The "Fight for $15 and a Union" had shifted the goalposts dramatically: whereas President Obama had recently called for a hike in the federal minimum wage to $9 per hour, the protests and strikes by fast-food workers around the country had roused the conscience of the nation, putting on stark display the immorality of billionaire CEOs profiting by keeping their workers unstable, insecure, and poor. What began as an organizing drive among black and brown fast-food workers in Brooklyn, coordinated by New York Communities for Change, spread rapidly across the country with the support of the Service Employees International Union. Seattle's move was a breakthrough in the campaign to reset the terms of the debate. From that moment onward, progressives could argue from a more principled and rational position: that the minimum wage should be set at a level that permits a worker to raise a family and live with dignity, not in poverty. We still are far from winning the argument. The federal minimum wage remains stuck at $7.25 per hour. But the American people support raising it significantly, and we now have robust evidence from many different cities where elected officials partnered with social movements to follow Seattle's lead—from New York City to Oakland, from Los Angeles to Chicago—that significantly higher minimum wages can reduce poverty dramatically and do not lead to significant job losses. More than 25 million Americans have seen their pay grow due to minimum-wage increases at the local or state level, with more than 10 million winning raises up to $15 per hour. And someday soon, when Congress is controlled by more compassionate elected officials, our federal policy will follow in the footsteps of Seattle and the other cities that blazed a trail forward.

Back in New York, the battle over workers' right to live with dignity was playing out under different political circumstances. Among the many ways in which America's brand of capitalism lags behind the rest of the rich world is our foolish failure to guarantee the right of workers to take a day off when they are sick. Although white-collar professionals, government employees, and unionized workers are generally allowed to take five or ten paid sick days every year, 40 percent of private-sector workers in America have no such protection. That means that they must either show up to work sick or give up pay and risk losing their jobs while they stay home to recuperate. It also means that working parents are forced to improvise whenever their sick children need to stay home from school. (We know how difficult this is firsthand: Carl has had to stay home from the germ factory that is day care at least ten times a year. We're lucky that Rachael has a flexible schedule, but most folks don't.)

Beginning in 2007, American cities began to try to address this problem with local laws that guaranteed workers the right to take a handful of paid sick days every year to care for themselves or their close relatives. The paid-sick-days movement was a particularly exciting one for progressives working at the municipal level, because it represented a clear opportunity to improve workers' lives through local legislation. One of the enduring frustrations for city council members and advocates like myself is that, in most American states, the authority of cities to pass local laws is severely constrained. Most cities, for example, are prohibited by state law from establishing minimum wages for private-sector workers or imposing new taxes to raise revenue. (In Washington State and California, cities are explicitly empowered to set minimum wages, which is one reason why Seattle and San Francisco were on the vanguard of the municipal minimum-wage movement. New York City was granted the authority to set a higher minimum wage only after labor unions and other progressive organizations put significant pressure on Governor Andrew Cuomo to amend the state law.)

However, the vast majority of American cities have the legal authority to guarantee the right to take paid sick days because the regulation falls under the general power to protect the public's health and safety. Keeping sick workers and sick children at home reduces the spread of disease. By 2012 the movement to guarantee paid sick days had racked up victories in San Francisco, Seattle (thanks again to Nick Licata's leadership), and Washington, D.C., and the battle had now reached New York City. A robust coalition of labor unions, public health advocates, community-based organizations, and feminist organizations were pushing for enactment through the city council. Their rallies and press conferences always had a good visual hook: rows of strollers, doctors and nurses in their scrubs, the icky mascot Germy, a reminder that nobody wants their cook or waitress to come to work while sick. My friend Emmanuel Caicedo of the Working Families Party had been tasked with coordinating the coalition, and Amy and I had joined the legal team and were responsible for drafting a proposed ordinance.

We faced two major obstacles. Mayor Michael Bloomberg was

fiercely opposed to any new protections for workers. And, frustratingly, he had a strong ally, Christine Quinn, in the Speaker's chair at the city council. The Speaker controlled which bills get to the floor and receive a vote—which meant that, in practice, nothing passed if it didn't have the Speaker's support. For more than three years Quinn had done the mayor's bidding and prevented a vote on the paid-sick-days ordinance. She did this even though the bill had the support of an overwhelming number of city council members—enough, most likely, to override a veto from the mayor.

Our coalition had two reasons to believe that now, in 2013, we might finally be in a position to overcome Bloomberg and Quinn's opposition. First, it was an election year, and Christine Quinn was running for mayor. (Bloomberg was term-limited out.) Guaranteeing paid sick days was enormously popular, especially among the Democratic primary voters who would determine her fate. Second, our allies on the city council had succeeded in building significant power, particularly through the creation of a progressive caucus. Of the fifty-one members of the New York City Council, forty-six were Democrats. But many of them, like Christine Quinn, were more accountable to the Democratic machine and the city's business lobby than they were to the middle- and working-class people who made up the bulk of Democratic voters in the city. Beginning in 2009 the Working Families Party had begun to try to change the balance of power within the council by electing genuine progressives to office and then organizing them into a caucus. By mid-2013 the caucus had eleven members and was led by Melissa Mark-Viverito of Harlem and Brad Lander of Park Slope, Brooklyn (who had come up with the idea of building Local Progress and enlisted the Center for Popular Democracy in staffing it). The caucus was challenging Christine Quinn for power and seeking to expand its membership in the upcoming election by winning many more council races around the city. The paid-sick-days fight was a perfect vehicle for that political objective because it highlighted how Quinn was blocking progressive legislation at the behest of Bloomberg and the business lobby.

One Thursday evening in February, I traveled uptown with my seventeen-year-old brother, Muki, and my comrades from CPD to attend a mayoral candidate forum we were cosponsoring along with a number of other groups from the paid-sick-days coalition. We passed various protesters and speechifiers as we entered the large church and took our seats near the back. Héctor Figueroa, the president of 32BJ Service Employees International Union, a union that represented janitors, security guards, and doormen throughout the city, welcomed the audience. He decried the widespread poverty in a city of such great wealth and highlighted the importance of the elections that were coming up later that year. Onstage, Christine Quinn was joined by a crew of candidates who were both more progressive than she was and were trailing her in the polls. The moderator probed the candidates about their positions on a series of policies that were in front of council—a living wage law for city contractors, reform of the police department's stop-and-frisk program, and, of course, the paid-sick-days ordinance. Public Advocate Bill de Blasio used his towering frame and baritone voice to decry the tale of two cities that was playing out every day in New York. He was strongly in favor of paid sick days, he said, and it was Christine Quinn's fault for blocking the measure. The other candidates piled on, to increasingly enthusiastic cheers, and then, when Quinn attempted to defend her actions by saying that the city's economy was not strong enough to accommodate a mandatory paid-sick-days law, the audience heckled and booed her. Muki and I were eager participants in raising the volume of opposition.

32BJ had been an important ally of Quinn in the preceding years, but that candidate forum in Harlem made clear to Héctor Figueroa that she had to change her ways. He had seen firsthand his members' enthusiasm for paid sick days and a bold, progressive agenda. His union would not be able to endorse her, Figueroa told Quinn after the forum, unless she moved the paid sick-days-bill to passage. It was a crucial turning point.

A few weeks later, sensing that our political power was at a peak, the coalition and our allies in the Progressive Caucus decided that it was finally time to unveil our secret weapon. For more than two years we had mused about the possibility of forcing a vote on the legislation through the use of an esoteric procedural move called a petition to discharge. This mechanism, which also exists in the U.S. House of Representatives, permits the sponsor of a bill to force an up or down vote on it on the floor of the full legislature, rather than keeping it bottled up in committee (the motion is literally to discharge the the committee from further responsibility for the bill), if she or he can get a majority of the legislature to declare its support for such a vote.

In February, I had been asked to draft a legal memo explaining the mechanics of the discharge petition, based on the published rules of the city council. They required that seven members of the council, including the bill's sponsor, sign their names to a petition requesting a vote on the legislation. A few days later there would then be a vote of the full body about whether or not to vote on the bill itself. That vote required only a simple majority for passage. Although the discharge petition had long been part of the council's rules, nobody could point to a single time that it had ever been used. Doing so would be an affront to the authority of the Speaker, and there had never been a sufficient number of council members who were willing to stick their necks out and risk the retaliation that would surely ensue.

Finally, however, with a super-majority of members signed on as cosponsors of the bill, public sentiment on their side, elections fast approaching, and a coalition of advocates demanding action, the leadership of the Progressive Caucus was ready to act. One weekend morning in mid-March 2013, as I was lounging about our Astoria living room, Brad Lander called my cell phone with a few hyper-specific questions about the discharge petition. What words had to be used? Was there any particular format? If he was about to go after the Queen, he didn't want to get tripped up by a technicality. I spent my day trying to find answers and sent over a proposed petition for the bill's lead sponsor and him to use.

Later that week, a flurry of frantic emails and text messages indicated that the deed was under way. Brad had shared the petition with the sponsor of the bill, who had to be the first signature on the petition to discharge. Brad had then signed in the third spot, leaving room for someone else to sign second. He was willing to be the gang leader but preferred that his signature not be the first one that Quinn saw when she read the petition. In the search for additional signatures, Brad approached Donovan Richards, a twenty-nine-year-old who had just taken office that month, filling an open council seat in Queens. Few politicians would have the courage to challenge authority so early in their tenure, but when Brad asked him to sign, Donovan was fearless: Why did he run for office if not to help protect New York's workers? he asked, echoing the sentiment that I had heard the year before from Judge Shira Scheindlin.

A couple of days later, when Quinn was shown a copy of the petition with twelve signatures on it, she knew that her bluff had been called. She could no longer block the rising tide of support for the law, not with the Democratic primary for mayor coming up in September, and the crucial support of 32BJ at stake. So she told the bill's sponsor and the coalition that she would negotiate a compromise and bring it up for a vote. The petition was never formally filed, but it had done the work we needed it to do.

The coalition had a number of key demands. We wanted all workers to receive five paid sick days every year, wanted them to be available for use in cases of domestic violence and on behalf of sick relatives, wanted stiff penalties for employers who violated the law, wanted viable enforcement mechanisms, and wanted workers to be given notice of their newfound rights. The Speaker was opposed to all of these demands.

Over the coming couple of months, Amy and I joined a team of five coalition negotiators who engaged in hand-to-hand combat with the Speaker's lawyers over every sentence in the proposed law. Amy and I were particularly adamant that the law should contain strong enforcement mechanisms. At Make the Road New York, we had seen how employers regularly violated minimum-wage and overtime laws with impunity because workers had no good mechanisms for enforcing their rights without fear of retaliation. (And I had seen the same problem at Columbia University, where the anti-sweatshop rules were going unenforced, and in the Chinese restaurant case in law school, where wage, hour, and housing laws had been ignored).

We were determined that the same thing would not happen with this new right. We also knew that the New York law would become a model for municipalities around the country, and we wanted to set a high standard. We drove the Speaker's lawyers crazy. They were totally unaccustomed to this kind of back-and-forth. For years, they had drafted laws the way they wanted and presented them to other council members or advocates as faits accomplis. But the power dynamics were different than usual, so there were real compromises within the negotiations.

In May, with an agreement finally at hand, the city council passed the law with overwhelming support, making Mayor Bloomberg's veto irrelevant. At the press conference at City Hall before the vote, our coalition and Christine Quinn were all smiles, pretending that there had never been bad blood between us. Half an hour later, public advocate Bill de Blasio stood alone in the same spot, giving his own press conference criticizing Quinn for having been the roadblock, congratulating the coalition on our win, and insisting that as mayor he would champion an expansion of the paid-sick-days law to even cover workers at the smallest firms.

I felt sorry for him that day. He had been our champion during the winter, putting crucial pressure on Quinn to come to the negotiating table, and now she was reaping the political rewards while he stood alone. But of course it was de Blasio who had the last laugh. New York voters understood that he was the real progressive in the race, and neither 32BJ's endorsement nor Quinn's newfound support for the paid-sick-days law could salvage her reputation. In September de Blasio closed an enormous gap in the polls and swept to victory. We got our paid-sick-days law and a more progressive mayor. Across the city, with the support of the Working Families Party and grassroots groups like Make the Road Action and progressive labor unions, insurgent candidates for the city council won resounding victories and the progressive caucus grew to twenty members when the new session began in January. With so many votes and the new mayor's support, the caucus was able to elect its own cofounder, Melissa Mark-Viverito, to the Speaker's chair. All of a sudden a city that had for twenty years been governed by the anti-worker, pro–Wall Street mayors Giuliani and Bloomberg was now being led by proudly progressive Mayor de Blasio and Speaker Mark-Viverito.

In the ensuing years the paid-sick-days movement rode the momentum from New York to victories in three dozen cities and multiple states, including Connecticut and then California. We still haven't passed a federal law, but tens of millions of workers are now protected by these state and local ones.

In between these exciting policy victories came the less glamorous but crucial daily work of building the Local Progress network: recruiting new members, establishing meaningful relationships with them, giving them the one-on-one support that they need, holding workshops and conferences—essentially, organizing these independent political actors into a collective institution. For the first three years of the network's existence we muddled through this work, struggling to achieve significant growth or generate deep buy-in from more than a couple dozen of the network's leaders. That began to change in the spring of 2015, when an organizer named Sarah Johnson told me she might be interested in coming to work for the project.

Sarah and I had met three years earlier when I volunteered on an insurgent state assembly campaign that she was managing. We stayed in touch and then, at the end of 2013, our paths crossed again. From her perch at the Working Families Party, Sarah had been in charge of the citywide effort to elect enough progressive city council members to permit the progressive caucus to control the chamber. She had supervised all the different campaign managers across the city who were trying to elect a crop of young, primarily black and brown progressives against more establishment Democrats. More than anyone else, it was because of her that the caucus grew from eleven to twenty members after that fateful fall election.

In the weeks after the election, Brad Lander reached out to both Sarah and me to see if we would come work with him and Speaker Mark-Viverito in the new council. Both of us were honored by the offer and intrigued by the chance to help implement genuine progressive governance in the city.

But our personal lives got in the way. Rachael was wrapping up her dissertation at NYU and had applied to university teaching jobs around the country. She had a slew of job interviews and ultimately received a plum offer to become a tenure-track assistant professor in the English department at the University of California, Santa Barbara. It was an incredible job in an absolutely gorgeous part of the country, and since it was the only permanent job offer she received, there really was not much to discuss. She was going to move to Santa Barbara. We could have managed a long-distance relationship for a year or two, but it seemed foolish to me to start establishing deep professional connections in the New York City government if my partner was going to be in California. Much better, we both decided, for me to continue working with community-based organizations and local elected officials from around the country. Amy and Andrew were more than happy to let me keep working for the Center for Popular Democracy from home in Santa Barbara as long as I was willing to travel frequently. So I thanked Brad for the job offer but told him I was moving to sunnier environs.

Sarah found herself in a similar position. Her husband finished his psychiatry residency in New York and got a two-year fellowship in Boston; rather than spend every weekend on Amtrak, she decided she wanted a job that could travel with her from Boston to wherever they ended up next.

Over a hipster brunch in downtown Brooklyn, Sarah and I talked about how we might work together to make Local Progress into something powerful. Unlike me, Sarah had been trained as a real organizer. She had years of experience building relationships with elected officials, getting them to work together on a shared agenda and navigating complicated coalition politics. I had been trained as a lawyer and policy wonk and been shooting from the hip ever since I arrived at the Center for Popular Democracy. Whereas I was improvisational and impulsive, Sarah was methodical and strategic. She would make a perfect collaborator, bringing to the project all of the skills and experience that I lacked. I was overjoyed when she called to tell me that she would take the job as my co-director.

Over the following year, I watched as Sarah and Brad refined our vision for the network, laying out a series of goals and strategies that would attract new members, funders, and allies. From them I began to understand that there were two very different ways of engaging in politics, particularly from the perspective of an elected official. The approach most culturally familiar to us conceived of the elected official as the protagonist, a leader who could achieve policy and political victories that also promoted his (it is still almost always a man's) personal career ambitions. But there was a different way to engage in politics. You could play it as a team sport. And in this version, elected officials worked in partnership with one another—and with constituents and activists outside of government—to build their collective power and advance a shared agenda. In this version the elected official saw her (in this case, it's often a woman's) role not as protagonist and leader but as one important player with a particular set of tools and powers who could help advance the coalition's shared political project. Community organizations could identify problems and generate public demand for action; policy experts could adapt the existing best practices to fit the local policy political and legal environment; political operatives could help organize the institutional and media drumbeat to demand action; and elected officials could be vehicles for that action, pushing legislation forward and demanding that their colleagues get on board.

It was this second version of politics, I realized, that had led to the minimum-wage victory in Seattle and the paid-sick-days wins in New York and elsewhere. Elected officials had not been the leaders of those campaigns. They had been genuine partners with the outside advocates who were generating and marshaling public support for the policy changes. It was no coincidence that the same local legislators who had helped win so many legislative victories were the ones who had sat around our Washington, D.C., conference table at the first meeting of Local Progress: they were interested in building the network precisely because they knew that they would be most effective as members of a team and a movement.

I took two important lessons from those victories in Seattle and New York: first, the team sport version of politics is dramatically more effective and enjoyable than the protagonist version. Second, elected officials are afraid of being criticized, and therefore going on the offensive with bold demands and creative tactics is usually a much better way to get things done than asking nicely and being patient.

Over the next three years I watched with admiration as Sarah transformed the network. She implemented a deliberate plan to prioritize the recruitment of black and Latinx elected officials, particularly black and Latina women. She hired new organizers to focus on strengthening our work in the South. And, most importantly, she transformed the network by empowering the elected officials to take on real leadership over our programming and strategy, which led to incredible buy-in and enthusiasm from them.

Three days after my ALS diagnosis, I called Sarah to give her the news. She was predictably shocked and, like most people, didn't know what to say. I was relieved, however, to know that Local Progress would be in excellent hands without me. I could take a few months off to get my bearings without worrying that the network would suffer. In the aftermath of the Trump election victory, funders from progressive foundations were eager to identify ways they could invest in resistance. Sarah and the elected leadership of Local Progress provided that opportunity, and in the ensuing months local elected officials from our network played a key role in the resistance to Trump's Muslim ban and Jeff Sessions's policy of attacking sanctuary cities.

By 2018, Local Progress had grown to over eight hundred members, ten staff, and a $2 million annual budget. On issues from worker rights to affordable housing and from police accountability to immigrant empowerment, the members of Local Progress are achieving many of the most important progressive public policy victories in the country. In Philadelphia, Council Member Helen Gym sponsored a law to guarantee workers a predictable schedule and fair workweek; in Austin, Council Member Greg Casar passed laws protecting residents from deportation and reforming the police department; in Minneapolis, Council President Lisa Bender and a crew of other Local Progress members passed a comprehensive twenty-year plan to combat climate change and racial inequity through smart housing, infrastructure, and budget policies; and members like Ayanna Pressley of Boston and Jesús "Chuy" García of Chicago have graduated from Local Progress into high-profile seats in Congress.

To be clear, victories at the local level have their limitations. Ultimately, access to five paid sick days a year—while important and valuable—will not transform anybody's life. And although raising the national minimum wage to $15 would bring millions of people out of poverty, our movement has won this reform only in a few big cities. Still, these victories have altered the national political discourse, laying the groundwork for broader transformations, and the lessons I learned about listening carefully, collaborating deeply, making bold demands, and acting decisively apply equally to federal politics. Americans deserve a political revolution, and I believe that day is coming.

CHAPTER SIX

FED UP

I settled down into my aisle seat in the small commuter jet. The warm sunrise bathed the mountains in gold and made the white Spanish architecture of Santa Barbara's tiny airport pop. I exhaled and smiled with anticipation. This trip, in late August 2016, would be one to remember for me and my colleagues at the Center for Popular Democracy.

I looked at my phone. A group text chain informed me that my comrades' flights had left on time from Philadelphia, New York, and elsewhere, but that the weather at O'Hare might create connection problems later in the day. An email confirmed that our press advisory had been blasted out to the in-boxes of most of America's economics reporters. I'd been neither subtle nor modest when composing it: "7 Federal Reserve Presidents and Governor to Meet with Fed Up Coalition in Jackson Hole. Officials to field questions in unprecedented on-the-record session with 120 community leaders." I scrolled through Twitter to see what people were saying about the upcoming

Fed symposium in Wyoming's stunningly beautiful Grand Teton National Park and whether we were getting any coverage.

A tweet from Binyamin Appelbaum, the *New York Times'* chief Fed reporter, announced that he had just published his profile of the Fed Up campaign, previewing the meeting we were about to have in Jackson Hole: "A 32-year-old lawyer decided liberals should pay more attention to the Fed. So he launched a national movement." The tweet was a shot of adrenaline straight into my ego. It vindicated years of hard work dating back to my clerkship with Judge Scheindlin; it cast me as both a visionary and a movement builder; it said that I was shifting national politics to the left. It was exactly the public recognition that I had yearned and fought for.

Yet I knew that, to the movement allies with whom I worked most closely, the tweet's grandiosity, exaggeration, and internal incoherence would be clear: Fed Up was a very clever "grass-tops" campaign, one that paired savvy media work and political relationships with a light level of community-based organizing to create the veneer of mass support. By definition, a "national movement" could never be launched by one person. So long as Fed Up was the tightly controlled effort of a Yale-educated white male lawyer, it would never approach the transformative political power that would be unleashed by a genuine mass movement of organized working-class people who care deeply about the politics of money.

I quickly read the accompanying article, which gave a pretty fair summary of the campaign's successes over the past two years while also acknowledging that we had not yet shifted America's monetary policy. And it certainly cast me as the hero. None of the dozens of working-class people of color who had given the campaign its legitimacy and its moral force were quoted.

I replied to Binya's tweet: "This tweet is too embarrassing for me to retweet. But thanks."

I took a deep breath, trying to savor the moment and to look at the other side of things. *Don't sell yourself short,* I thought. *Be proud of what you've created. The Federal Reserve is the most powerful economic policy-making body in the country, but progressives have ignored it since the 1970s. We have had decades of growing inequality and flat wages, and yet there has been no concerted political effort to change the policies of the institution most responsible for this status quo. You've changed that. And as a result of the campaign's work, the Federal Reserve is talking about race and inequality for the first time ever. Fed policy makers and economists and reporters are questioning whether we could actually push for genuine full employment. The Democratic Party platform is once again highlighting the importance of the Fed. And because of you, the next president, Hillary Clinton, has said that the institution must be made accountable to the public and not to Wall Street.*

It may not actually be a national movement, but it's a pretty damn impressive political accomplishment. Not bad for four years of work. And you've got a whole career ahead of you to build on this. Enjoy the moment. You've earned it.

The small jet took off and circled over the vast Pacific blue. The early-morning sun covered our whole plane in orange warmth. I looked down at my picturesque new home of Santa Barbara. Rachael and I had been there for less than the two years but it already felt deeply comfortable. Although my success with Fed Up was making me proud and hopeful, its significance was dwarfed by a different recent development in my life: three months earlier, Rachael had given birth to a wonderfully chubby boy, whom we named Carl King, in honor of my mother's father—a proud, stoic, clever journalist and translator who went by Carol or Carl or Charles, depending on whether he was living in Romania, Austria, England, or Israel during those inconceivably tumultuous decades from 1920 to 1998. We gave Carl his mother's last name because, well, screw the patriarchy.

The weeks leading up to Carl's birth had been serene and contemplative for Rachael and me. We had each pushed to finish various work projects by her thirty-eighth week so that we would be ready for an early arrival. But our little man bided his time until the forty-second week, which meant we spent all of May trying various old wives' tricks—leisurely walks, spicy dinners, loving sex—to coax him out. Rachael was incredibly uncomfortable, but we both tried to cherish those days, filled as they were with quiet anticipation and the knowledge that everything would be very different very soon. When the time came, we took one final walk, one mile from our home to the hospital.

The first months of Carl's life were like a fairy tale (though with a bit less sleep for Rachael than she would have liked), aided by our employers' humane paid-family-leave policies, our supportive families, and Carl's generous appetite. We quickly mastered the five-*S*'s system for soothing: Swaddle him, sway him on his side, shush in his ear, and give him a pacifier to suck. I swaddled my little burrito very tightly, swayed emphatically, and shushed with all my might, and Rachael happily assented to my claim of soother in chief. We shared the premonition that I might end up being the "fun" parent because I had the sense of humor of a four-year-old boy—or maybe an eleven-year-old on my mature days. Rachael was profoundly satisfied with our lives: her first book was on track for publication with a prominent press (and tenure would follow soon thereafter), her baby boy was healthy and happy, and she had a partner who would be a dedicated, involved father—something she had never had herself.

About a month after Carl was born, I resumed working from home and held him in my arms as I joined my first conference call from our sunny back deck. It really was the perfect work-life balance. The perfect life.

As the plane gained altitude, I inserted my earbuds and clicked "play" on Phosphorescent's *Muchacho*. The album's soaring hymnal celebration matched my mood and my moment. I had climbed to a new vista. An expanse of new adventures and obstacles and pleasures and accomplishments spread out before me. I was the author of my own story, and it was going so well.

Later that day, as we pulled into the Jackson Lake Lodge for the third year in a row, I and my campaign deputy, Shawn Sebastian, were relaxed and confident. I'd like to think it was something like what defending champions feel warming up for the first game of the playoffs. We knew the court intimately (we'd held about three dozen press conferences and meetings with Fed officials since 2014) as well as the referees (we had a good relationship with nearly every reporter who would be at the event); our opponents had already agreed to play by our rules (Shawn was going to moderate the meeting with Fed officials, so we could tailor precisely all the topics of discussion); our team was well prepped and our game plan tight; and with the *New York Times* story in our back pocket, we were already up 10 points.

The "First Amendment space" just outside the lodge's entrance was our home court, the only place on these Federal lands where we could lawfully make noise or hand out literature. There, the campaign's field manager, Rubén Lucio, was coordinating a team of people to put together the frames and brace for a beautiful fifteen-by-fifteen-foot forest-green banner that would tower over our proceedings. It would provide the backdrop for our photo op, a gut punch that fused our messages on economic and racial justice: "Full Employment for Black + Brown." As Martin Luther King Jr. said just before his death, when he was organizing the Poor People's Campaign to fight for full employment: "If a man doesn't have a job or an income, he has neither life nor liberty nor the possibility for the pursuit of happiness. He merely exists."

Like cheery barn raisers ready to build a new and more just world, Rubén's team hoisted the banner behind our podium. CNBC,

Fox Business, and two other outlets had set up their TV cameras; reporters were milling around with their notebooks, ready for the show to start. Meanwhile, our motley crew of 120 low-wage workers, students, retirees, economists, and professional organizers gathered around wearing our patented bright green T-shirts. This year our two messages were meant to lay the groundwork for pushing reform legislation through the U.S. Congress in the new year and continuing to pressure the Fed to appoint someone other than white male bankers to leadership roles: "We Need a People's Fed" and "Who Does the Fed Represent?" We looked good.

For the third year in a row, we had crashed the Fed's exclusive and remote getaway. A bunch of low-wage people of color were inserting themselves into debates that, with a few exceptions, had for a hundred years been reserved for financiers and insulated bureaucrats. As they ricocheted off the walls of the Jackson Lake Lodge, our raucous cries of "This is what democracy looks like!" actually felt authentic and transformative.

Our press conference employed a central practice of community organizing: making sure that the people most impacted by public policy are the ones deciding what solutions to pursue and voicing demands. Like previous Fed Up events, this presser featured powerful personal testimony and argument from workers who deserved more than the American economy was currently offering them. Maria Rubio, a human rights lawyer and refugee from Honduras, spoke with ferocity about her inability to make ends meet as a cleaning lady in New York City and the Fed's statutory and ethical duties to ameliorate the situation. And, because we also wanted to prove our policy chops, we had one of our campaign's best economists, Josh Bivens from the Economic Policy Institute, explain why the U.S. economy was still not at full employment and why the Fed should continue keeping interest rates as low as possible. The cameras rolled and the reporters scribbled dutifully.

But the main event was still to follow. We wrapped up the press conference and filed into one of the large meeting rooms on the ground floor of Jackson Lake Lodge. The competition had moved onto the Fed's home court, but we had all the momentum and knew that we were dramatically better prepared.

At a U-shaped table, ten members and staff from the campaign sat down with nine of the Fed's seventeen most important decision-makers; the rest of our coalition sat in the audience fifteen feet away. TV cameras, reporters and Fed staff were scattered around the room. We had prepared four questions for the Fed officials, each coming from a different powerful Fed Up leader—but these were long questions, three to five minutes each, filled with argumentation and evidence, and punctuated with the challenge that Fed officials justify the unjustifiable: Why should banks like Morgan Stanley be permitted to literally govern the Fed, even as it bails them out and enriches their CEOs? Why should 80 to 90 percent of the Fed's policy and governance positions be occupied by white people and dominated by male bankers and CEOs, rather than a more diverse set of leaders from across the American economy and society? Why, in the face of inflation that was beneath its target and wage growth that remained stagnant, was the Fed intentionally trying to slow down the economy? And would the Fed commit to studying questions of inequality, racial discrimination, and full employment in order to show that its leaders cared about these issues? (This last one was an intentional softball that had its intended effect: Minneapolis Fed president Neel Kashkari immediately agreed to our request, and has since then launched major public research initiatives on precisely these questions and become the most outspoken advocate at the Fed for genuine full employment.)

"Fed Faces Its Critics at Jackson Hole," the *Financial Times* headlined its August 26, 2016, story on the event.

**Policymakers Accused of Compromising Interests
of Poorer Citizens in Rare Meeting with Activists:**

It was an event far removed from the esoteric academic debate that for decades has dominated gatherings of senior central bankers and academics at Jackson Lake Lodge.

On the eve of their annual symposium in Wyoming, Federal Reserve officials found their plans to tighten policy under assault from community activists, who accused them of compromising the interests of poorer citizens in a fight against an illusory threat of inflation.

In a meeting with the Fed Up coalition attended by 11 top US Fed officials on the eve of the Jackson Hole symposium, central bankers insisted they had no desire to halt the recovery but that they needed to act to prevent risky imbalances from emerging down the road.

However, in a packed and occasionally heated gathering in a sweltering hotel meeting room in Grand Teton National Park on Thursday, community activists argued that the Fed's leaders needed to better understand the plight of ethnic minority Americans on low wages.

Rod Adams, an organiser from the Neighborhoods Organizing for Change in Minneapolis, said that while the economy had recovered for white citizens, African-Americans and Latinos were still lagging behind with higher rates of joblessness.

"You will be leaving us behind," he said, accusing the Fed of "pulling the ladder right up after you have climbed it."

He added: 'I don't want to be sacrificed in your war against an inflation enemy that isn't here."

As the meeting ended and we started filing upstairs to enjoy the beautiful evening sun setting against the majestic Grand Teton

Mountains, I ran into Binyamin Appelbaum, the *New York Times* reporter who had written the complimentary profile the previous day.

"What'd you think?" I asked him.

"I thought it was pretty incredible," he said, explaining that reporters almost never get Fed officials to engage so extensively with criticisms of their policies. "Congrats."

It had taken me nearly five years to earn those congratulations. The seeds of Fed Up had been planted in the fall of 2011, when I visited the encampment of Occupy Wall Street a few blocks away from the federal courthouse where I was working. The Occupy movement burst suddenly onto the American political scene, giving voice to the broad and profound dissatisfaction with the financial and corporate control of our economy and politics. And although it quickly dissipated in the cold of winter, the movement left a new consciousness and critique in the minds of millions of citizens and activists, including myself. The Wall Street financiers who had crashed the economy were made richer than ever before; the millions of families who had lost their homes and the workers who had lost their jobs were left impoverished and despondent. This was no way to run an economy or a society.

It was with that mind-set that, in the beginning of 2012, I read a series of blog posts and articles by Matthew Yglesias that would shape my thinking and my work for years to come. Yglesias argued that if progressives wanted to build a more equitable economy, we had to start paying serious attention to the Federal Reserve. This was the narrative—the worldview, really—that I internalized after digesting his arguments:

For large swaths of the American public, personal financial security has always been an unattained dream. *How will I pay the rent next month? Is the new boss going to fire me? Will we ever be able to save enough for the kids' college?* These are the recurring fears for scores of millions of working and middle-class people, in addition to the millions more who live on the margins of society, unable to find any stable work.

This insecurity persists, despite America's tremendous wealth, because of our gaping economic inequality and the absence of strong social welfare programs. For more than forty years, the fruits of the American economy have gone only to the richest in society; indeed, our public policies have taken money away from the 99 percent and shifted it to the CEOs and financiers who pay for the campaigns of the politicians who write those rules.

This story has gained increasing notice since the Great Recession, spurred by the mic checks of the Occupy movement, the colorful marches of the Fight for $15, and the bellicose clarity of Bernie Sanders's presidential campaign. But it is an old story—as old as American capitalism itself. Who benefits from the sweat, labor, diligence, and ingenuity of America's workers? And who is left behind? These questions have dominated America's politics and public discourse for two centuries, with only occasional breaks to focus abroad.

Scholars of American history and politics believe that the strength of the economy, more than any other factor—including the quality of the candidates—determines the outcome of our presidential elections. "It's the economy, stupid" was the crystal clear slogan for Bill Clinton's winning 1992 presidential campaign. And it summarizes so much of our shared political history: from the mass mobilizations of farmers and factory workers in the final decades of the nineteenth century through the enormous transformations of the New Deal, which aimed to bring shared prosperity to a society riven by despair, and into the retaliation of the Reagan Revolution, which again sought to entrench the power of the owners of capital. Indeed, America's original sin and continuing crime—slavery and the oppression of black people—has always been about stealing and reappropriating the fruits of labor. And although our political discourse sometimes forgets it, the fight for women's liberation is about more than abortion or birth control: it's about whose labor gets compensated, and how fairly.

That much I knew already, but it was here that Yglesias opened my eyes: despite the central importance of the economy to our lives and society, since 1978 progressives have largely ignored the tremendous influence that the Federal Reserve wields over the shape of our economy. Although elected officials, journalists, and active members of civic society understand the centrality of economics to the welfare and happiness of the country's residents, few of them understand the role of the Federal Reserve in setting that economic course, and even fewer think of the Fed as an important site for political struggle. Nobody considers the politics of abortion or affirmative action without thinking about the Supreme Court, but policy makers and commentators regularly forget about the Fed when they discuss economics.

For far too many political observers and participants, "the economy" is a mysterious creature shaped by forces outside of any decision-maker's control: technology, complex global relationships, the whims of financial markets, and the sentiments of consumers all, in this story, determine whether we have "economic growth" or a recession, whether unemployment goes up or down, whether factories close or the price of the dollar goes up.

The reality, however, is that the economy is something built by humans. We set the rules that govern the relationships between workers and their bosses, between corporations and their competitors, between investors and startups and banks, between rich countries and poor, and within the financial markets. Although economics is by no means a science, the general course of our national macroeconomy is largely up to the decisions of policy makers. We can decide whether workers' wages will go up or be stagnant, whether recessions will rob families of their homes or not, whether small businesses will be able to access loans or not, whether corporations will be able to monopolize an industry. And no entity has more power over these questions than the Federal Reserve.

In general, even those political actors who do think about the Fed treat it as a technocratic institution that makes expert decisions about how to build a strong economy. They rarely appreciate the fact that every day the Fed is making decisions that are fundamentally political—i.e., fundamental to the structure and shape of our body politic. Who has money, who can get it, and at what price? Who will be unemployed, who will find work, and at what wage? These questions are political, not just economic, because they address the most fundamental political question that any society faces: Who has power and who doesn't?

The Fed is our nation's central bank. It is a bank to the commercial banks, facilitating lending between banks and providing emergency loans so as to prevent runs on banks and the financial collapses that they can cause. (These powers were on vivid display during the financial crisis of 2008, when the Fed and the U.S. government bailed out various Wall Street firms—and did so, to the detriment of the public, without imposing major restraints on the banks' ability to commit malfeasance again or providing restitution to the millions of people whose lives the banks had upended.) In its capacity as the nation's central bank, the Fed sets the rate of interest that one bank must pay to another for short-term cash. This rate, called the federal funds rate, serves as the baseline for most other lending in the United States, including mortgage, car, student, and small business loans. That's why the Fed's interest-rate decisions are so important: they underlie the prices that we pay for many of the most important and expensive goods and services we rely on. And, consequently, they have an enormous impact on the course of the entire American economy.

This line of thinking struck a deep chord within me because it tied together my interests in economics and politics. I had enjoyed majoring in econ as an undergraduate, mainly because it allowed me to learn about the workings of the macroeconomy: how the taxation and spending choices of Congress could stimulate or stifle growth; how the Federal Reserve's decisions about interest rates could impact global trade and the unemployment rate; how, in essence, and for better or for worse, the course of our economy could be set by politicians in Washington, D.C. Now I saw how my compatriots in the progressive movement had failed to recognize this important reality and that there were tremendous human costs to that oversight.

I also thought there was a chance I could do something to fix this problem. I was going to start a job in the fall at the Center for Popular Democracy, a brand-new advocacy and policy shop that would work with community-based organizations around the country to promote economic, immigrant, and racial justice. It was run by the type of people who would be open to innovative new campaigns and might enjoy launching an effort about Federal Reserve policy.

In September 2012, CPD held an open house in its quirky brownstone in Bushwick to celebrate its recent founding. I was scheduled to finish my clerkship and start working there a month later, and was eager to go celebrate with the progressive New Yorkers who would soon be my colleagues and comrades. Over cocktails and finger food, I mentioned the idea of a monetary policy advocacy campaign to Paul Sonn, who was a role model for the kind of advocate I hoped to become: he was a veteran lawyer and policy expert at the National Employment Law Project who had authored many of the most important minimum-wage and hour laws around the country over the past twenty years, and whom I had met during law school when I was working to draft a new living wage for New Haven. He started nodding his head and murmuring, "Yeah, I really like that . . . Uh-huh, uh-huh . . . That's interesting." And he started asking the kinds of smart, challenging questions that progressive activists around the country would ask me repeatedly over the next two years as I tried to get Fed Up off the ground:

Since Fed officials aren't chosen via public elections, how could we influence their policy choices? How might we get activists excited about the dry, esoteric topic of the Fed and monetary policy? Since interest rates were already at zero in the wake of the recession, what else could the Fed do to improve the economy?

Paul was excited about the idea and suggested that we talk with Dean Baker, a lefty economist who had foreseen the housing collapse, coauthored a book (with Jared Bernstein) entitled *Getting Back to Full Employment: A Better Bargain for Working People*, and was always eager to challenge neoliberal conventional wisdom. I had read Dean's commentary over the years and was looking forward to seeing what a big shot like him would think about my idea. So late that night, when I got home to my Astoria, Queens, apartment, I wrote up a summary for Paul to forward to Dean. Two days later we got Dean's response: "Hi Paul, I think this is a fantastic idea. In many ways Fed policy swamps whatever else we might try to do in terms of promoting employment and decent wages. The right understands this, which is why the current debate on Fed policy goes from the center-right to the extreme right." Dean said he was eager to move forward on the proposal. I was pumped: Dean Baker was a legit economist, and if he and Paul both liked the idea, then maybe it could actually work.

A month later, I showed up for my first day on the job. I sat down for a check-in with my boss, Amy Carroll. She had been the legal director at Make the Road New York when I spent my fellowship year there and had recruited me to join her at the Center for Popular Democracy when she moved over to help found it earlier that year.

Like at many start-ups, the staff at CPD were running a hundred miles an hour, trying to prove impact, identify new revenue streams, and scale up quickly enough to survive. They had wanted me to start months earlier, but I had been committed to my clerkship through October. So Amy was excited for me to start and take some of the workload off her plate.

We talked about the exciting projects that I would delve into: the fight to pass a paid sick days law in New York City, guaranteeing the right of workers to take a few days off every year to care for themselves or their loved ones; the launch of a new network of progressive local elected officials from cities around the country; the idea of passing an enhancement to New York State's minimum wage law to better enforce the prohibitions on wage theft and underpayment. At the end of the meeting I told her about an idea for another campaign we might want to run: pushing the Federal Reserve to adopt innovative and expansionary monetary policies that would create jobs and raise wages. With a maternalistic smile, Amy asked me to elaborate. I would go on to deliver this pitch hundreds of times, but even at that early date I began with the claim that full employment matters tremendously.

In the three decades after the end of World War II, the United States experienced consistently strong economic growth that translated into more and higher-paying jobs, significant reductions in poverty, an expanding middle-class, and major reductions in racial economic inequality. But since the mid-1970s all of those trends have reversed. Wages have stagnated, the American middle class is shrinking, 20 percent of American children live in poverty, deaths of despair are on the rise, egregious racial and gender pay gaps persist, and wealth inequality is out of control: the four hundred wealthiest Americans have more wealth than half of all Americans combined. What happened?

Although there are multiple culprits, none is more significant than the American government's abandonment of its commitment to genuine full employment. Economists of different worldviews disagree about the meaning of "full employment," but I subscribe to the simple notion that in a wealthy country and a healthy economy, anybody who wants to find full-time work should be able to do so—or, at least in an aggregate sense, there should be as many job openings as there are job seekers. Some people may be unemployed as they transition between jobs, but long-term unemployment should be negligible and there should be no consistent unemployment due to a lack of demand for workers in the economy.

It's obvious why having a stable, good-paying job is fundamental to any individual family's dignity and well-being. But why is full employment so important to a healthy society? And what does it have to do with the rising inequality and economic weakness over the past four decades? Here's the key: in a full employment economy, workers reap the benefits of their labor. But in an economy with less than full employment, workers are at the mercy of employers and as a result are paid less than their work is worth.

In an economy with high unemployment, there are many job seekers for each job opening. When an employer posts a job opening and receives one hundred applications, perhaps thirty people have the skills and experience that she is looking for. And with thirty qualified applicants to choose from, she's under no pressure to raise the wage she was planning to pay or offer generous benefits. There is, to use the term coined by Engels and Marx, a reserve army of labor, destitute and desperate to work. But in a full employment economy, where there are as many job openings as there are job seekers, workers are in a very different bargaining position. They can ask their bosses for raises and leave for better employment if they don't get them, and employers looking to hire new workers need to offer higher pay.

This is the intuitive and obvious relationship between full employment and higher wages. It's why a full employment economy creates broadly shared prosperity, whereas a high unemployment economy promotes inequality and poverty. Under full employment, workers have bargaining power, and they can demand wages that reflect their productivity. But when unemployment is high, as it generally has been since the mid-1970s, it is the owners of capital who reap the rewards of workers' higher productivity; they don't need to reward workers' efficacy and ingenuity with commensurate wages.

[[art: insert EPI productivity pay gap graph; TK]]

The exception that proves the rule is that in the late 1990s, when unemployment finally fell quite low, inequality began to shrink and wages grew significantly—especially for low-wage workers and workers of color.

As of 2012, when I laid out this idea for Amy, the average American worker was more educated and efficient than she had ever been. And yet the median worker's wage hadn't risen meaningfully in decades. This helps explain why the Federal Reserve's choices have such profound impact on the shape of our economy and our society. By deciding whether or not to speed up or slow down the economy— by lowering or raising interest rates, respectively—the Fed has an impact on the economic fortunes of almost everybody in this country. By making it easy to borrow money and promoting job growth, the Fed not only radically transforms the lives of unemployed people (and their families) but it also strengthens the bargaining position for all workers, facilitating higher wages and more stability in employment.

The bottom line? CPD should launch a campaign to push the Fed to do whatever it takes—including via innovative expansionary monetary policy—to get back to genuine full employment.

Amy smiled and nodded and listened. Looking back, I think there were at least three strands of thought going through her mind:

- *What the hell is "innovative expansionary monetary policy"? Is he trying to put me to sleep?*
- *The chutzpah on this kid is incredible. I need him to get to work on real shit, pronto.*
- *This is exactly the kind of creative campaigning that I founded CPD to do. Maybe I can teach Ady how to ask the right questions to develop this proposal into something interesting.*

I had laid out a good argument for why the Fed should pursue full employment, but I still needed to tell a comprehensible story about *how* the Fed should do that and how *we* could plausibly get the Fed to do it. Over my first months at CPD, Amy and I talked through those questions, and quite soon she had identified the crucial element that was missing from my analysis and my proposal: race.

In America, race and economics are inextricably intertwined. Black labor has never been compensated fairly in the United States; indeed, uncompensated black enslaved labor was the central foundation for the global trade and Industrial Revolution that propelled America toward two centuries of prosperity. White Americans have always reaped an unfairly disproportionate share of the economy's fruits and black Americans its pits. The Great Recession exacerbated this reality, costing millions of black families their homes, life savings, and jobs.

In 2012, while the unemployment rate had begun to significantly fall for white Americans, it remained outrageously high for black workers. "Last hired, first fired," rang true in the black experience, because the scarcity of jobs always facilitated and exacerbated the intentional bigotry and unconscious biases of employers and the structural racism built into our society. Bigoted employers don't need to hire African-Americans if there are unemployed white applicants, and unless they are self-aware and proactive, strong social science evidence shows that even non-bigoted white employers will, for example, unconsciously discriminate against applicants with stereotypically black names. In addition, structural racism means that even superficially nondiscriminatory behavior will redound to the benefit of whites: if a white boss hires his nephew or a young woman who went to the same college, that perpetuates white prosperity at the expense of black.

Amy's insight was this: if the Federal Reserve were to decide that the economy had recovered and didn't need any more extraordinary help, it would be exacerbating and reinforcing these racial disparities. African-Americans and Latinos would be left farther behind.

So my framing would matter. A campaign pitch about the Federal Reserve and creative expansionary monetary policy would be met by glazed-over eyes and silence. A campaign about jobs and wages would be met by nodding heads and smiles. But a campaign about combating racial and economic inequality by delivering full employment to all communities? That might actually get some people excited.

I wrote up a two-page campaign proposal. It laid out some ideas for how we might begin to affect Federal Reserve policy. We would run a series of popular education workshops for low-wage workers in each of the twelve cities where the Federal Reserve has a regional bank. We would teach the workers about what the Fed was and why it mattered to their lives. And then we would organize a set of escalating pressure tactics designed to highlight how Fed officials were harming working-class people. We would lay out a series of policy reforms that the Fed could adopt in order to promote more job creation and wage growth. And we would demand that the Fed reform its governance and ensure that its leadership better represented the diversity of the American people.

But how could we hope to influence the decisions of such an insulated and distant institution? First, we would put monetary policy on a human scale, bringing decision-makers face-to-face with the workers whose lives they were affecting. By holding meetings with Fed presidents and by taking them on tours of local communities, we could start to shift their understanding of the economic reality by showing them that the same economy that was delivering prosperity to Fed officials and everyone else within their social and professional circles was woefully failing large swaths of the country.

Second, I realized that there was a robust corps of journalists covering the Fed whom we could use to help disseminate our message. Economic data and Fed news releases are dry stuff; we could help the reporters spice up their coverage by giving them human-interest stories, colorful protest imagery, and a bit of controversy and narrative tension.

Third, I hypothesized that although Fed officials were formally insulated from public opinion—i.e., we couldn't vote them out—they prided themselves on being fair and open-minded technocrats who examined the evidence and made equitable decisions that served the public interest. Their reputations and pride would be damaged if a movement of struggling black and brown workers made the credible case that their policies were exacerbating racial and economic inequality.

Over the next eighteen months I had a dozens of informal conversations with my supervisors at the Center for Popular Democracy and organizers and policy wonks from allied institutions. The idea was met with interest and support, but also with healthy skepticism.

The central doubt was whether we could plausibly interest low-wage workers in so esoteric a topic. Federal Reserve interest rate decisions were made far away from the communities in which my organization and our allies worked. And although they have had an impact on all of our lives, that impact was obscure and indirect. How could we get busy people to spend their precious time organizing around this issue when other topics—like a local school closing or another police shooting—felt so immediate and close to home?

By the spring of 2014, I was getting quite dejected by my inability to get a campaign off the ground. In the middle of one workday, from the third floor of Casa Kent, I got on the phone with my father and shared my frustration. "What would count as success?" he asked me.

"I suppose if I could actually convince some people to take action to pressure the Fed, that would be a success," I said, "even if we have no impact on their policies." My father told me to work toward that goal.

As I searched for answers to the good questions that my comrades were asking, I also needed to find the answer to another foundational question that plagued every nascent political campaign: Where was the money? This campaign would require staff and travel, and that would take real dough. My supervisors were willing to let me dabble in this work in my spare time, but if I wanted to make it a core part of my job, I would need to raise the money to pay my own salary.

In mid-June 2014, while in San Francisco for an unrelated meeting, I got a phone call from an old friend from law school. Shayna Strom had recently left her job at the White House to work at a new foundation that was being set up by Dustin Moskovitz, the Facebook cofounder who had been Mark Zuckerberg's roommate in college. The foundation's staff was trying to decide where to make their initial investments and had apparently identified monetary policy as a good opportunity to have a big impact on Americans' well-being.

Their offices were just a mile away from my hotel. Could I come over to meet with Shayna and her coworker, Alexander? Yes, of course I could.

Over beers on the Embarcadero, Alexander, Shayna, and I bounced around ideas for what this advocacy campaign might look like. I learned that Alexander's interest in the Federal Reserve had been piqued by the same Matthew Yglesias articles that had inspired me. He had interviewed a number of economists over the past year, all of whom thought that trying to influence Federal Reserve policy was a very good idea, but none of whom had been able to lay out a plausible theory of how one might go about accomplishing that goal. Now, finally, Alexander was talking to an organizer who was laying out a game plan.

A week later Alexander and I got on the phone and he shared with me the good news: he could give me a short-term $100,000 grant to continue exploring the idea and try to get it off the ground. Finally, I had a breakthrough.

Back in New York, I shared the good news with my new coworker, Shawn Sebastian. I'd been introduced to Shawn a couple months earlier by two mutual friends. He had recently graduated from NYU School of Law and was looking to start a career in progressive politics. He said he could come volunteer at CPD for three months, supported by a modest stipend from NYU. I was happy for the help.

Together, we began planning a meeting to get the Fed Up campaign off the ground. We invited leaders from eight community-based organizations around the country to come to Washington, D.C., for a daylong meeting. We would use some of Alexander's money to pay for the travel. I asked Shawn to put together a presentation modeling what a popular education workshop might look like, so that the community organizers could get a sense for how they might pitch this campaign to the their memberships.

It was time to finally answer in simple, accessible language the important questions about how the Fed's policies actually influence the economy and how we could actually impact the Fed's policies. This was new terrain for Shawn, so we went through the arguments step by step, trying to make them clear and relevant.

First, we had to explain how the Fed influences the economy and the financial situation of working families. Once again we went for the human scale. Here's an example:

A young couple is looking to buy a home. The price for a newly constructed house in a nearby development is $300,000. With a 3 percent thirty-year fixed mortgage, the monthly payments would be $1,265. But at 5 percent those mortgage payments would be $1,610—that is, 27 percent higher.

If interest rates are low, and the couple can get the 3 percent loan, the local economy will see a series of positive consequences: perhaps a dozen local companies and contractors will be enlisted to build the home, providing jobs for laborers, electricians, plumbers, etc. Those workers will in turn have higher wages for the month, which they'll spend at supermarkets, retailers, and other businesses. So $300,000 that would otherwise be sitting in a bank's vault (or, more accurately, on its ledger in a Federal Reserve computer) will instead be pushed into the local economy, creating jobs and raising wages.

If interest rates rise to 5 percent, however, the story looks different. In one scenario the $350 increase in monthly mortgage payments is simply too much for the couple, so they choose not to buy the house. That's a loss for all of the workers and business owners who would have benefited from the spending that would have come with construction of the house.

But imagine that they are able to scrounge up the extra $350 in monthly payments, so they decide to take out the mortgage even at the higher interest rate. There are still significant consequences for them and the local economy: as a result of the higher interest rate, they have $350 less in disposable income—every month. Maybe that means they no longer go out to the movies or a restaurant for date night; maybe that means they don't buy a new car for a few more years. Whatever the specifics, the higher interest rates likely mean approximately $4,200 less in consumer spending every year—which means $4,200 less in profits and wages for the businesses that they otherwise would have patronized.

And that only represents the impact of interest rates on mortgages and new home construction. If the couple has student debt, credit card debt, or car loans, then they will be paying more interest on those every month, leaving them with even less disposable income.

This emblematic story explains the power and importance of the Federal Reserve's monetary policy decisions. The impact of a 1 or 2 percent change in the Federal Reserve's interest rate reverberates throughout the American economy, which features 1 million to 2 million new homes being built every year; $1.45 trillion in student debt owed by 44 million borrowers; over $1.2 trillion in car loan debt; and about $750 billion in credit card debt owed by about 175 million credit card holders. And that's not to mention the importance of low interest rates for small businesses to borrow and invest in new workers and capital.

So where's the rub? Why doesn't the Fed always keep interest rates low and promote genuine full employment? Why, for example, did the Fed raise interest rates from 2015 to 2018?

The answer from Fed officials and conservative economists is that it needs to slow down the economy in order to keep inflation low. If unemployment gets too low and workers are able to bargain for significantly higher wages, this line of thinking goes, firms will need to raise their prices significantly; workers will then demand higher wages to offset their higher cost of living, and a dangerous upward price-wage spiral will wreak havoc on the economy.

The most conservative members of the Federal Reserve—like

Kansas City Fed president Esther George—were making this argument loudly beginning in 2011. (Indeed, various Fed officials were publicly fretting about inflation in 2007 and the beginning of 2008, just as the entire U.S. economy was collapsing.)

But worrying about excess inflation in America's current economy is a bit like the fire chief refusing to put out a blaze because he's worried about flooding. For the past decade, inflation in the United States has been consistently under 2 percent—the rather arbitrary and very low target that the Fed set under former chairman Ben Bernanke. Meanwhile, despite it being the longest "recovery" in history, wages have barely grown at all. That is to say, employment rates and wages have been lower than the Fed's goals, and inflation has also been too low; the economy, in short, has been too weak. And all of this has happened against the backdrop of decades of stagnant wages for most workers.

So what motivates Fed officials to keep the economy weaker than it could be? First, the Federal Reserve is alone among major U.S. policy-making institutions in that it is not fully public. Its governance structure is convoluted and esoteric—intentionally designed to ensure that the Fed is accountable to the interests of America's major financial institutions rather than the broad American public. Second, most Fed officials received their training and came of age in the 1970s and 1980s. Their formative economic experience was the high inflation and of the '70s and the "heroic" decision by Fed chair Paul Volcker to tame that inflation by jacking up interest rates and creating a major recession in the United States, throwing millions of people out of work. Which is to say, they're still fighting very old battles instead of grappling seriously with the new world there we're in. And third, Federal Reserve leaders are a wealthy and largely white group of people who work and socialize with other white and wealthy people and are legally accountable primarily to an even whiter and wealthier group of people. And so their perspective on the economy is very different from that of the average American.

And yet, in the beginning in 2012, with Congress controlled by a Republican Party that had long ago stopped listening to reason or caring about the welfare of the broad American public, it seemed to me that the Federal Reserve represented the most powerful economic policy-making body that might actually be impacted by reason and advocacy.

At that initial meeting in D.C., Shawn's presentation was a huge hit. As the meeting closed, I called the question: Should we launch this campaign? The Federal Reserve was holding its annual conference in Jackson Hole, Wyoming, in three short weeks. We could crash the exclusive confab and make a splash, but we had to make the decision immediately. Organizers from St. Louis, Washington, D.C., Kansas City, and Minneapolis all gave an enthusiastic thumbs-up. Why not give it a shot? they asked. What have we got to lose?

But I had an embarrassing personal dilemma. All year long, Rachael and I had been looking forward to a week of backpacking in Glacier National Park, and we had scheduled it for the week before the Jackson Hole event. I couldn't go on vacation and prepare our team of protesters at the same time.

Shawn came to the rescue. Over the coming two weeks, he prepped eight brave adventurers, teaching them all about the Fed; booked flights and hotels; and printed the signs and bright green T-shirts—featuring the slogan "What Recovery?" on the front, and graph showing wage stagnation on the back—that would become our campaign's signature. Our friends at the Economic Policy Institute connected us with Ylan Mui, a Fed reporter, who previewed our trip by profiling Ce-Ce Butler, a McDonald's worker who was part of our special-ops crew.

When we landed at the remote Jackson airport for that first trip to the annual meeting, the article had already drawn attention. Esther George, the president of the Federal Reserve Bank of Kansas

City, who was hosting the meeting, had reached out to Ce-Ce and invited her to meet that very day.

Only a few hours before she was scheduled to open her biggest event of the year, George sat down with all ten of us, listening as we each explained why we were there. Every other member of our group told her about their family's economic struggles and why they needed her to pursue stronger economic growth. My family was upper-middle-class, so I chose to highlight how I felt her fears of inflation were overblown and why I thought she needed to focus her energy on job creation. At the end of the meeting, we snapped a photo and shared it on Twitter.

A couple of hours later, as the Fed officials and their interlocutors began filing into the conference space for the opening dinner, my nine comrades and I formed a receiving line twenty feet away from the door. "What recovery?" read our most prominent sign. "Want to understand labor market dynamics?" read another. "Ask a worker." Federal Reserve chair Janet Yellen, with her shock of white hair and diminutive frame, smiled in surprise as she walked by us. I ran to catch her before she went inside. As I placed my hand on her shoulder and thanked her for her advocacy on behalf of working families, the news photographers snapped away furiously. The photo of the two of us was splashed across the front page of the *New York Times* business section the next morning and the talking heads on cable news wondered out loud whether security had been too lax in letting me get so close to her. We gave interviews to all the assembled reporters, who were intrigued by the novelty of protesters at the Fed's meeting. One of our contingent, Reginald Rounds, was ecstatic when we listened to the long interview that he had given to the BBC. His voice carried particular force because he had traveled from his hometown of Ferguson, Missouri, which had just been engulfed by an uprising against police brutality and racial economic oppression.

As the news articles piled up, all featuring our central message that the economy wasn't strong enough for communities of color and working families, my boss Andrew texted me from New York: "The press coverage is insane!" My theory was being proven right: with so little colorful narrative at the Fed meeting and so many reporters who cared about it, we could get our message heard loud and clear with even a minimum amount of political theater. And on Friday evening, as our trip wound down, we got another piece of good news: Michelle Smith, Janet Yellen's right-hand woman, emailed me to say that Yellen would be happy to host a meeting back in Washington, D.C., since she hadn't had time for a sit-down in Wyoming. We were off to the races.

Four years earlier, when we moved from New Haven to Queens, Rachael had spent the summer in China on a language fellowship. I had done all the packing and driven our belongings into New York, enjoying the novel challenge of steering a midsize U-Haul over the Triborough Bridge, through the midday traffic, and around Astoria's myriad potholes. This time it was her turn. When I got back from Jackson Hole, our entire apartment was in boxes. And in what we felt was the ultimate sign of our newfound class status, UCSB had agreed to pay for our moving costs. I was more than happy to let a trio of burly men carry everything down the two flights of stairs and into an enormous orange truck.

We sat on the carpet in the empty apartment, filled with anticipation for our new life out west. Rachael's five years of hard work in graduate school had paid off handsomely with a dream job, and my two years of scheming and proselytizing about the Fed had been vindicated. We traveled to the Upper West Side to say goodbye and spend the night with my father and stepmom. For our final dinner, we decided to go back to the taqueria on Amsterdam Avenue where I had taken Rachael for our first date. It had been twelve years since we arrived in New York City for our first year at Columbia. All of sudden we were entering our thirties and moving to California.

The next week, camped out at my mother's house in Pasadena while we waited for our furniture and looked for an apartment in Santa Barbara, I had a follow-up phone call with Alexander, the funder who had given us the $100,000 seed grant. He was excited about the results of our trip to Jackson Hole, and particularly amused that so much of the press coverage had mentioned our bright green T-shirts. Of course, I told him, it's all about the T-shirts. He asked me to send him a budget for 2015.

Twenty-five of us gathered in Washington, D.C., in mid-November for our meeting with Janet Yellen and the other governors. We identified three people to share personal stories about life in a weak economy, and another six people to present each of our demands to the Fed. Twenty-four hours before the meeting with us, we blasted out a press release announcing the formation of the Fed Up Coalition, which would be bringing the voices of everyday Americans into the Federal Reserve. We scheduled a press conference on the steps of the Fed for the next day, just before we would go inside the headquarters.

That night, while prepping in my hotel room, I got a phone call from Michelle Smith, Yellen's consigliere. She was not happy. She had set up the meeting thinking it would be an anodyne listening session. We were using it to launch a public campaign aimed directly at her boss. Her colleagues inside the building were urging her to call off the meeting, she told me. I asked her not to do that. The working-class folks who had taken time away from their families and jobs to travel across the country wouldn't be very happy if Yellen canceled the meeting at the last minute, I said, hinting at the prospect of embarrassing publicity in that unfortunate event. Michelle decided to keep the meeting but punished us by canceling the planned group photo with Yellen that they had previously agreed to.

All of the major newspapers sent reporters to our press conference the next day. We told our stories and previewed our policy demands, which included a call that the Fed use a transparent process for filling the open presidencies at its Philadelphia and Dallas banks, and that it not repeat its usual formula by selecting a white male corporate executive. After we were done pontificating, we scarfed down some empanadas before filing into the Fed's enormous white-marbled headquarters. We were escorted into the ornate conference room where the Fed's policy makers meet every six weeks to set interest rates. Three dozen Fed staffers sat in the audience and around the back wall, while most of our contingent took seats around the central table. At the appointed hour, Janet Yellen walked in with three of her deputies—Vice Chair Stanley Fischer and Governors Lael Brainard and Jerome Powell. Over the next hour we ran through our game plan, telling stories and laying out policy demands. When Kendra Brooks of Philadelphia recounted how she had lost her job and then her home, I thought I saw Janet Yellen's eyes tear up. Fischer thanked us for laying out our demands so clearly, Brainard and Powell each reiterated our argument that the economy was still not strong enough, and Yellen thanked us for our time and our perspective—without committing to do any of the things we asked. As the meeting ended, Anthony Newby, the executive director of Center for Popular Democracy's organizational partner in Minneapolis, turned to me and said, "That was an amazing piece of organizing, brother."

The successful meeting with the Fed dispelled the nagging doubts about our ability to interest working-class people and community-based organizations in this work. And the glowing press coverage that we received for launching the campaign made it clear that we could immediately impact the national debate about Fed policy. When Alexander called to tell me that he would give us a $750,000 grant for the following year, we had everything we needed to run a proper campaign.

I flew home to Santa Barbara, logged into CPD's employee portal, and requested three weeks of vacation in December. It had been an intense year, and I was ready for a long break to clear my mind. Rachael and I had been renting a cute bungalow by the ocean, but we were eager to take advantage of America's absurd mortgage interest tax deduction laws and buy a place of our own. After two months of diligent searching, we put an offer down on a beautiful, cozy, three-bedroom Depression-era cottage on the city's Westside, five hours after it came on the market. Although someone else had outbid us by $10,000, the owner was taken by the charming letter that Rachael had written to accompany our bid, and escrow closed a few days before Christmas. (Rachael's dissertation was on the role that letters played in the rise of eighteenth-century literary genres, and her expertise certainly was paying off.) My father, stepmom, and brother flew in for the holiday from New York; Rachael's mother, sister, and sister's boyfriend arrived from Rhode Island; and my mother and stepfather drove up from Pasadena. We had a Christmas feast in the rented bungalow, and on December 26 we cleaned it out and moved our belongings into our new home. On New Year's Eve we stayed up playing cards and getting drunk on champagne and cider. Our future was bright and getting brighter.

Over the next eighteen months, the Fed Up campaign continued to shape the national discussion about Federal Reserve policy by rinsing and repeating our formula. Shawn and I traveled to the Federal Reserve cities around the country, where we held popular education sessions with our partner organizations and their members. Using the money from Alexander, we provided them with grants that would pay for an organizer's time. They built small, local coalitions of allied organizations, often including labor unions and community organizations. Those coalitions requested meetings with the local

Federal Reserve presidents, where we would repeat the approach we had taken with Janet Yellen in D.C. William Dudley, president of the Federal Reserve Bank of New York, initially refused to meet with us, so we called Pedro da Costa at the *Wall Street Journal* and told him that we would be protesting outside Dudley's offices. His story ran the morning of our protest; in the middle of it, our lead organizer got a phone call from Dudley's deputy offering to schedule the meeting and apologizing for any miscommunication.

The following August (2015), knowing that a repeat of our small protest would not generate the same surprise and attention at Jackson Hole, we brought one hundred workers and organizers to the Fed's symposium and announced our intention to hold our own counter-conference. The Nobel Prize–winning economist Joseph Stiglitz supplied our event with the star power it needed, Obama adviser Jason Furman dropped by to tell us he thought we were doing important work, and even Lael Brainard, the Fed governor, sat quietly in the back of the room during one of our sessions. The press coverage was even better than in year one.

But were we actually making any difference? It was hard to know. The Federal Reserve had not raised interest rates once since the beginning of our campaign, but no one could say whether our pressure had affected its decisions. Only a few weeks after our initial Jackson Hole protest, the Fed had created the Community Advisory Council—with the explicit aim of focusing on issues that mattered to working-class families—and had appointed some good people to it. But we didn't know whether that council had any influence, either.

By the spring of 2016, however, it was at least clear that we had significantly shifted the political discourse about the Fed. Using some of the new money from the big grant, I had hired a young policy wonk named Jordan Haedtler to lead our advocacy in Washington, D.C. Jordan was soft-spoken, hardworking, and charmingly nerdy: he sang in barbershop quartet competitions on the weekends and spent his vacations visiting presidential libraries. He quickly got to work building relationships with the staff of the Democratic members of the House Financial Services Committee and the Senate Banking Committee, which had jurisdiction over the Fed. Janet Yellen was required by law to testify twice a year in front of each committee, which presented us with valuable, predictable opportunities to advocate for full employment and more diverse and representative governance. In advance of each hearing, Jordan worked with our economist allies to draft recommended questions, with accompanying background information. He then gave the questions to the Democratic staffers and organized our community partners to call their members of Congress and urge them to highlight our priorities during the hearings. (They were often happy to oblige; it wasn't as though they had other constituents calling on them to ask different questions during these gripping affairs.) Simultaneously, Jordan and Shawn (and eventually Rubén Lucio and Victoria Ruiz, a punk rocker activist from California) organized delegations of working-class folks to attend the hearings in person. This meant travel and very early mornings to get in line for a coveted seat in the small hearing room, but our work paid off handsomely: at each hearing, Yellen was peppered with a dozen questions from progressive Democrats, many of whom publicly thanked our activists for showing up in bright green T-shirts and noticeably changing the ambiance in the room. This was a stark change from previous years, in which the hearings had been dominated by Republicans excoriating Yellen and her predecessor for doing too much to promote job creation and not enough to prevent inflation.

Our crew of Latinx and black activists were particularly effective—in partnership with the many black members of the House Financial Services Committee—at forcing Yellen and the Fed to grapple with racial inequalities. In the July 2015 hearing, Yellen gave this unsatisfactory response to a question one of our allies posed about racial disparities in the labor market: "So, there really isn't anything directly the Federal Reserve can do to affect the structure of unemployment across groups. And unfortunately, it's long been the case that African-American unemployment rates tend to be higher than those on average in the nation as a whole." She was washing her hands of any responsibility for the problem, so we quickly released a statement laying out the argument that Yellen was wrong—that full employment actually makes it harder for employers to discriminate and the Fed needs to be acutely attentive to the people who its policies are harming the most.

Then, on Martin Luther King Jr. Day in January of 2016, the respected economist and recent Fed president Narayana Kocherlakota published a blog post criticizing his former institution for having failed entirely to grapple with race. He read through the most recent publicly available transcripts from Fed deliberations (from 2010) and found that although African-American unemployment was a whopping 15.5 percent or higher throughout the year, "there was no reference in the meetings to labor market conditions among African Americans." This was the powerful evidence we needed linking our two central demands: with not a single black or Latinx person among its nineteen key decision-makers, the Fed simply didn't have the understanding or the perspective to set policy that reflected the interests of all Americans.

With Kocherlakota's powerful critique in hand, we started pushing to get the Democratic Party behind a reform agenda for the Fed. Jordan worked with his contacts in the offices of Representative John Conyers and Senator Elizabeth Warren to draft a letter to Janet Yellen urging her to prioritize diversifying the Fed's leadership. The message was clear: Fed Up was behind the Democratic Party's newfound attention to the Fed, and ignoring our demands would mean risking the ire of Congress. We got 127 members of Congress to cosign the letter, including the entire Congressional Black Caucus and heavy hitters like Maxine Waters and Chuck Schumer.

Simultaneously, I was engaged in an ongoing courtship of the policy team on the Hillary Clinton presidential campaign. She was trying to fend off an unexpectedly strong challenge from Bernie Sanders in the Democratic primary and was eager to prove her progressive bona fides. Sanders had long been a critic of the Fed's subservience to Wall Street, and I figured this was our best chance to get the next president on the record as supporting Fed reform. If she expressed support, it would be a powerful signal to congressional Democrats that they should work with us to craft and pass legislation in the New Year. Shawn, Amy, and I had visited the Clinton campaign's bustling downtown Brooklyn headquarters to meet in a bland, windowless conference room with her policy director, Jake Sullivan, and three economics advisers all named Mike. We were pleasantly surprised that the Clinton team agreed almost completely with our substantive policy proposals. The problem, they explained, was that the political and communications teams on the campaign didn't think voters cared much about the Fed and were reluctant to use scarce bandwidth talking about this issue. It became clear over the ensuing weeks that we would have to find some way to force the Clinton campaign to issue a statement.

On a Thursday in mid-May, I got up early so I could help with the media rollout of our congressional letter to Yellen. I brewed a pot of coffee and sat down with my laptop at the two-person high-top table in our kitchen, looking out a picture window on our back deck, modest backyard with potted succulents and an explosive pink bougainvillea, and the sun rising over the Santa Barbara mountains in the southeast. Rachael was still sleeping, her belly propped up with pillows, her due date three days away. Our lives were about to get so much richer and more joyous, our nights a good deal less restful, and our parents a lot more present. I couldn't wait. But I also cherished this peaceful moment alone, with the warm cup of joe between my palms, sweet and milky and going down easy.

Jordan and Shawn had blasted out a copy of the letter and begun following it up with pitch calls to a few dozen Fed reporters. They told me that they were getting a good response and we could expect solid coverage. I texted a link to one of the Clinton campaign's Mikes. He told me that this was a good time to try to get Clinton on the record supporting us. Could I get some reporters to call the campaign for comment? I quickly jumped on the phone with the *Washington Post*'s Ylan Mui. She had given the Fed Up campaign our first-ever article two years earlier and it was time to return the favor. She was excited at the prospect of scooping Clinton's first comment about the Fed and thanked me for the tip.

A couple of hours later, Ylan's article posted online. The headline was perfect: "Hillary Clinton to Support Federal Reserve Change Sought by Liberals," it said, crediting us with moving her. The quote Ylan got from the campaign was even perfecter: "Secretary Clinton believes that the Fed needs to be more representative of America as a whole and that commonsense reforms—like getting bankers off the boards of regional Federal Reserve banks—are long overdue." It was everything we wanted and more. Fed Up had been calling for legislative reforms to the Fed for only five months. Now the presumptive next president of the United States was calling them "long overdue"!

"Fuck yeah!" I texted Mike. "It's a pleasure doing business with you." Over the course of the morning, more and more articles popped up, linking the congressional letter, Clinton's statement, and the Fed Up campaign's advocacy. Over email and phone calls, our coalition celebrated our most impressive victory to date. We had moved the power brokers of the Democratic Party to embrace a dramatically more progressive vision for the nation's central bank. I thought back again to the modest goals I had set on the phone with my father two years earlier. "When we fight, we win!" goes the union chant. It felt so true.

A month later, when she again went to testify in Congress, Janet

Yellen had a different perspective on the question of racial disparities in the labor market: instead of saying they were not the Fed's business, she highlighted them in her prepared remarks and said they should inform monetary policy choices. Embarrassed by Kocherlakota's finding, the Fed adopted a practice of describing racial disparities at the beginning of each policy-making meeting; within the year the Fed would launch major research projects on race and the economy and appoint the first-ever African-American regional Fed President: Raphael Bostic, an economist with expertise in housing discrimination. It was now clear that our campaign was having an impact on Fed policy.

Three months after the Clinton campaign endorsed reforming the Fed, I would board that sunny flight to Jackson Hole, happier than I had ever been before: proud of my work and my role in society, in love with my wife and our newborn son, ready to embrace every ounce of the joys and challenges that stretched out in front of me. And then, one month after that, on October first, 2016, Rachael and I had our fateful brunch with my friend Katy, where I complained that my left hand didn't seem to be working properly.

CHAPTER SEVEN
PROGRESSION

Over the previous fifteen years, Michelle Smith had been the adviser to three successive Federal Reserve chairs, setting strategy and solving the political problems of the most powerful economic policy makers in the world. And now she was waiting for me, standing just outside of the majestic conference room where the Fed's leaders meet to decide how they will steer the global economy.

In May 2017, trying to retain a semblance of normalcy despite my diagnosis with ALS seven months before, I joined a fifty-person delegation from Fed Up traveling to Washington, D.C., to once again meet with the most powerful woman in the world, Fed chair Janet Yellen, and her sidekick, Vice Chair Stanley Fischer. As in previous Fed Up meetings, most attendees were unemployed or working low-wage jobs. A few were economists at D.C. think tanks, and a handful were professional organizers and rabble-rousers. Most were black or Latinx; a few were Asian. And a handful were white.

Once again we were going to push the Fed's leaders to keep interest rates low in order to promote the creation of more good jobs and higher wages. And we would urge them to appoint African-American and Latinx leaders to crucial decision-making positions, to finally diversify the lily-white institution that had deprioritized the needs of people of color for so long. But we also had a new plea, with a very different flavor: Please don't leave the Fed now and give President Donald Trump another seat to fill; sacrifice a few years of your retirement and help our country survive his tumultuous reign.

"It's so good to see you, Ady," Michelle said, smiling broadly and shaking my hand, both of us wordlessly agreeing to pretend that we hadn't spent the past week jousting over the details of this parley, with Michelle threatening to cancel the meeting, and me threatening to tell the press that the Fed had gone back on its word after dozens of poor people had requested time off from work and arranged child care while they traveled to Washington.

I had been fretting over this precise moment ever since we had scheduled the meeting six weeks prior. What would I tell Michelle when she saw me? Did she already know about my ALS, word trickling through the tight-knit Fed press and bureaucracy? Should I just pretend that everything was okay?

"Good to see you, too, Michelle," I said. "Thanks for having us."

"What happened to your leg?" she asked me, looking at the black brace that connected my shin to my shoe. I decided not to get into it. "It's just a medical issue."

"But you're okay, right?"

I wasn't in the mood to lie by saying yes. And the truth was, I didn't even want to keep it secret. I wanted her to know my pain. To ease my burden a little bit by sharing it. This disease sucks. It's my personal tragedy. But if Michelle Smith knew, and Janet Yellen knew, and if they both felt sorry for me and agreed that it was a tragedy, then maybe that would be a sign that I was an important person. Maybe it would be a sign that I wasn't about to just flicker out into darkness; that when I died in a couple years, half a century before the actuaries had thought I would, at least I would have left my mark on this world.

"No, unfortunately not," I said, my voice quivering noticeably. "I was diagnosed in October with ALS. Lou Gehrig's disease." I paused for a brief instant. Did she know what ALS was? I hadn't in September. Most people hadn't.

"I'm so sorry, Ady," she said, but it wasn't clear to me from the tone of her voice whether she knew that I was facing a pretty quick and certain death sentence or whether she just understood from my answer that something was seriously wrong

"Thank you. But that's not why we're here," I said quickly, to cut the tension and move us on to other matters.

It was already 2:02 p.m., our meeting was supposed to start at the top of the hour, and the tight agenda that I'd painstakingly curated and prepped was on the verge of disintegrating. We had a minor clusterfuck of a problem: thirty minutes earlier, Reggie Rounds, one of the three low-wage workers who was slotted to give testimony during the meeting, had gotten into a heated argument with the Fed's chief of security, and we'd been told that he posed a threat to Yellen and Fischer and couldn't come in.

I introduced Michelle to Jennifer Epps-Addison, the thirty-five-year-old president of the Center for Popular Democracy network who was standing right beside me, and whose husband was back home in Los Angeles, battling progressive multiple sclerosis. "Jennifer was right there when the argument happened," I said.

"I saw it all," said Jen. "Reggie didn't cuss, he didn't raise his voice. All he said was 'The Fed is the people's bank; now let us in.' And your security officer overreacted."

Suddenly, Janet Yellen walked up. I shook her hand. Jen shook her hand. And then, for three precious minutes, the two of us—activist lawyers with fancy credentials and fulfilling jobs in the movement whose hopes for happy lives had recently been destroyed by incurable neurological diseases—tried to convince the most powerful woman in the world that, rather than re-creating in miniature America's obsession with over-policing the behavior of poor black men and then precluding their political participation, she should instead order her security guards to let into our meeting a chronically unemployed man from Ferguson, Missouri—whom she had met on two occasions before—so he could once again plead with her to set global economic policy that would prioritize his need for a job over the interests of the Wall Street financiers who had dominated Fed policy discussions for one hundred years.

Holy fuck. This was my life.

Our negotiation was inconclusive. Janet said little. Michelle said they would see what they could do but that we should start the meeting and maybe they would let Reggie in soon. We gave a copy of Reggie's testimony to the St. Louis organizer who had brought him; she could read it on his behalf if necessary. The last dozen of our group were let in through security.

I went to the bathroom. I threw cold water on my face and patted it dry with a paper towel. I came out, and the hallway was almost empty and suddenly uncomfortably quiet; our delegation of fifty, plus a few dozen Fed staffers, had taken their seats inside the Board of Governors' room.

Only Janet Yellen and Stanley Fischer remained outside. And as I limped from the bathroom toward the conference room, I could see the two of them speaking quietly, watching me intently from forty feet down the hall. Did they know that I was dying? Did I finally matter? Could our stories sway their decisions?

In May of 2017, other than my leg brace and my limp, I still looked healthy. At the Hyatt Regency Washington on Capitol Hill, where CPD was holding its annual gala, I stood around chitchatting about the early atrocities of the Trump regime, half listening to the speakers onstage. I could no longer manage to hold both a drink and a plate of food at the same time, but otherwise I was a normal partygoer. Some old friends from law school came and said hi, commiserating about my ALS and telling me about their newborn. I had been on my feet for six hours, and I was ready to leave. I grabbed my coworker Sarah and we headed out. On the escalator I told her that, for the first time ever, I was feeling out of breath.

"Is that something that happens to people with ALS?" she asked me.

"Yes," I told her. "That's how ALS kills you." She rubbed my back, and we rode the rest of the way up in silence.

This was the unrelenting rhythm of ALS. A new part of the body became weak, a new symptom appeared, a new task became difficult or impossible. Sometimes you saw it coming, but sometimes you didn't. Sometimes you'd made preparations, and you could mitigate the damage, but sometimes you hadn't, or sometimes you couldn't. In the ALS community, this series of physical declines is referred to, unironically, as "progression," which is exactly the wrong way to describe what is happening. My disease is advancing, I am decaying, and yet we refer to the pace of my "progression."

The days when a new symptom appeared were the worst, I told the psychiatrist at Cedars-Sinai. Not only did the new symptom immediately make my life more difficult, but it was also a sign of things to come: it was another damaging data point in the scatter plot that would predict my paralysis and death. Some people lived with ALS for more than a decade; others died within a year. Each new symptom gave me more bad news about where I was on that spectrum.

The shrink, well versed in the mindfulness that I was trying to embrace, advised me to develop a routine on which I could rely in those difficult moments: Spend the evening doing something enjoyable with Rachael, like cooking a favorite meal or watching a reliably good show. Notice the cloud in the sky and then let it float by. Bring your attention back to where you want it.

Riding that escalator with Sarah, I thought about what my new symptom meant. Every few months, when I visited the ALS clinic, the nurses had me blow hard into a small handheld device that measured the volume of air in my lungs and the force with which I could push it out. The machine took that information, combined with my age and size, and spat out a percentage. The week after my diagnosis, my forced vital capacity was at 103 percent of what would be expected in a healthy man my age and size; it had declined to 80 percent by the spring of 2017. As my diaphragm became weaker and weaker, that number would continue to fall. Eventually, I would face a daunting choice: get hooked up to a ventilator that would breathe for me—but prevent me from speaking or eating—or let my breath become air.

But I wasn't there yet, I told myself. Carl's first birthday was only three days away, and we had invited most of Southern California over to our house for barbecue ribs and cupcakes. I said goodbye to Sarah and turned my eyes homeward.

A month later my father and I put away our work for the day and headed out for a late-afternoon constitutional. He had been a regular visitor from New York ever since Carl was born, and my diagnosis eight months earlier had only made his visits more frequent. The Westside of Santa Barbara is a quiet residential neighborhood, made up of modest two- and three-bedroom single-family homes that are insanely expensive by the standards of most American communities. Passing the assorted California cottages and Spanish stucco houses, we looked with admiration at the carefully constructed gardens. My favorites were the ones filled with elaborate cacti and colorful succulents.

In the two years before Carl was born, Rachael and I had delighted in taking weekend excursions to the nearby garden centers, from which we assembled our own collection of drought-resistant plants. I had spent half a dozen happy weekends digging up the grass in our front yard and replacing it with an elaborate mix of yuccas, agaves, echeverias, salvias, and an olive sapling for good measure. At Santa Barbara Stone, I loaded up the trunk of our Civic with large crimson sandstone tablets. I chiseled them into stepping-stones and arranged them into two pathways leading through the garden, blissfully unaware that the small succulents and ground covering that I placed nearby would completely conceal them within a couple years. Sweat dripping off my forehead, dirt coating my forearms, I took unadulterated pride and pleasure at this improvement of my land—a pleasure that was only enhanced by the refreshing shower and indulgent afternoon snacks that followed.

Now, walking with my father only eighteen months later, I was in no shape for gardening. On my left I wore a brace to help mitigate my foot drop. On my right I carried a hiking pole from REI that helped me keep my balance. I had fallen about a dozen times over the preceding year, doing varying degrees of damage. I planted the cane in sync with my left foot—every other step at times, or every fourth step if I was trying to move quickly. My father and I passed the local elementary school (cue the cloud overhead, asking if I would live to see Carl play in that yard, and watch that cloud pass by) and began to ascend a long hill. It wound left and then right; after a mile the sidewalk ended, and we walked in the street until we got to a dead end and a chain-link fence. This had been the turnaround point on my regular quick-and-easy 2.5-mile runs, which I had favored when I didn't have the time or energy to drive to the shoreline for a more ambitious excursion. The climb had tired me out, but I told my father we should push ahead past the fence and into a hilltop park. I repeated our mantra: *Do what you can, while you can.* For the final ascent—a thirty-yard, very steep pitch—my father held my left hand and we marched up together, one deliberate step at a time.

At the top of the hill, we sat on a bench admiring the 180 degrees of Pacific blue beyond the golden surrounding hills. Catching our breath, we reflected on how much had changed since we had first started coming here only two years before. We both knew that this was the last time I would muster the strength to walk up to this plateau. The sun was setting on a gorgeous day, and on my life as well.

On the steep descent, my father grasped my arm with both hands, determined not to let me tumble down. There he was, a sixty-three-year-old man, watching his son's body decay every month in front of his eyes.

On July 17, I got in our Civic and drove to the UCSB Children's Center to pick Carl up. He was the biggest and oldest in his class of ten students, and I usually found him playing outside with various push-along toys or in the dirt patch that his teachers let him turn into a mud pit. He had started walking at ten months, in March. Now, four months later, he was gaining speed and confidence, while my walk was slowing down and becoming wobbly. I grabbed a plastic bag with his lunch and dirty clothes, picked him up, and walked out to the car. With Carl on my hip, I pressed the remote unlock button, opened the rear passenger door, and stepped off the curb to put him in his seat.

Suddenly I was falling backwards, and then I was on the ground. My butt was sore and Carl was crying, but both my arms were wrapped around him, and I knew he hadn't been injured. Two strangers walked up to help. One put Carl in his seat; the other helped me to my feet. I buckled him in and kissed him and told him we would drive home. Pulling out of the parking lot, I cried and cried, apologizing to him and bemoaning my lot in life.

At home, Rachael tried to comfort me, but she knew there was no good way to reduce the sting. Via text, a friend tried to commiserate by telling me that she, too, had once fallen while carrying her child. But the comparison was meaningless. I knew that this would be the last time I could carry Carl in my arms. ALS was destroying my ability to be a good father.

That summer marked the end of our attempt to return to a "normal" life like the one we had before my diagnosis. Within a few weeks of my fall, I no longer felt safe picking Carl up out of his crib or putting him onto his changing pad. As my left hand became weaker and weaker, and as Carl became more interested in performing impromptu backflips, Rachael took over 100 percent of the diaper changes as well. Every task that I could not do was one more task for her. I was in charge of bath time, until I could no longer safely pick Carl up out of the tub; we muddled through for a couple more months, Rachael putting him in and taking him out, until I could no longer get myself up off the floor without help, at which point I resigned myself to observer status. Sitting on a chair in the bathroom, teaching Carl the words to "Yellow Submarine" while Rachael washed and dried him, was certainly a version of fatherhood—but it was less than he deserved, and far less than I had planned to provide.

Rachael remained upbeat and hopeful. Yes, I was disabled. Yes, our lives were a bit harder. But she could pick up my slack. We had each other and we could, at least for now, make our days enjoyable. Focus on right now, she would remind me. Best to leave the future blurry.

That summer, Republicans in Congress tried to make good on their long-standing promise to repeal Obamacare. Across the country, countless activists showed up at the offices and town halls of their members of Congress, beseeching them not to gut the regulations that protect people with preexisting conditions, or the funding that makes Medicaid available to millions of families. In Congress, the wheelchair-bound members of ADAPT, a disability rights organization, disrupted business as usual, occupying members' offices, and preventing hearings from proceeding. Time and again, Senate Majority Leader Mitch McConnell and House Speaker Paul Ryan announced that they had sufficient support to pass their legislation; time and again they delayed the vote when it became clear that their claims had been premature.

I watched the proceedings with trepidation and more than a little regret that I was not helping the resistance; it was particularly discordant for me to sit out a battle over health care. Instead, I continued working on Fed Up and Local Progress, the two projects that I had founded years earlier. My comrades and I had grappled with the question of whether and how to continue the work in the face of the new political landscape in Washington. Trump's attacks—on Muslims and immigrants and health care and the environment and on and on—were fierce and unrelenting. We certainly understood and shared the desire to fight back. (Local Progress did help dozens of cities and counties around the country adopt "sanctuary" policies to protect immigrants, and local elected officials rushed to the airports along with activists on the day the Muslim ban was announced.) But we also knew that there was a cost to getting distracted. The American economy had become radically unequal in recent decades precisely because progressives had ignored the Federal Reserve and let the 1 percent write the rules. Municipal governments from coast to coast were dominated by corporate interests and machine politicians precisely because progressives had failed to do the organizing necessary to take power in the bluest parts of America. Fed Up and Local Progress were beginning to effectively address these needs, and Shawn and Sarah and I were loath to shift our attention away from them.

On Wednesday, July 26, I traveled to sweltering Austin, Texas, for the sixth annual Local Progress national convening. Tarsi Dunlop, Sarah, and the rest of the team had done all the work to prepare for a great conference; I had helped to plan a panel or two but had largely eased into my role as an éminence (prematurely) grise. I marched around the conference with my REI trekking pole, putting on a good face for the 150 local elected officials who had arrived from around the country. My voice cracked during my introduction of our keynote speaker, former congresswoman Donna Edwards—who had recently been diagnosed with multiple sclerosis, a cousin of ALS—but the gathering was mainly filled with hope.

But it also felt like a bit of a sideshow, because back in Washington, D.C., the Senate was finally about to pass a Trumpcare bill that had already passed the House. On Friday night, after filling up on Texas barbecue and saying goodbye to my compatriots, I retired to my room, where I turned on C-Span. Republican senators Susan Collins and Lisa Murkowski had announced that they would not support the Republican bill, but we needed to find one more no vote. All eyes were on John McCain, who was now battling brain cancer after spending years battling the two men—Mitch McConnell and Donald Trump—who would benefit the most from his yes vote. Early in the morning, my screen glowing in the dark, I watched McCain stride onto the Senate floor and turn his thumb toward the ground. It was the latest in a series of unexpected last-minute victories that had preserved Obamacare. Supreme Court chief justice John Roberts had been the unlikely savior five years earlier; now it was McCain's turn. The next morning, as we closed out the conference in Austin, our collection of activists and local elected officials were ebullient, suddenly optimistic that our national resistance might yet see us out of this dark era.

Three weeks later, it was time for my second major event of the year: the fourth annual Fed Up protest-cum-conference in Jackson

Hole, Wyoming. Once again, others on the Fed Up team did all the heavy lifting, and I joined them there, with my cane and leg brace, mainly to be a pretty face.

This year the Federal Reserve symposium was infused with much more politics than it had been in a long time. Janet Yellen's four-year term as chair was coming to an end, and everyone was speculating about whom Donald Trump would pick to be the next chair. We were hoping that Trump would nominate Yellen for another term, which would accord with tradition—each of the last three Fed chairs had been renominated by presidents of the opposite party (Ronald Reagan renominated Jimmy Carter's pick of Paul Volker, Bill Clinton and George W. Bush both renominated Reagan's pick of Alan Greenspan, and Barack Obama renominated Bush's pick of Ben Bernanke). Yellen indubitably deserved a second term. She had entered her chairship as the most qualified official ever to assume the post, and her four years had been wildly successful: the labor market had continuously gotten better, inflation was stable and low, and Yellen had made no blunders that spooked financial markets. Under any normal president, her renomination would have been a virtual certainty, not least because her successful stewardship of the economy would be incredibly helpful to the president's reelection prospects.

But Donald Trump was no normal president, and neither tradition nor basic managerial principles nor even rational self-interest seemed to guide his decision-making process. As he would later tell Lou Dobbs, Trump—like a hyperactive mutt who pisses on every tree—was primarily interested in leaving his mark on the Fed. The rumored favorite was his chief economic adviser, Gary Cohn, the Wall Street banker. We weren't sure what Cohn's approach would be to monetary policy, but we were pretty confident that he would work hard to roll back regulations on the financial sector, putting the American economy at risk.

So we developed a strategy to oppose Cohn in the hope that if we defeated him, Trump might select Yellen instead. Recent news had been dominated by the white supremacy rally that had taken place in Charlottesville two weeks earlier, featuring Nazi flags and deadly violence. Trump had refused to condemn the event, saying instead—with Cohn standing right behind him—that there were some "very fine people" involved. Reporting indicated that the Jewish Cohn was unhappy with Trump's comments, and we worked to drive a wedge between them. We issued press releases saying that if Cohn did not have enough integrity to criticize Trump's tolerance of Nazis, then he would not make for an independent Fed chair. On Friday, just as we were preparing for our press conference, Cohn issued a statement saying that the Trump administration "can and must do better in consistently and unequivocally condemning" white supremacists, neo-Nazis, and the Ku Klux Klan. Our ploy had worked. Trump resented being criticized by his underling, and within a couple weeks Cohn was out of the running for Fed chair.

During our trip to Jackson Hole, I mainly played the role of senior adviser. I was proud to see the rest of the Fed Up team run an effective workshop for our members and a playful and smart press conference about the self-dealing and corruption inside the highest echelons of the Trump administration. I walked around the Jackson Lake Lodge gingerly, making small talk with Fed officials and reporters and accepting their warm wishes with a smile on my face.

The world, and my life, were so much worse than they had been twelve months before.

In September, Rachael and I dropped Carl off with his grandparents on the East Coast and flew to Italy for a ten-day vacation. My favorite cuisines were Italian and Indian, but our trip to Japan had set a high bar. I was eager to dig in. We began in Umbria, where a friend of Rachael's mother let us use his vacation home. A local cook arrived to prepare our first dinner: runny scrambled eggs baked with shaved truffles; *cacio e pepe* pappardelle with more truffles; veal scaloppine accompanied by aromatic eggplant Parmesan; rounded out by a rich tiramisu. We were off to a great start.

We spent five days traipsing around the scenic towns of Umbria. My legs were strong enough to carry me down the cobblestone streets of Spoleto and Gubbio, past the medieval stone buildings with their low doorways and colorful facades. But they were too weak for me to climb staircases with no handrail, so I waited in the plazas while Rachael visited inside the museums and palazzos. In the evenings, I ordered pasta for both my *primi* and *secondi*; since Rachael was kind enough to give me bites of hers, that meant I could try at least three varieties every meal.

Back at the villa, I sat at a desk overlooking the lush hillscape, opened my laptop, and began writing this memoir. Since shortly after my diagnosis, Rachael and I had talked about what I would leave behind for Carl, how he would get to know his father. I also wanted to leave something behind for the progressive movement: some lessons, some reflections, some strategies—*something*. But did I have a story or insights worth sharing? I didn't know if anyone would want to publish my reflections, let alone read them. But Rachael told me to worry less about my audience and more about myself: the important question was whether I would enjoy writing. And there was only one way to find out.

The next morning we continued our tour. The cathedral at Orvieto was jarringly ornate. We sat with the other sightseers and admired the facade, overflowing with biblical narrative in bronze and gold and stone and glass. Inside, our eyes were pulled upward—past the black and white stripes of basalt and travertine, past the glowing semitranslucent alabaster and the colorful glass—to the heavens. In the chapel, we chuckled at the frescoes of fire and brimstone on the ceiling and then indulged in chocolate and pistachio gelato from the adjacent shop.

In Assisi, I struggled to walk up the hill to the magnificent basilica, built in the thirteenth century to honor the recently deceased, widely beloved Saint Francis. Step by slow step we went, letting all the other pilgrims overtake us. No, there was no elevator to the Upper Basilica, we were told. So I grabbed the wooden railing with both hands, pulling myself up the stairs glacially and sideways. Moments later, inside the nave, my droopy tired foot caught a small lip on the floor. Without the strength or coordination to adjust my footing, I went speeding down a wooden ramp, tumbling onto the smooth marble floor below. I had to calm the well-intentioned onlookers who rushed to quickly hoist me on my feet. After I caught my breath, we walked around the room carefully, admiring the frescoes depicting the life of Saint Francis, thinking about the centuries of pilgrims, both crippled and not, who had come before us. We tried desperately not to let the fall ruin our day, not to let my progression ruin our trip, not to let ALS ruin our lives.

In Rome, we took a golf cart tour of the city's highlights; in an earlier life, visiting Mexico City and Edinburgh, Marrakech and Shanghai, Rachael and I had always walked as much as possible. Each stop was more crowded than I had remembered from my last visit fifteen years before. But the al dente spaghetti carbonara made me cry, the richly bitter cappuccino made me feel alive, and on our final evening, when we sliced into an enormous ball of buffalo mozzarella and its milk came flowing out, I knew that I was spending my final years just right.

CHAPTER EIGHT
LIFTOFF

I spent most of November 2017 sitting in the living room in a $2,000 leather power recliner that my father and I had recently bought so that I could breathe more easily while I slept propped up. My supervisors at the Center for Popular Democracy had happily granted my request to take the last two months of the year off in order to make progress on my memoir. But then I discovered the ten-minute matches on Chess.com and indulgently lost myself for the entire month in international competition against similarly mediocre players. I would begin to play when Rachael retired to the bedroom around nine thirty, and then, suddenly realizing it was three a.m., I understood why all of my opponents were from India. By Thanksgiving, I had developed proficiency with the Scotch opening, thrusting both of my center pawns into the middle of the board and hopefully ending up, five moves later, up a pawn or dominating the center with my queen. But by then I had also sated my appetite for hedonistic frivolity; it was time to get back to work.

But I could not focus on my writing. It seemed irresponsible to reminisce about the simpler times of years past while Donald Trump and his Republican Party were burning down Washington, D.C. I had largely avoided resistance work over the past year, opting to keep my focus on the Federal Reserve and municipal policy making, but I could avoid it no longer. The stakes for our country were too high and my time remaining was too short; if I wanted to contribute to the defense of American democracy, then I had to join the battle that was raging. "This is our moment in history," Senator Elizabeth Warren said in a video that I had produced with Local Progress earlier in the year. "Not the moment we wanted, but the moment we are called to." I decided to take her advice.

I called up Jennifer Flynn Walker, a veteran organizer who had cut her teeth as an AIDS activist in New York City using transgressive tactics to help drug users and homeless people win unlikely political victories that dramatically improved their lives. Jen was responsible for leading the work at the Center for Popular Democracy to fight back against the Trump administration, so she had spent much of the past year traveling around the country, training newly politicized folks in disruptive protest techniques, and had spent the rest of it bringing those people to Washington, D.C., to throw sand into the gears of the Republican machine. Throughout the summer, she and her army engaged in asymmetric warfare against the occupying forces, using pointed questions and cell phone cameras as their primary weaponry. Everywhere the Republican members of Congress went, they were confronted by constituents decrying their agenda and demanding answers to impossibly simple questions. "My son is twenty-three and cannot find a job that provides health insurance. Why are you promoting a law that would kick him off of mine?" "My daughter has asthma and I have diabetes. Do you really think that the health insurance companies should be allowed to deny us coverage because of these preexisting conditions?" "I rely on Medicaid to keep me alive. Why are you trying to destroy the program?"

All around the country, activists trained by Jen and others like her were turning themselves into bird-doggers, hounding politicians at town halls and other public places and sharing videos of their encounters with local news and social media. In July their hard work had paid off and Trumpcare had gone down to an unlikely defeat. But now, in early December, it looked like the K Street lobbyists had successfully circled the wagons around the entire Republican Party and were about to score a multitrillion-dollar tax cut windfall at the expense of the 99 percent of us.

I told Jen I was ready to enlist in her campaign, and she told me she was planning a day of action on December 5. Come to D.C., she said, and let's go after some vulnerable Republicans. Speaker Paul Ryan enjoyed a twenty-three-seat majority in the House, so if Democrats stayed united in opposition, he could afford to lose some but not too many of his members. Our strategy was to target the Republicans in swing districts who were facing serious challenges in the midterm elections that were eleven months away. Many of these were from suburban districts in California, Pennsylvania, New York, and New Jersey that Hillary Clinton had won and that would actually see their taxes go up under the Republican plan. We decided that I would help target Orange County's Darrell Issa, a two-time convicted carjacker who had profited nicely when his business burned down only weeks after he had boosted his fire insurance by 400 percent; he was now the wealthiest member of Congress.

I bought my plane ticket and asked my father and brother to join me in D.C. for the day. It was going to be an important first for me: in over fifteen years of activism I had never engaged in civil disobedience. It was embarrassing, frankly, like being a film critic who had never watched Fellini, or a chef who had never poached an egg.

On the chilly morning of December 5, about two hundred of us gathered in a public park a mile south of the Capitol, where Jen and two other organizers split us up into groups and gave us marching orders. We hopped on buses for a short drive and then calmly filed through security at one of the House office buildings. We then began paying visits to Republican members of Congress, occupying the hallways, using the human mic to tell personal stories about how the tax scam would make our lives more difficult and dangerous. I walked through the hallways slowly, leaning on my cane and holding my father's hand. My voice was already getting softer and slower, so I saved my breath and let other people do the mic checking. At one early stop I pointed out to my father a hijabi Palestinian-American woman who was being taken away in handcuffs. "That's Linda Sarsour," I said, pointing out one of the cochairs of the Women's March, an unapologetic Brooklynite who had helped forge Communities United for Police Reform. "She is probably the most prominent Muslim activist in the country."

By midafternoon our numbers had dwindled to about twenty-five people; the rest had either already been arrested, or had gone home. I was slated to be our final arrestee. So, after walking about three miles through the various halls and passageways, I found myself standing in front of Issa's office, mic checking with a small company of comrades. My six-foot-four-inch, twenty-two-year-old brother, Muki, gave me all the amplification I needed, bellowing out my comments over the heads of everyone else. My father stood fifteen feet back, nervous about how the cops might treat me but grateful to be part of the action. Next to me stood our field commander, Jennifer Flynn Walker; my Fed Up partner Shawn Sebastian; one of my longest-serving CPD coworkers, Julia Peter; and an old ally from my access-to-medicine days, the Yale Law School professor Amy Kapczynski. Live-streaming it all was MoveOn.org's Washington director, Ben Wikler, a pal with whom I had shared many strategic bull sessions over the years.

The police were very patient with us, letting me and Jen speak for fifteen minutes before our chanting and banging on Issa's office door became too much for them to tolerate. They gave us three warnings, during which everyone who didn't want to be arrested was directed down the hallway. And then, one by one, my comrades were placed in plastic handcuffs and escorted to the elevators. The police had a harder time knowing what to do with me, because without a free hand to hold my cane, I wouldn't be able to walk. After consulting with his supervisor, my arresting officer simply walked beside me. Ben's video showed me wobbling down the hallway like an al dente linguine. "Show me what democracy looks like!" shouted the chant leader. "This is what democracy looks like!" replied our supporters. As I passed Ben and his camera, I tried an advanced move, holding my cane up victoriously without breaking stride, hoping that I wouldn't pay for the image with a painful fall.

I was put in a paddy wagon along with the other practitioners of civil disobedients and driven to a vehicle repair garage in the back of a police station that had been repurposed to process mass arrests. The mood inside was jubilant. We had come from all over the country to resist our government's greed and racism, and we basked in the warmth of righteous solidarity. About two hours later I paid a $50 fine and was released onto the street, where my father was waiting along with a small welcoming committee. We walked just one short block back to the Capitol Skyline Hotel, which Jen Flynn had cleverly made our base of operations. Outside the hotel, I stood and spoke to Megan Anderson, whom I had met earlier that day. She had traveled from Cincinnati to be there, an effort all the more impressive because she was almost completely paralyzed below the neck from spinal muscular atrophy, a motor neuron disease related to ALS. We talked about how moving the day had been. I finally allowed myself to get emotional, to acknowledge the tragedy that infused my activism that day. "There is a higher purpose," Megan said. "I think you will see that there is a reason you are here today." The spirituality of her comment was foreign to me (and I bristled at the idea that there was some purposive intentionality behind my ALS), but it reminded me of my aunt Deb's comment a year earlier that I would "make meaning" out of my disease. Megan and I shared some tears, and then I went inside to eat and rest.

The next day I was flying home to Santa Barbara, with a transfer in Phoenix. I did not know that it would be the most consequential flight of my life.

I sat in the lobby of the Capitol Skyline Hotel, peeved that Amanda Shanor was already an hour late. She was an old friend and mentor from law school—the one who had first advised me to go get a job at Make the Road New York—and we were supposed to be catching up a bit before she took me to the airport. She finally arrived and put my suitcase in her sports car as I carefully maneuvered down the steps out of the hotel. My frustration only grew as we drove south to DCA, because she was insisting on holding her cell phone, looking at Waze, and driving stick shift, all at the same time. I begged her to let me do the damn navigation, but she refused. As she missed one turn and then another, my bemused outrage turned genuine. She was going to make me miss my flight! She dropped me off curbside with about forty-five minutes to go before takeoff. I didn't want to schlep my bag through two flights and a transfer in Phoenix, so I shuffled toward the bag drop as quickly as was prudent, regretfully avoiding the moving walkway because I was worried it would trip me up. The agent at the counter tagged my bag and said that I had made it with only thirty seconds to spare. Flashing my cane, I jumped to the front of the line at security and scurried down to my gate. They were in the middle of boarding, and I again walked up to the front. The gate agent signaled for me to stand in front of a woman with large sunglasses and a stylish coat with a puffy collar.

She was talking on the phone with charisma and confidence.

"Yeah, look, I'm disappointed, too. I definitely thought we could make it go viral. It's a great video. Sometimes Twitter works in mysterious ways."

I love eavesdropping. After she hung up, I shamelessly started bragging to her. "I had my first viral moment on Twitter yesterday," I told her.

"Oh?," she said politely.

I told her that Ben Wikler's video of my arrest had gotten 2,000 retweets and tens of thousands of views.

"Very cool! My friend Linda Sarsour got arrested protesting yesterday as well," she said. We made the obligatory comment about what a small world D.C. is, and then she said something very interesting. "You know, Jeff Flake is on this flight."

My eyes lit up.

Flake was a conservative Republican senator from Arizona who had never met a corporate tax cut that he didn't love. But he was one of the few Republicans who had dared to criticize Trump during his first year. There was a glimmer of hope that he might vote against the tax scam.

"You should talk to him about it," the woman said.

"Okay," I replied, "but you have to film it." She eagerly agreed and told me that he had already boarded ahead of us. As we walked down the gangway toward the plane, she filmed me introducing myself to the camera and explaining why I was in D.C. and what I was about to do. "On this plane is Arizona senator Jeff Flake, who voted for the tax bill even though he said he cared about the deficit and he cared about working people and people like me. So when I get on, I'm gonna ask him: Why did he vote for the tax cut bill?"

As I walked down the aisle of the plane toward my seat, I saw him sitting in the first row of economy. His bronze tan and perfectly coiffed hair stood out among the sea of regular travelers. I stopped, stuck out my hand, introduced myself, and asked him why he was planning to vote for the tax bill (after it was revised to match the House version). He said it would help economic growth. I explained why I disagreed. Sixty seconds passed. A flight attendant walked up to me, asked me if I was okay, and told me that I had to take my seat because they needed to board the plane and I was blocking the whole aisle. I told him I wasn't okay: I was very sick and I needed to get answers from the senator about his vote. Flake offered up a solution. "I'll come back and talk to you. How's that?" he offered.

I found my seat near the back of the plane. My new friend showed me the video she had shot of me hunched over Flake, leaning on my cane, making him increasingly uncomfortable. It was a solid piece of bird-dogging, but more important was the promise he had made to keep the conversation going. And now we had time to prepare!

We asked the man seated next to me if he would be willing to exchange seats with her and he happily traded up for her window seat. Then she sat down and we started introducing ourselves properly. Her name was Liz Jaff and she was a Democratic Party political operative. She had grown up in South Africa and been in college in Cape Town when Senator Barack Obama visited the country in 2007. She had interviewed him for her student newspaper and had fallen in love, so she emigrated to the U.S. and showed up uninvited at his Iowa headquarters. She was so warm and enthusiastic that they let her staff the front desk, greeting volunteers and other visitors. Later she worked in Obama's White House and then got involved with the effort to modernize the Democratic National Committee's tech systems. I told her about my work, which triggered recognition: Liz's fiancé was a policy wonk, and he had told her about my Fed Up campaign. We played the name game, comparing notes on mutual acquaintances, both surprised that we had never crossed paths before.

And then we got down to work. We needed a strategy for my conversation with Flake, and we were only going to get one take. Liz logged onto the on-board Wi-Fi and started texting with her friend

Winnie Wong, a socialist activist with a solid Twitter game. Liz came up with a brilliant hashtag on her first try: #FlakesOnAPlane. Working with Winnie, we started trying to build anticipation about our upcoming conversation. My coworker Shawn Sebastian tweeted out enthusiastically "This is kismet. @AdyBarkan, who has ALS, is on a flight with @JeffFlake and he's asking how Flake could vote for a tax bill that will take healthcare away from 13 million people and cut Medicaid. Stay tuned!" I'd never heard the word "kismet" before. I looked it up. Destiny. The stakes were high, and I didn't want to disappoint Shawn.

On Twitter, I solicited ideas for what questions I should ask Flake and what arguments I should make. A young immigrant asked me to push Flake on his support for DACA, the program that allowed undocumented youth to obtain work permits and authorization to stay in the country. Flake was a supporter of the program, and we wanted him to use his leverage over the tax scam to force Senate Majority Leader Mitch McConnell and/or Donald Trump to renew DACA, either through legislation or executive action. Liz and I were both worried about getting good-quality audio, so we tested different options and figured out that if she held up the microphone on her earbuds near my mouth, my words would be quite clear. An hour passed and Flake still hadn't come by. We agreed to give him another hour and then go up and talk to him.

Pushing Flake on his vote seemed worthwhile because he was one of the only Republicans who had expressed serious concerns about the tax bill. In order to defeat it, we needed to find three Republican no votes. He had been giving noble speeches recently about American democracy and good governance and had decried the opaque and rushed process by which the Republican leadership had authored the legislation. Could I convince him to make his vote match his rhetoric? Could I marshal all of my policy expertise and my emotional personal story to sway this hard-line conservative "deficit hawk" into voting with the Democrats? In high school I had been a champion debater and an award-winning thespian. But this was no weekend tournament. Millions of Americans would lose their health insurance and thousands would die if this bill became law. I sat quietly and laid out in my mind all of the different arguments that might appeal to him.

Thirty minutes later, after the drinks cart had passed, the senator walked down the aisle and stopped at my row. Liz began to film on her phone, holding the mic as far as she could into our conversation to try to overcome the loud jet-engine background noise. I began our conversation as I usually do when I'm talking to a powerful person who can give me what I want: by sucking up. I told Flake that we all admired his bravery in criticizing Trump and the secretive Senate bill-writing process. Then I summarized for him my personal story and asked him why he would put my health care at risk for the benefit of millionaires and billionaires. Because the tax cut would dramatically increase the Federal deficit, it was going to trigger enormous automatic cuts to Medicare and other crucial programs; these cuts would be allocated by a White House official who had repeatedly expressed his disdain for Medicare disability funding. This bill, I told Flake, would put at risk my access to a ventilator and the other medical care that I would need if I wanted to stay alive to watch Carl learn to read or shoot a basketball. He tried to assuage my fears by pointing out that Mitch McConnell and Paul Ryan had promised to waive these automatic "paygo" cuts. I laid out the many times that those two men had already lied about the tax bill, claiming it would be deficit-neutral and wouldn't raise taxes on anybody. He correctly noted that paygo had been triggered many times in the past but never actually implemented. We were descending into seriously esoteric debates, and I could sense that I was missing an opportunity to land an emotional gut punch. So I pivoted to a new topic.

Why not use this tax vote as an opportunity to demand a solution for Dreamers? I asked him. He explained that he was working hard on finding a fix and was confident there would be one by March. I told him that it was a mistake to give up his leverage now in exchange for promises of future action. He was unwilling to take a hard negotiating stance, he said. He thanked me for the conversation and tried to end it. I wouldn't let him. I asked him about the Children's Health Insurance Program. I asked him if he was happy with the process by which the tax bill had been written. "No, none of us are happy with the process. It's a lack of regular order that's been going on for years now. It's been pretty dysfunctional, the whole Senate," he replied. I had finally broken through, found an argument that resonated with him. I decided to press my case.

"So why not take your stand now?" I pleaded, my voice becoming more intense. He smiled with embarrassment, leaning back, unable to respond. I pushed. "You can be an American hero; you really can. If the votes match the speech . . . Think about the legacy that you will have for my son, and your grandchildren, if you take your principles and turn them into votes. You can save my life." (I've thought about that sentence some, since of course even by voting no on the tax scam he could not actually keep me alive. But if he did vote no, saving many other lives, he would be giving my life the kind of purpose we are all seeking).

"Well, thank you," he said, reaching to shake my hand and make his escape. I wasn't quite finished. "Please, please remember this conversation," I pleaded, moving my emotional appeal into sixth gear. He tried a bit of flattery himself, saying "You're very read up on everything, aren't you?"

I decided not to reveal that I was a lawyer and a professional activist, opting instead for some hyperbole: "My life depends on it." I moved to my closing argument. "I need you to make your votes match your principles, Senator—and for the rest of your life, you will be proud if you vote this bill down. You will be proud. And on your deathbed, I promise you"—my voice cracked with emotion at the thought of my own not-too-distant deathbed—"you will remember voting no. This is your moment to be an American hero. Please, we will all be watching you. Please. Thank you." I shook his hand again and let him go. He turned around and walked to his seat. I turned to Liz, who stopped recording.

"That was incredible," she said. I asked her if she had captured it all. She was optimistic, but we immediately plugged her buds into our ears, rewound the tape, and watched the exchange from the beginning. I was relieved that everything was fully audible. Liz knew that she had social media gold on her hands. She tried to upload it to Twitter, but the Gogo Inflight didn't cooperate. So we alerted her 2,000 followers and my 200 that we had just had a very good conversation, and the video would be forthcoming after we landed. We spent the rest of the flight getting to know one another, gossiping about Democratic politics, and deciding that we should start a super PAC together to elect progressive people to local office.

Down on the ground in the Phoenix airport, Liz chopped the video up into seven bite-size pieces and tweeted it out. I boarded my connecting flight to Santa Barbara and sat quietly on the plane, reflecting on the intense trip. I thought back to my conversation with Megan Anderson, the disabled activist from Cincinnati, and to the new word that Shawn had taught me. Megan had said that there was a reason I was in D.C. Maybe they were right. Maybe it was kismet.

Rachael had stayed up late, waiting for me to get home and following the action on Twitter. What a crazy coincidence, she said. She agreed with Liz that it had been a pretty incredible interaction, but we had a new and pressing problem on our hands. The air was burning my lungs. Nearby forest fires were racing through the mountains, saturating Santa Barbara in smoke and ash. It was unhealthy for everyone, but little Baby Carl and I were at particular risk. My lung capacity was already diminished, and this felt unbearable. We went to bed, agreeing to leave town the next day if things hadn't improved.

Morning came, the air was still terrible, and Liz's video was going viral. A reporter from the Intercept was the first to reach out for an interview. Rachael got in touch with a friend from grad school who lived two hours north, in San Luis Obispo; yes, of course, he said, we could go stay with them for as long as we needed. I poked around on Twitter and played with Carl while Rachael packed up. I contacted a mentor from college who now edited the opinion page of the *Washington Post*. He said he would gladly take an op-ed. Our neighbors were not planning to evacuate and they agreed to watch our two cats while we were gone. We got in the car and started driving.

By midafternoon I was camped out on our friend's sofa in SLO and news outlets around the country were writing about #FlakesOnAPlane—including CNN, HuffPost, the *Hill*, and ABC News in Phoenix. The Arizona Democratic Party tweeted out a photo of the second-story marquee outside their headquarters, which now read: "Sen Flake / Listen to Ady / you can be a hero." My coworkers at CPD jumped into action, pitching reporters, producing highlight videos, and figuring out a plan for escalating the pressure on Flake and the Republicans.

By Saturday afternoon I had decided that I needed to build on the momentum and go back to D.C. Jennifer Flynn Walker was already planning the next day of mass civil disobedience for Wednesday, December 13. This time, though, I wouldn't be flying alone. On the advice of a Twitter comment, I asked Rachael if she would like to come along and bring Carl. It would be more fun together and would make for some serious political drama. The tax scam was going to harm tens of millions of families, so we decided to put our whole family in the limelight to make the stakes crystal clear. *NBC Nightly News* sent a film crew to tell my story and show us preparing for the return journey.

The fight was already beginning to take a toll on my body. I found it impossible to sleep lying flat on our friend's guest bed, so I spent four uncomfortable nights propped up on the sofa, trying to get a little rest in between the scheming and organizing. We booked one-way flights to D.C., posted a fund-raiser online, reached out to Jeff Flake's and Susan Collins's offices to request meetings, circulated a press release, and got ready to escalate.

The Republican tax bill was a central priority for the donors who represent one of the key pillars of the party's structure. And in recent decades almost no one has been better than Mitch McConnell at enforcing partisan discipline, ensuring that no senators cross party lines to undermine his agenda. We knew, therefore, that there was tremendous pressure on Flake, Collins, and the other senators to vote for the tax bill. And we knew that our only hope of swaying their votes was to bring enormous counterpressure to bear. We would have to drive thousands of phone calls into their offices, get local papers to editorialize against the bill, and show them that the proposal was very unpopular with their constituents. None of us had any illusion that my conversation with Flake alone would convince him to vote against the bill. Kismet might open up some opportunities, but it is organizing that takes advantage of them. So we shifted into high gear, because we hoped that the conversation might finally stimulate our base to start fighting hard. During the earlier debate over Trumpcare, Republican members of Congress had been overwhelmed by phone calls and protests—just enough to convince Collins, Lisa Murkowski, and John McCain to vote no and kill the bill. But the resistance to the tax bill was much weaker. Dramatically less pressure was being applied, probably because people did not see the bill as a threat to their families. Sure, they assumed, it might further enrich the monied interests, but it wasn't going to take away people's health care.

We were all hopeful that my advocacy might be a spark that could change this dynamic. By making the tax bill about health care and by personalizing it so vividly, I was trying to convince the base that the law was a threat to them, to our social safety net, to our democracy. As Jen Flynn Walker explained to me, our hope was not that Flake or Collins would be persuaded to vote against the bill simply because a few dozen people got arrested in front of their offices; rather, we thought that the arrests would force the news media to finally pay attention and convey our message to the general public. Civil disobedience has a way of focusing the mind, clarifying the moral stakes, and shifting the discourse away from abstract policy toward specific human stories.

I began using my Twitter account to lay out this theory of change. Every day since the Flake encounter, I was gaining a few thousand new followers. I tried to use that platform to change the conversation about the bill, to clarify what it meant for my family and yours, for our economy and our society, for our government and our democracy.

It was, as much as anything, a coming-out party for me. Until that week I had not been public about my ALS. For more than a year, Rachael and I had avoided saying anything about our new life on social media. We had been open about the disease with anyone who we interacted with, but we had never broadcast our news to the hundreds of friends and acquaintances with whom we did not regularly interact. (I had hoped to post a message on Facebook at the six-month or one-year anniversary of my diagnosis, but I could never figure out exactly what to say. It felt too momentous. I let the dates come and go, using Facebook less and less.) In the days after the #FlakesOnAPlane video went viral, we received a stream of emails, phone calls, and text messages from people who had only just heard the news. It was too exhausting to become newly sad with each well-wisher. Instead, I tried to respond constructively, telling them that we wanted to use the disease to fight back against the Trump agenda and asking them join us in D.C., make a contribution, or call their members of Congress.

A number of close friends took me up on the invitation to come make a final stand in Congress with us. My college buddies Sim and Jeremy came down from Boston and Philadelphia. Our new nanny-share friends from Santa Barbara, Mona and Jia-Ching, brought their baby, Layaal, all the way across the country to gallivant around Capitol Hill with Baby Carl. And Katy, the childhood friend who had first diagnosed me with ALS, told us that she had a few days off and offered to accompany us out to D.C.

We arrived on Tuesday evening and checked into our new home away from home, the Capitol Skyline Hotel, where my bosses had splurged to book us the (modest) suite. A power recliner and a manual wheelchair were waiting for me in the living room. In the lobby, I had a joyous reunion with Liz Jaff, my new partner in bird-dogging. We spoke to a couple reporters and then watched the returns come in from the special U.S. Senate election in Alabama. Our mood went from energized to ebullient when it became clear that Democrat Doug Jones would pull off the stunning upset. All of the momentum was on our side, and I was filled with optimism that we would be able to defeat the bill. Jones's win meant that the Republican margin in the Senate would shrink to 51 to 49 once he took office in early January, and they would only be able to survive one defection on the tax bill. But in order to get there, we had to continue gumming up the works. And we intended to do just that, starting in the morning.

Jen Flynn Walker had choreographed an elaborate dance of controlled chaos for the day. Rachael kicked off our advocacy by talking about our smoke-induced evacuation from Santa Barbara in a speech in the hallway outside the office of Representative Mimi Walters, a California congresswoman who had voted to reduce funding for the prevention of forest fires but found plenty of money to pay for massive corporate tax cuts. When Rachael finished, Jen Flynn took over the human mic and a couple dozen protesters sat down in the middle of the hallway, chanting, "Kill the bill, don't kill us!" Jen escorted

Rachael past the police officers while our first wave of disrupters took their arrests.

Back at the hotel, I ate a bacon egg and cheese on an everything bagel and gave a few interviews to reporters. My friends prepared a half dozen framed photos of me, Rachael, and Carl that we planned to give to the Republicans whom we would lobby that day. Then they shuttled me over to the Senate, where I was greeted by a dozen friends and family. My uncle Yochai, who had been an important role model for me, came down from Boston with his two sons. Brad Lander, the Brooklyn council member with whom I had founded Local Progress, brought his high schooler Rosa. We exchanged hugs and I tried not to burst into tears. My extended community was coming together in support of me and our shared hopes for the country. I could feel that something special was happening.

In the bright, airy lobby of the Hart Senate Office Building atrium, I sat down with leaders from the Women's March—Linda Sarsour, Bob Bland, Winnie Wong—plus Ana Maria Archila (one of the co-executive directors at the Center for Popular Democracy and a longtime leader in the immigrant rights movement) and Liz Jaff, to shoot a video about what we were doing that day. A few dozen comrades surrounded us, cell phones in hand, trying desperately to inspire others to join our battle. We talked about the assault on working families that this bill represented, about how it undermined our democracy and the social fabric of our country. And we talked about our hopes for a different world. We were trying to change the tenor of the debate, to speak in a different register, to transcend the quotidian partisan rhetoric in favor of a more profound discourse.

After we were done, Jen Flynn announced that it was time for us to go meet with Senator Susan Collins. A handful of Maine residents had come down and Senator Collins had agreed to give us fifteen minutes of her time. About two hundred supporters escorted us to her office and waited in the hallway as we went inside, accompanied by a *New York Times* reporter and a couple of live streamers. In the lobby of her office, we reiterated our theory of change: the only way that Collins might vote no is if we reach her on an emotional level. "If Senator Collins actually saw you as a human, saw me as a human, then she wouldn't pass any of this," I said to one of the Maine activists, well aware that the *New York Times* reporter was scribbling in his notebook. A standoff ensued when the reporter and videographers tried to sit in on the meeting. Collins's staff insisted that they leave, and we finally relented.

Once the senator came in, however, the leader of the Maine delegation began live streaming from her iPad, and everyone who had been kicked out watched our conversation on Facebook from the other side of the door. The activist women began explaining to Collins how this bill would harm them; Collins listened intently and then began reciting a mind-numbingly boring explanation of minor tweaks that she had negotiated in exchange for her support. I tried to bring the conversation back to the fundamentals, arguing that the bill would put Medicare at risk and severely damage the private insurance market. Collins showed us a letter that Speaker Ryan and Senate Majority Leader McConnell had sent her, promising that they would pass technical fixes that would protect consumers from excessive premiums. As I had done with Jeff Flake, I pointed out the many ways in which the Republican leadership had been lying about the bill, and argued that it was foolish to give her vote now in exchange for a promise of action later. Back and forth we went, long after the fifteen-minute mark.

Finally, our field commander burst through the doors. "Ady, we have to wrap up this meeting," Jen Flynn said. "Time is running out, figuratively and literally." She meant that we had to move on to other offices and that our hundreds of protesters in the hallway were getting antsy. After the senator's next apologia, I turned around in disgust and told my handler to wheel me away. Out in the hallway,

I told our assembly that Collins was unwilling to use her power to protect the health care of her constituents; Jen took this as her cue and led a new round of chants. My optimism from the previous evening began to melt away: Collins did not seem open to voting no. I watched as the police arrested another few dozen comrades and then headed over to the Russell Senate Office Building, where a handful of Arizonans and I had a meeting scheduled with Jeff Flake. With Collins an apparent yes vote, we would definitely need to sway Flake in order to kill the bill.

But when we got there, we were told that the senator was on the floor voting on some unrelated matter. We would have to wait. This was a problem. I had assumed I'd be arrested outside of John McCain's office after our meeting with Flake. Soon the reporters and TV cameras would be going home for the evening, so we didn't have time to dilly-dally. The young Arizonans started singing and chanting in the hallway, and I joined them. The police shouted out their first warning, telling everyone to disperse or be arrested. Sitting in my wheelchair in the crowded hallway, I had trouble seeing what was going on or communicating with anyone about what we should do. I began to ask for a mic check, but suddenly, after the cops' second warning, Jen Flynn swooped in and wheeled me away. The visuals weren't good here, she said, and I should wait for the grand finale.

A contingent of about thirty people remained. We walked toward John McCain's office. He was our final hope for a Republican no vote. He was back home in Arizona, being treated for brain cancer. I had written a comically long speech addressed to him, pleading that he not make his final act the destruction of our health insurance system. It highlighted the ways in which Mitch McConnell had spent the last two decades undermining McCain's priorities, including campaign finance reform and the norms that had long governed the Senate. And it reminded McCain of Trump's attacks on his military service. My hope was to deliver the speech, get arrested, and then try to get him a video of it. We turned a corner and I saw, up ahead, the majestic columns and high ceiling of the Russell Building's rotunda. That setting would make for a far more compelling end to the day than another crowded hallway.

I directed everyone to come into the rotunda, and we formed a semicircle. Rachael stood next to me, holding Carl in her arms. His toddler friend Layaal and her parents gathered close. Megan Anderson put her wheelchair on my other side.

A guitarist started strumming "This Land is Your Land" by Woody Guthrie, which I had specifically requested for the occasion. Singing together creates powerful bonds and memories, and yet we do far too little of it in our movement—resorting instead to tiresome chants. I wanted this day to be different. Guthrie's anthem had long been a touchstone in my family. It weaves together beautifully themes of solidarity, injustice, struggle, and natural splendor. It's a song about loving America while insisting that she become a radically more just nation. Plus it just makes for a great sing-along. Someone handed out the full lyrics to the song, including the later radical verses. Brad stood in front of me, live streaming. So did my uncle, his eyes welling up with tears. I had to look away so as not to lose all control. We put our fists in the air and Carl sucked his thumb, soaking in the intense experience. The police began to move in, but Jen Flynn ran interference, begging them to let us sing for a few minutes. They obliged.

After we were done, I began mic checking my speech addressed to John McCain. I got a few sentences in before the police lost their patience. Over the din of the police bullhorn, with people being arrested left and right, and others escaping behind police lines, I had no hope of actually delivering my epic monologue. So we sang a few more choruses and offered up the obligatory chants. When the police came to arrest me, I stood up from my wheelchair, looked at the TV cameras and cell phones in the balcony above, and raised a framed photo of my family, trying desperately to focus attention on the heart of the matter. The police officer took my arm and walked me out to the elevator.

A few hours later, after I had paid $50 fine and been released from lockup—after my friends and family had finished eating Indian food out of to-go containers in our hotel suite, and after Rachael had gone to sleep—I sat in my recliner and tried to catch my breath. It had been a whirlwind day. A whirlwind week. A whirlwind year. A few months earlier, when my therapist had asked me whether ALS was giving me anything—in addition to taking so much away—I had struggled to answer. The best I could come up with was that it had created more time with friends and family over the past year and had let me skip some passport control lines on vacation. But now I had a different kind of answer. As I sat in the hotel room contemplating the possibility that I could use my ALS to block the tax bill—or at least gin up enough resistance to make the vote politically damaging for the Republicans—I realized that I had a better answer to his question. ALS was giving me newfound power at the very moment that it was depriving me of so much strength. My voice was growing softer, but I was being heard by more people than ever before. My legs were disintegrating, but more and more people were following in my footsteps. Precisely because my days were numbered, people drew inspiration from my decision to spend them in resistance. Precisely because I faced such obstacles, my comrades were moved by my message that struggle is never futile.

Sitting in that armchair late into that night and the nights that followed, I began to understand just what it was that I was doing in Washington, D.C. Of course, I had come to try to defeat the tax bill. But I was in search of so much more. I was in search of a legacy and in search of a personal story that ended in something more than tragedy. It was through collective struggle, I began to realize, that I could find my personal liberation. I could transcend my dying body by hitching my future to yours. We could transcend the darkness of this moment by joining the struggles of past and future freedom fighters. By coming together in pursuit of a different world, we could tell a different story about who we were—who *I* was. We could, in the words of my aunt, "make meaning" out of our time on earth— make meaning even out of my ALS.

The battle over the tax bill was reaching its final crescendo. Both the Senate and the House had passed similar versions of the bill. But they needed to pass identical versions, so we had one last bite at the apple. It was Thursday morning, December 14, and we expected the House and Senate to vote on Monday and Tuesday. That meant we had four days to generate as much opposition as possible. We scheduled our last stand for Monday, December 18, my thirty-fourth birthday. I spent Thursday and Friday being pushed around Capitol Hill, doing interviews on CNN and MSNBC, filming messages to the base with Senators Elizabeth Warren and Bernie Sanders, and trying everything we could to encourage people to come for protests on Monday. (I had previously worked with both Warren's and Sanders's staffs on Federal Reserve policy but was only now beginning to develop a personal relationship with the senators themselves). Doug Jones's victory in the Alabama Senate race showed the tremendous danger that Republicans would face during the upcoming midterm elections. Our hope was that if we filled the halls of Congress, we might scare a dozen members of the House into voting no. Or perhaps we might break through to the conscience of McCain or Flake or Bob Corker or Murkowski. And if that didn't work, we would turn to plan B: actually defeating the Republicans in the midterms. If we could make the tax bill politically toxic—precisely by highlighting its enormous human consequences—then perhaps we could make sure that there would be no affirmative Republican legislative agenda for the final two years of the Trump presidency.

Over the weekend my coworkers from the Center for Popular Democracy and I made a last-stitch effort to enlist the institutional center-left in the fight. There are innumerable think tanks, advocacy organization, and labor unions in Washington, D.C., with many thousands of staff between them. But very few of these institutions were putting significant effort into defeating the tax bill. We spent Saturday and Sunday trying to change that, hoping that we might convince at least some of these allies to empty their buildings on Monday and send all of their staff into Congress to join our protest. This was our best chance to sow dissension within the Republican Party and undermine their electoral prospects. Our weekend effort was wildly unsuccessful. Our requests came too late and fell on ears that were too uncomfortable with transgressive direct action. Although they sing the praises of the workers and civil and women's rights movements of bygone eras, too many professional advocates are unwilling to adopt the very tactics that made those movements powerful.

Monday morning arrived, bringing with it my birthday and some of my closest friends. Sim had managed to trade shifts at his Boston hospital and came down wearing his lab coat. Jeremy took the train over from Philadelphia. In my hotel room, the three of us put on matching black T-shirts with a simple message: "Democracy!" We shooed away some of the people who were milling about and insisted on quiet. I picked up the landline and called in to Pod Save America, the political podcast hosted by former Obama administration staffers who were trying to help mobilize the resistance. We talked about the tax bill, I gave them a hard time about the strategic errors of the Obama White House, and we established a friendly rapport that would help promote my activism repeatedly over the following year. Michael Nigro, a photojournalist from BuzzFeed News, arrived with his cameras to follow me around for the day; the portrait he took of me that night, fist raised in the air, would become my favorite.

Our coalition had decided that our closing argument should emphasize the impact that the tax bill would have on health care. It was the issue that voters cared about most. So we began the day with a press conference featuring nurses, doctors, and patients talking about Medicare and Medicaid. Sim stood behind me and spent the day wheeling me through the halls of Congress, nearly a dozen years after we had first occupied an nineteenth-century neoclassical building together.

Nisha Agarwal, the New York City commissioner for immigrant affairs, had come down to D.C. as well. She had helped found the Center for Popular Democracy back in 2012 and had gone into the De Blasio administration filled with hope that she could model for the rest of the country what a pro-immigrant local government looks like. She was charismatic, strategic, and unabashed about her ambition to change the world. But then she, too, was struck by fatal misfortune before even turning forty: glioblastoma, like Senator McCain. Unlike me, however, Nisha had decided to remain intensely private about her brain disease. But a second aggressive surgery to treat her cancer in mid-2017 had gone awry, causing a stroke that initially left her unable to speak or move. She was recovering—slowly—and saw in our protest against the tax bill the opportunity to speak publicly about her struggles and our broader, collective struggle. In a *New York Times* profile of her trip down to D.C., Nisha argued that the tax bill was prioritizing the needs of the 1 percent at the expense of medical research that could help find a cure for her cancer.

She and I and a few hundred other protesters spent the day visiting the offices of swing senators, speaking to reporters, trying to highlight the human costs of the legislation. We ate birthday cake outside of Senator Collins's office, strategized with Nancy Pelosi, and tried to encourage optimism among our troops. In the afternoon,

Megan Anderson and I rolled up to Senator Lindsey Graham, who was giving an interview to a bank of TV cameras about his friend John McCain, who was back home battling cancer. I began to speak with him, but he took one look at me and ran away. I recounted the story the next day at a major press conference organized by Pelosi, in a clip that would be viewed over 2.5 million times on Facebook. Graham's behavior was emblematic of the entire tax scam, which was being passed without public hearings, without testimony from patients or tax experts or medical professionals, without any genuine engagement with the American people. Graham was afraid to acknowledge my humanity, because doing so would make his position untenable. The Republican agenda was too damaging to the American public to survive an honest accounting, too damaging to survive genuine public debate and scrutiny. Graham and McConnell and the rest of them knew that their argument was a losing one, and so they did their work behind closed doors and ran away from those of us trying to pry them open.

But although we clearly had the better argument, we had failed to build enough power. Our efforts over the weekend had failed to generate a significantly higher turnout than on previous days. Enthusiasm on Twitter and last-minute scrambling were no replacement for deep, deliberate organizing. Without huge, disruptive crowds, we had little hope of scaring enough Republicans into voting no. Our messaging began to shift. If this government was unwilling to see our humanity, unwilling to promote the public interest, then we would have to replace it with a different government. It was time for the American people to rise up, I said—not just over the coming days and weeks, but over the months between now and November.

We returned to the Russell Rotunda for one final hurrah, where over one hundred of us sang and chanted and took arrest. We had lost this fight. Trump had his first major legislative victory. But we had our message for the upcoming midterm election. The Republican Party had sold out the American people in favor of their corporate donors.

Rachael and I bought our plane tickets home. ALS was continuing its daily assault on my body. Carl's hair was continuing to grow longer and curlier, his vocabulary broader and more entertaining. My newfound notoriety created new opportunities for activism and only heightened the difficult choices I faced about how to spend my precious, limited time.

Back in Santa Barbara, on December 21, we confronted a new, untimely loss. Our beloved cat, Dante, who had lived with us for ten years in three states on two coasts, had gone missing during the evacuation. He had warmed our laps during countless winter evenings, but we would have to face the new year without him. We bought one of the few remaining Christmas trees, hung Carl's stocking over the mantel, and snapped a photo of the three of us. I tweeted it out with the most hope that I could muster: "It's been a hard year for many families, including ours. And next year will bring a new wave of challenges. But we're here together now. So we're going to cherish this moment, enjoy this day. And we'll do it again tomorrow, thankful for what we have. May you find peace, too."

CHAPTER NINE

RESISTANCE

As soon as the tax bill was signed by President Trump, I began to look around for the next political struggle. There were some major policy questions in front of Congress, and the midterm elections were only ten months away. I had a new platform from which to influence national political discourse and I wanted to make use of it quickly—not only because there were urgent issues to address, but because my body was rapidly deteriorating and I knew my platform would soon disintegrate as well. Whatever mark I wanted to leave on the world, whatever legacy I wanted to leave for myself—for Carl to remember me by—I had to leave it now.

On the day before Christmas, from the comfort of my Santa Barbara living room, I called up Ana Maria Archila. She and I talked through the contours of the immigration debate that was about to dominate national politics. When Congress reconvened in the new year, there was going to be a major battle over the program called Deferred Action for Childhood Arrivals, or DACA, which President Obama had created to give nearly a million young undocumented immigrants authorization to work and live in the United States. Trump was threatening to end the program and dishonestly demanding that Congress reestablish it through legislation. Although there were bipartisan majorities in both the House and the Senate in favor of permanently codifying DACA, the Republican leadership was committed to satisfying its racist and xenophobic base by letting the program expire or, at the very least, holding the young immigrants hostage in exchange for an even more militarized border and a more restrictive immigration system. Nevertheless, we had some hope that we could overcome their callousness because they needed Democratic votes in order to pass essential spending legislation before January 20; if Democrats held firm, they could trade their support on the budget in exchange for fair floor votes that would make DACA permanent.

I asked Ana Maria what CPD was doing on DACA and how I could help. She told me to call up her old mentee, Cristina Jiménez, who was the executive director of United We Dream, the country's largest immigrant youth membership organization and the driving force behind the creation of DACA. Cristina would understand every nuance of the current debate and would know how we could best be useful. We connected two days later, our respective stomachs full from holiday feasting.

Cristina explained to me that she and her coalitions had two chief objectives. First, the movement needed to shore up support from Senate Democrats for taking a tough bargaining position. If they held together in support of a filibuster to the budget legislation, they could shut down the government and create a political crisis. This was the leverage they had to demand a floor vote from Majority Leader Mitch McConnell. But not all Senate Democrats were quite ready to go to bat for the undocumented immigrant youth. That needed to change. Second, Cristina explained to me, we needed to force some Republicans in the House to express support for DACA. There were about two dozen Republicans in swing districts who had many immigrant constituents, and Cristina hoped to pressure them to support DACA—or, if they resisted, unseat them in November.

We made a plan. We would kick off the new year with a bang, holding a protest outside the office of California Democratic senator Dianne Feinstein; she was an establishment Democrat who was being wishy-washy about this fight but was also facing a serious primary challenge and couldn't afford to alienate immigrant communities or the progressive base. If we could force her to take a strong stance, it would send a powerful message to Senate Minority Leader Chuck Schumer and the rest of the caucus. Cristina would organize immigrant youth and allies and I would bring along a couple of Hollywood celebrities and movement allies whom I had built relationships with over the preceding month. We got to work and scheduled our protest for January 3 in Los Angeles, hoping to set the tone for the whole year.

On the evening of January 2 we got some good news. Our press release previewing the following day's protest had done the trick, scaring Feinstein into releasing a strong statement saying that Democrats should not vote for a funding bill without a corresponding vote on DACA. Ana Maria, Cristina, and I celebrated over texts and email: there is nothing more gratifying than having your demands met even before you hold your protest! We decided to go through with the action anyway, tweaking our message slightly and saying that we needed the rest of the Democratic caucus to reiterate Feinstein's position.

The next afternoon the three of us met up at a coffee shop near Feinstein's office along with a few dozen immigrant youth, the actors Alyssa Milano and Bradley Whitford, and the Women's March leaders Linda Sarsour, Bob Bland, and Winnie Wong. Rachael was flying out of LAX early the next morning, so she and my dad came along for the ride; my childhood friends Katy and Nate Smith came to support us, too. And we also had some uninvited guests. A crew of white nationalists were occupying the corner outside Feinstein's office, and they had apparently already punched somebody before we arrived.

We gathered at a corner a block away and gave speeches to the assembly of network TV cameras and live streamers. Feinstein's staff had asked if we would come up to meet with them, so we marched our company down the sidewalk to the battlefield, Alyssa pushing my wheelchair while I held hands with Cristina and Ana Maria led our chants. When we got to the corner across the street from Feinstein's office and the hateful counterprotesters, Linda and most of our large group stayed behind while eight of us crossed the street under police escort. The cops had suggested that we enter the building through a back door, but we insisted on our right to go through the front door like all of the senator's other constituents. So the cops accompanied us as we marched straight past the white nationalists, who screamed in our faces. They were frightening, but their presence mainly served to highlight the stakes and contours of the debate. Whose side were Senators Feinstein and Schumer going to be on?

Upstairs, a group of five undocumented youths told their stories and demanded that Feinstein hold strong and pressure California's House Republicans to support DACA. Her staff reiterated her newfound resolve, to our satisfaction. We tried to wrap up relatively quickly because we knew that our crew was working hard down at street level, trading chants with the MAGA hats. Back downstairs, we closed out the proceedings by declaring our protest a success and announcing that we would soon take our fight to Washington, D.C.

Back at home in Santa Barbara, I had different new battles to fight. It had become too difficult for me to dress myself in the morning, and Rachael had her hands full getting rambunctious Baby Carl and herself out the door. So I reached out to a local nonprofit that connected me with a freelance home health aide named Poppy. She was middle-aged, going on sixteen, with glitter on her temples and jeans that she had hand-painted with colorful figures and patterns. Every morning from eight to ten a.m., she would come and help me get dressed, make me breakfast, and play with Carl if Rachael needed a moment. Over avocado toast (obviously), Poppy told me how she had gotten involved in caregiving: as a young woman in the '80s she nursed her brother, who was dying of AIDS in small-town Minnesota. Her story reminded me to be grateful that ALS is not accompanied by excruciating pain or oppressive social stigma, that suffering is universal, and that our deaths can leave behind beautiful legacies.

New symptoms were coming on fast. I found myself increasingly short of breath, and the pulmonologist at Cedars-Sinai told me that my forced vital capacity had continued its steady decline. He wrote a prescription for a ventilator and told me to use it whenever I needed help breathing and at night whenever possible. A few days later I got an email from the company that provides such devices: my health insurer, Health Net, had denied coverage based on the absurd claim that a ventilator would be "experimental." It is in fact totally standard care, one of the only things shown to marginally extend life expectancy. I took to Twitter, calling out Health Net for its ridiculous behavior. A few thousand retweets and eight hours later, the respirator company emailed me back. "You must know some pretty powerful people." Health Net had reversed its decision, faster than ever before.

Our college friends Sim and Davida were visiting the weekend that a pulmonary therapist brought over the ventilator and showed us how to use it. My doctor friends pelted her with difficult questions, and I tried to get used to having a machine rhythmically blowing air into my mouth. Sim assembled a shower chair for me, because the suction grab bars that I had installed a few months earlier were no longer sufficient to keep me safe.

Around the same time, a different medical device provider came over to deliver a power wheelchair. It was an incredible machine, with an incredible price tag of $35,000. Luckily, we had navigated the insurance bureaucracy and it didn't cost me a dime. The wheelchair had a very comfy seat and back, which would prove crucial once I started sitting in it for twelve or more hours a day. It tilted back and elevated up and moved in all sorts of creative directions to allow me to stretch or stand up or hang upside down if I needed to. But I wasn't yet ready to become a person who uses a wheelchair, so I put the device in the garage and tried to appreciate my final months of walking around.

The worst news of the month came from my neurologist, Bob Baloh at Cedars-Sinai. He was investigating an early-stage stem cell treatment that might slow down the pace of ALS progression. He had also come up with an innovative clinical trial: rather than treating some patients and leaving others with placebos, he was injecting his fetal stem cell concoction into the spinal cords of all the patients in the study, but only in locations that would impact one leg for each patient. He planned to assess the differential between the two legs in order to determine whether the treatment was working. For a year I had held off on enrolling in his study in the hopes that Dr. Baloh might eventually agree to give me a more comprehensive solution. I wanted him to work his magic throughout my spinal cord, including in the upper regions that control breathing functions. We could apply for permission to conduct a single patient clinical trial, I would find a way to raise the money, and I would marshal my political contacts to help get the FDA's permission, I told him. During late 2017 he expressed some openness to the idea, saying only that he needed a bit more time to do pre-clinical work and get his colleagues on board. I was optimistic. But in January, Dr. Baloh burst my bubble, telling me that he wouldn't be able to move forward before September at the earliest, and that my breathing would likely not be strong enough to tolerate spinal cord surgery at that point.

This news was a particularly hard blow because it was the last medical intervention that I believed had a chance to arrest my ALS. The edaravone that I had brought home from Japan had clearly not done the trick, and neither had the various supplements or vitamin shots. Also useless were the drugs in clinical trials that the Boston doctor Merit Cudkowicz had spoken about hopefully: masitinib, tirasemtiv, and NP001. These were all failing their studies. If Baloh was unable to move forward quickly with a full-body stem cell treatment, then I was surely headed for complete paralysis. Maybe future generations of ALS patients would benefit from meaningful medical advances, but they would come too late for me. On this front, acceptance was turning out to be a wiser course than hope.

In between DACA machinations, breathing-machine disputes, and depressingly glacial scientific progress, I at least had good news on my book project. Two literary agents had reached out to me during the tax fight to see if I had ever considered writing a memoir. Yes, I gleefully replied; I even had a sample chapter for their review. After some interviews and reference checks, I signed with Ms. Rachel Sussman of New York City, and we landed on a working title.

By the end of January, I had a ventilator to help me breathe, a wheelchair to move me around, a home health aide to take care of me, no more hope of a medical breakthrough that might help me, a literary agent to sell my book, and a national platform from which to bloviate and organize. Life and death were both moving quickly, and my daily existence was very different from what it had been only two months before.

My health insurance company denied a claim of mine for the second time, telling me that I was too ill to benefit from edaravone, the Japanese drug, which had recently been approved by the FDA. This time I decided not to get outraged on Twitter. Instead, I would take my complaint to their doorstep. I wrote up a series of ten questions for Health Net—Why was my claim denied? What process was used to evaluate it? How many claims have you denied this year because they sought "experimental" treatment? How many times have people appealed your denial? How many times have you reversed your decision?, etc.—and printed out a hundred copies. A friend from Santa Barbara drove me down to Health Net's corporate headquarters in the suburbs of Los Angeles, where we were met by my mother, my protest comrade Jen Flynn Walker, and a two-person film crew from the online news outlet NowThis.

We walked/rolled around the Health Net offices, handing out my list of questions and asking employees if they could help us get answers. Finally a public relations representative came out to speak with us. We sat down in an empty conference room and started going through my questions. He couldn't—or wouldn't—answer a single one. Two days later, NowThis released a three-minute video documenting my fruitless excursion that got over 8 million views. I published an op-ed in the *Nation* describing my experience and arguing that it was time to dispense with our wasteful, inefficient, infuriating for-profit health insurance system in favor of a single-payer Medicare-for-all program. Health Net again reversed its decision, but by then it was too late. They had messed with the wrong dying activist one too many times. A consumer rights lawyer reached out to me, and within a couple days we had made plans to file a class action lawsuit against the company.

The political battle over DACA was also heating up, and I was eager to get back to Washington, D.C., and throw my support behind the brave undocumented youth who were risking deportation by engaging in creative and transgressive acts of civil disobedience. (Eight years earlier, in law school, I had written an unorthodox paper about the immigrant rights movement that theorized about the First Amendment rights of undocumented immigrants to do precisely this—make their political claims more powerful by announcing their status at protests—so I was eager to witness these acts of democratic constitutionalism firsthand). Donald Trump and his white nationalist movement were seeking to expel as many brown people as possible from America. White people like me have a particular moral obligation to resist his agenda, and I was excited that Cristina Jiménez and her crew at United We Dream wanted me to join their fight.

But I could no longer travel alone. I needed a chaperone. So I called up Nate Smith. He and I had met twenty years earlier in Algebra II during the fall of freshman year of high school. Neither of us had known anybody, so we had started eating lunch together. He was quiet and intelligent, far less willing than I to break rules or challenge authority, much better read, and a good bit more disillusioned with the consumerist McMansion society we were growing up in. I listened to the Beatles, he listened to the Ramones, we listened to Dylan together. I ran the 400, he threw shot put. I fell asleep almost every morning in AP Chemistry; he stayed awake and set the curve on the exam. When we went to see *High Fidelity* in the theater, he had to explain to me both meanings of the title's double entendre, and most of the film's musical references. By senior year we had shed our adolescent awkwardness. He was elected class president on the strength of his hilariously sarcastic campaign video (promising to expand the lunch options so vegetarians would no longer have to eat their textbooks, etc.), and I was only slightly offended that he hadn't asked me to be his campaign manager. When he and I "established" the Middle Aged Motor Association (MAMA) student group (which had a membership of two), our friends over at the yearbook happily played along and dedicated a half-page spread to photos of us splayed out provocatively on the hoods of his puke-brown 1984 Camry ("El Tigre") and my navy-blue 1988 Cadillac Sedan DeVille. God, I loved that boat.

After getting his BA from Harvard, Nate took a predictably

counter-culture path and became a fancy Los Angeles cook. But that road offered offensively low pay and long hours, and in 2018 he was preparing to change careers by getting a master's in software engineering. But all his classes were online, so when I called him to see if he would like to accompany me on an excursion back to our nation's capital, he didn't hesitate.

We spent our first night together at a hotel outside of LAX, where he helped me get undressed, adjusted, and readjusted the many pillows that we used to prop me up in bed, and fiddled endlessly with the masks on my ventilator. He schlepped my bags, helped me walk down the airplane aisle when I had to pee, and delivered me safely to my new home away from home, the Capitol Skyline Hotel. I introduced him to my many comrades at Center for Popular Democracy and the charismatic leaders of the Women's March. He had majored in government and was up-to-date on the day's political news, but he had never seen the sausage-making from up close. He liked many of the people he was meeting but was a bit surprised by the ad hoc nature of our work. Neither of us knew just how much ad hoc politicking lay in store for him.

At a church near the Capitol, Nate helped me up onto the stage, where I sat with immigrant leaders and members of Congress. A thousand activists from across the eastern seaboard jammed into every corner of the nave. All of the other speakers delivered their remarks from the podium, but when it was my turn, I sat next to it in my uncomfortable manual wheelchair. Holding the microphone up to my mouth was too tiring, so I depended entirely on the strength of the audience's voice, repeating each of my mic-checked lines in booming unison. When our program was done, we marched ten blocks in the light drizzle. Then the United We Dream students filled the halls of Congress with their bright orange knit beanies and their T-shirts demanding a "Clean Dream Act Now!" They marched from office to office, pouring out their humanity, challenging the members of Congress to justify their callous cruelty. At the end of a long day we congregated back in the Russell Building rotunda, where dozens of immigrant youth strapped enormous bright, cardboard butterfly wings to their backs and others unfurled gorgeous artwork from the balcony. Their choreographed dances and songs, worthy of any stage, gave voice to their desperation and their dreams. Nate wrapped an orange bandana around my forehead and we joined them in a tight circle, where I pounded my cane on the ground to the rhythm of their clapping. Once again the police took us away. Once again our pleas failed to move the Republican leadership. Trump, McConnell, and Ryan were unwilling to permit an up-or-down vote on DACA. If the undocumented youth were to receive some stability and peace of mind, then other immigrants and border communities would have to pay a steep price. We flew home, inspired and dejected at the same time.

In March we would try one last time. Trump had announced that the DACA program would terminate on the fifth, so hundreds of us gathered on the National Mall. Muslim and Jewish religious leaders locked arms with Latinx youth; Nate pushed my wheelchair, and once again I held Cristina's hand. At the intersection between Congress and the House office buildings, one hundred protesters sat down and blocked traffic. I went inside with the imams and rabbis. I stood up out of my wheelchair. Two of the most prominent Muslim leaders in America took my arms. Step by careful step, Omar Suleiman, Nihad Awad, and I walked down the corridor, toward the pack of flashing and rolling and live-streaming cameras. When we got to Paul Ryan's office door, I lifted my cane and knocked—quietly at first, but louder and louder as it became clear that his staff would not even face our delegation. "If you do not disperse," the police bullhorn blared, "you will be subject to arrest." It was the first time in memory that Muslim-American religious leaders had engaged in civil disobedience, a testament to Linda Sarsour's hard, careful organizing and her commitment to multiracial solidarity.

Although our pleas again fell on deaf ears, the courts stepped in and declared that the Trump decision to end DACA was arbitrary and capricious. The urgency to find a legislative solution dissipated, and with it the little hope we had of winning for the immigrant youth citizenship. Late at night on a phone call debriefing the struggle, Cristina Jiménez told me and Ana Maria Archila and others that it was time to turn our attention to the elections. Only a new balance of power could make life more secure for her people.

From D.C., Nate and I headed north to Baltimore, where we met up with Liz Jaff to figure out how we could help deliver that new balance of power. Of the 197 Democrats in the House of Representatives, about 90 belonged to the Congressional Progressive Caucus. I was slated to receive the caucus's "Activist of the Year" award at its annual conference, where many movement progressives would gather to scheme about the election and make plans for its aftermath. Liz and I sat in a lounge outside the main auditorium, batting around ideas for how we might help flip the House to Democratic control. If we raised enough money, maybe we could run ads about the importance of health care and the threat posed by Republicans to families like mine. Or maybe we could raise money for voter registration and mobilization by community-based organizations like those in the Center for Popular Democracy network. Someone told us about an upcoming special election for a House seat in Arizona. It was a heavily Republican district, but the Democratic candidate was strong, and—who knows? we thought—maybe anti-Trump sentiment was fierce enough to make an upset possible. We decided to take a field trip to Phoenix. As the conference came to a close, Representative Keith Ellison of Minneapolis presented me with my award. I mic-checked a twenty-minute speech, condemning the cruelty of the Trump administration and the cowardice of the corporate Democrats who had run the party for far too long. As I rattled off the long list of Progressive Caucus members who would chair House committees under a Democratic majority—Maxine Waters on Financial Services! Jerry Nadler on Judiciary!—I wondered what path America would take in November. The polls were looking pretty good, but, of course, they had looked good in 2016, too. And it didn't seem like luck was something I could be counting on.

Back home in Santa Barbara, Nate and I began making arrangements for our April excursion. We would spend a few days in Arizona trying to influence the media narrative and excite the Democratic base; then we would travel to Atlanta and Athens, Georgia, to support two bold candidates who were running in Democratic primaries and schmooze with high-dollar donors at the Democracy Alliance conference; and then we would wrap up at CPD's quaint farmhouse in New York for the organization's quarterly staff meeting. The logistics would be extra complicated this trip, because we decided it was time for me to start using my power wheelchair. At each stop, we would need to rent a wheelchair-accessible van, along with the usual recliner and an accessible hotel room.

Special elections matter in large part because they are bellwethers for the national mood. Donald Trump and the Republicans in Congress were exceptionally unpopular. But would that translate into electoral victories for the Democrats? The special election in Arizona's Eighth Congressional District would tell us a lot about what would be coming in November. Surprisingly, however, national Democrats were not investing heavily in the race. They probably thought it was unwinnable because its voters had chosen Trump by over 20 percentage points and its former Republican congressman by an even larger margin.

Liz Jaff and I had competing theories for how we might impact the midterms. I believed that the key would be getting more Democrats to actually come out and vote. Midterm elections are famously low-turnout affairs; many people (especially young, black, and brown people) who vote for Democrats in presidential elections fail to show up for the midterms. If we could motivate more of them to take this election seriously, then we could win back the House and maybe even the Senate. Liz looked at things differently. She knew that one of the key reasons Trump had won was that suburban and working-class white people had flipped from voting for Obama in 2012 to voting for Trump in 2016. Our goal, Liz thought, should be to convince these voters that the Republicans were hurting their families. To make the case, there was no example more powerful than health care and no messenger better than me. And Arizona's Eighth Congressional District was the perfect laboratory to test her hypothesis: it was home to one of America's first planned retirement communities, Sun City, and had enormous numbers of senior citizens. Senior citizens who vote. Senior citizens who depend on Medicare every day. The candidates in the race fit our narrative perfectly. Our opponent was a standard-issue Republican troglodyte with bleached-blond hair and an avowed commitment to repealing Obamacare, regardless of how many people that would hurt. The Democrat, Hiral Tipirneni, was a charismatic public health doctor who knew how to talk about public policy in simple language that resonated with voters' lived experience. And, of course, Phoenix was the one place where I actually had some name recognition, at least among political reporters—the *Arizona Republic* had published a play-by-play of my entire eleven-minute conversation with Jeff Flake—so my upcoming campaign excursion might actually generate some local headlines. That, at least, was our theory.

Nate drove up to Santa Barbara and we headed to our picturesque airport. Rachael gamely agreed to join us for the Arizona portion of our trip, and she took Carl out of day care for a few days so he could come, too. Liz met us in Phoenix, bringing along a scrappy film crew from People's Television, a production company based out of SoHo founded by a radical named Nicholas Bruckman. Nick and his team would follow us around for a few days and then produce some hard-hitting thirty-second ads that Liz would try to get up on television in the crucial final days before the election.

Phoenix sprawls. Dozens of miles of single-family homes and cookie-cutter strip malls, splayed out on a mind-numbing grid. And then dozens of miles more. At a retirement community, we visited a monthly Parkinson's group meeting, where I talked about my battle with ALS and why the special election was so important for protecting our access to health care. Rachael and Carl and I knocked on a handful of voters' doors, giving Nick the B-roll shots he would need for our political ads. We stopped by the local Democratic headquarters and gave a pep talk to the volunteers, telling them that their efforts would set an example for activists all around the country. With Nate's and Rachael's steady support, I made the exhausting effort to get in the hotel swimming pool with Carl, to Nick's effusive gratitude. Then, at eleven p.m.—with marijuana stoking our creative embers and suppressing our better judgment—Nate and I made the decision that we should all wake up in six hours, go buy red T-shirts at Walmart, and join the thousands of students and parents and teachers who were demanding a real investment in the state's public schools, the latest in a wave of bold teacher strikes that had won unlikely victories in conservative states that year. Liz and Nick were game, and I was lucid enough to let Rachael and Carl sleep in.

The following day was our main event. At seven thirty a.m., in an antiseptic office park in the municipality of Surprise, Arizona, the chamber of commerce was holding the only candidate forum of the election. We had purchased a block of tickets in the hope that we might re-create a #FlakesOnAPlane moment. Nick Bruckman and his crew were not allowed to bring in their professional equipment, but they each had high-resolution iPhones at the ready. Our hosts knew we were coming: four police officers stood guard at each door, the machine guns in their hands more appropriate for Fallujah or *Grand Theft Auto* than a polite civic breakfast. The friendly neoliberal moderator asked straightforward questions of each candidate while the chamber's officers watched us like hawks, expecting a disruption at any moment. We didn't oblige.

Instead, when the Q and A session was over, I rolled up to the Republican, State Senator Debbie Lesko, and asked why she wanted to strip me and those Parkinson's patients of our Medicare. Neither she nor the congressional Republican leadership wanted to cut Medicare or Medicaid, she insisted. I expressed grave concern that she didn't even know about her party's central legislative agenda and promised to send her the evidence that very day. It wasn't a Jeff Flake home run, but Liz and Nick got the footage they needed. Nick's editor spliced together my conversation with Lesko against the crystal clear headline from the *Washington Post*: "Ryan says Republicans to target welfare, Medicare, Medicaid spending in 2018." Our video made the rounds on Twitter and the *Arizona Republic* published a long article about my attempt to influence the election, including via what Liz audaciously promised would be a six-figure ad buy.

I kissed Rachael and Carl goodbye and thanked her for taking time off of work to join this expedition. Nick and his crew flew home. And Liz, Nate, and I flew to Atlanta for a meeting of the biggest Democratic donors in the country to try to make good on her bravado.

The Democracy Alliance was founded by wealthy Democrats after the 2000 election in order to build political infrastructure to help win elections and advance progressive priorities. I had been invited to give a seven-minute plenary talk in the ornate ballroom at the luxury hotel where the DA was holding its biannual meeting. I prepared some inspirational remarks, but it was Liz who had brought with us a secret weapon with which to introduce me: a three-minute cinematic epistle from me to Carl, weaving together our family's struggle with ALS, my activism during the tax bill fight, and the importance of the upcoming midterm election. Nick had produced an incredibly powerful video, complete with a soaring orchestral score, and as I rolled out onto the stage, I looked out over a sea of teary-eyed millionaires.

Over the next twenty-four hours, Liz told everyone and their mother about our trip to Arizona and the opportunity to score a stunning political upset. She shook the trees for donations, climbed into the branches to shake them some more, and then got out a chain saw and swung it around wildly until she had raised a cool $100,000. Back in New York, Nick and his editors pulled together two thirty-second advertisements featuring images from our recent trip and urging voters to vote for the Democratic doctor. We wired the money over to the TV stations and to Facebook on Thursday evening, which meant voters would see them for a full four days before polls opened on Tuesday. I was glad that other politicos were finding our work valuable but nervous that it wouldn't make a difference.

Meanwhile, my speechifying duties complete, Nate and I woke up before dawn and drove east to the Town House Café, a restaurant famous for feeding civil rights activists back in the day, right off the courthouse square in the town of Covington, Georgia. There, I poured loads of salt on my grits and eggs and listened as an old-timer recounted the month he spent in jail because the white city government refused to let him and his comrades pay bail for their sin of protesting segregation. Our hosts were Richard Dien Winfield, a University of Georgia philosophy professor, his righteous wife, Sujata, and their adult children. Winfield was running for Congress on a transformative platform: a guarantee of access to a decent job for anyone who wants it, enhanced free Medicare for all, a $20 minimum wage, free child care and university, and free access to legal services for civil and criminal matters.

Winfield and I bonded over our shared opinion that the job guarantee in particular had the potential to transform America's economy and society. The central concept was simple. Any U.S. resident who wanted one could get a job, funded by the federal government, that paid a fair wage, included good benefits, and provided a useful service to the American people: installing solar panels and retrofitting homes; building public housing and mass transit; caring for young children, the elderly, and disabled people; creating public art; rejuvenating local parks; teaching summer camp; and on and on. Done correctly, a good-jobs guarantee would largely eliminate poverty in the United States. It would directly and radically improve the lives of long-term unemployed and "unemployable" people—particularly the black, Latinx, and Native American workers who suffer from both structural and malicious discrimination. It would combat gender inequities by giving women an alternative if they are being underpaid or mistreated in their jobs. It would empower all private-sector workers to demand raises and form unions by dramatically reducing the costs of being fired. It would facilitate a just transition to a carbon-free economy. It would strengthen our economy's long-term trajectory and people's daily lives by creating transit, energy, and communications infrastructure. And it would enrich Americans' lives by funding child, elder, and special-needs care. Sounds pretty good, huh?

The job guarantee was also a crucial intervention into American politics. America's founding sin and its continuing greatest failure is the racialized inequality that has been built into our economy. And as the 2016 election made clear, the Democratic Party has struggled to imagine an agenda that addresses race and class at the same time. This failure left open political terrain that could be occupied by the racism and corporatism of Donald Trump. This was the insight that Amy Carroll had introduced to Fed Up, turning it from a good but wonky idea into something that grassroots activists could connect to. It was also a key insight of Martin Luther King Jr. and Bayard Rustin. The 1963 March on Washington was billed not only as a march for civil rights but a march for "jobs and freedom." I continue to believe this combination is central to a politics that can unite a race analysis with an inequality (or class) analysis, transcend the dilemma that Liz and I had debated in Arizona, and inspire a movement big enough for the change we need. That was why I had traveled to rural Georgia. A job guarantee can address race and class at the same time, uniting all the various interest groups within the party around a common vision for shared prosperity. I believed that a victory by Winfield in the general election, or even just in the primary, would help us place this issue at the center of the Democratic Party's agenda.

Over the course of twelve fascinating hours, Winfield and I spoke about his platform with progressive activists in Oxford, white Republican residents of a trailer park in Monroe, black residents of a public housing complex, and union leaders at a United Steelworkers Hall. I urged the activists to pour their hearts into this campaign because of how it would transform the contours of acceptable political discourse in our country if Winfield could win on such a platform in a southern Republican stronghold. Everyone we spoke with enthusiastically embraced his vision for a more equitable economy. Not a single one worried about budget deficits. I gave Winfield some pointers about his canvassing rap and spoke with his staff about their field program, which was disappointingly small. After the union meeting ended, Sujata pulled me close and told me something about my legacy and my country and my son. I began sobbing and buried my face in her shoulder until I was ready to look up and say good night. As Nate drove us over dark country roads back to Atlanta, I was filled with a sense of hope and purpose and deep, permanent loss.

Both the Arizona doctor and the Georgia philosopher lost their elections that spring, but their efforts foreshadowed good things to come. Tipirneni lost by only 5 percentage points, a massive swing in a district that Trump had won by 22. If Democrats could create a wave even half that big in November, they would win dozens of seats and take control of the House. Winfield did not win his congressional primary, but only a few weeks later a young democratic socialist named Alexandria Ocasio-Cortez won hers running on an equally bold platform in New York City, shocking the Democratic establishment. I had publicly supported her primary challenge to the incumbent corporate Democrat, and had made a small donation, but was as surprised as everyone else when she won. In Congress, Ocasio-Cortez has already become the most prominent advocate for a Green New Deal, with a job guarantee at its center. Her vision is brilliant because it marries a wildly popular proposal—decent jobs for everyone—with a crucial policy intervention: a just transition to a carbon-neutral economy. In order to preserve the planet, America must find a new reservoir of political will, and the Green New Deal represents the best path I've heard to reach those salutary waters.

"Faster! Faster!" Carl said, the first time we put him in my lap and I rolled my wheelchair down the sidewalk. Once I resigned myself to using the wheelchair, and we resigned ourselves to paying $28,000 for a *used* wheelchair-accessible van, my world expanded. I could once again go to the zoo, accompany Rachael to pick Carl up from day care, and go down to my beloved shoreline. Watching the college boys and svelte grandmothers and jolly parents running on the paths I knew so well was no longer infuriating. Oftentimes it wasn't even sad. Instead, I was just happy to be out in the fresh warmth.

That spring we celebrated Carl's second birthday, my signing of a book contract, and the publication of Rachael's book, *Writing to the World: Letters and the Origins of Modern Print Genres*. In her research into the new literary genres like the newspaper, novel, and biography that emerged in the eighteenth century, Rachael had had a profound insight: their early iterations were all heavily dependent on letters (correspondence) for their structure, and that, she argued, was because the familiar genre of the letter was helping readers transition from the old world of manuscript to the new world of print. It was a brilliant piece of scholarship that guaranteed her a successful career as an English professor. Knowing that we would soon lose my income, her success brought us important peace of mind for the long term.

Although Rachael's career was flourishing, life at home was becoming more difficult for her. Carl was in prime toddlerhood, making constant, not-always-rational demands on her. In the evenings, after a full day of teaching and research, Rachael needed to feed us dinner, get Carl bathed and asleep, and then repeat much of the process with me. I could no longer brush my teeth, shave my face, or clean myself after using the toilet. I needed help getting out of my wheelchair, into my pajamas, and into the living room recliner, where I slept. Could she please bring me a bottle of water? Oh, my laptop needs to be plugged in: Would she mind? Oops, I dropped my phone: Could she come get it? During the nights, uncomfortable and too often short of breath, I moaned and grunted loudly, using increasingly elaborate handholds and maneuvers to turn myself over. It woke her up and kept her awake. With each month, as my symptoms worsened, Rachael's duties expanded, her personal time vanished, and our romantic partnership morphed into more of a unidirectional caregiving one. In the early weeks after my diagnosis, Rachael had urged us both to stay in the moment and enjoy the good life we still had; as our lives became harder, that strategy became more difficult to execute.

In the spring of 2018, we also welcomed into our home a set of new faces. The filmmaker Nicholas Bruckman told us that he wanted to make a documentary about me, so Rachael and I let him and his cinematographers record our domestic life, warts and all. My first home health aid departed for a full-time job but found for me an incredible replacement: Laura, a middle-aged sailor who lived on her small boat in the Santa Barbara marina and brought dignity and purpose to every small act of caregiving. I was grateful for her emotional intelligence, because ALS forced us to become so intimate so immediately. I also hired a new personal assistant to watch over me during the day and help me keep working and writing.

Aiyana Sage was in her late twenties and had moved to Santa Barbara because she loved the laid-back, crunchy, earnest, creative artist community she had found here. She typed fast, paid attention to details, cooked a delicious roast chicken, designed beautiful social media graphics, made Carl laugh, and didn't make me feel embarrassed when I needed her to unbutton my pants in the living room and then empty my plastic handheld urinal.

Meanwhile, my comrades and I had developed a theory for how we might impact the midterm elections. We would replicate our Arizona adventure in swing districts across the country, trying to inspire more progressives to volunteer on campaigns and shooting advertisements to persuade voters that the Republican Party was bad for their health. I had been invited to give a couple major speeches in Detroit and Minneapolis in July, so Liz Jaff and I began to plan a three-state road trip through Minnesota, Wisconsin, and Michigan. But our appetite for narrative drama soon got the best of us, and after spending a few days examining lists of competitive House races, we decided to embark upon a six-week, twenty-state trip, from California to Maine, in a wheelchair-accessible RV. The audacity of the excursion was precisely the point. I would try to set an example for others to follow, throwing my whole body and soul into the election. If the stakes for our democracy were in fact monumental, then nothing less would be appropriate.

There were a thousand and one details to work out. First, we identified thirty congressional seats held by Republicans that Democrats could plausibly win; we focused on the tier 2 races that were more difficult than the tier 1 "toss-ups" where the Democratic Party was already heavily invested. Our goal was to broaden the playing field, creating more opportunities for upsets and a higher likelihood that we could win the 218 seats necessary for control of the House. Liz made a budget and started working the phones in search of funding. Helen Brosnan—a scrappy twenty-three-year-old feminist and democratic socialist with a vulgar sense of humor and an infectious laugh—designed an event calendar with community-based organizations and resistance groups in each of our target congressional districts. Nate flew up to Seattle and dropped $70,000 on one of the two wheelchair-accessible RVs for sale west of the Mississippi. There were RV campgrounds to reserve, T-shirts to design, press releases to write. We've decided to call this the Be a Hero tour, as an allusion to my plea to Jeff Flake that he put country above party. And Liz filed the paperwork for the Be a Hero PAC, which would help us do the work.

Most concerning to me was the state of my voice. Every week it was softer, my diction more jumbled. Would I be able to inspire my audiences into action? Would I even be understood? I made a backup plan. Jennifer Epps-Addison, the president of the Center for Popular Democracy network who had been by my side during the conversation with Janet Yellen, agreed to join us for long stretches of the trip. She was a former public defense attorney and worker organizer, and had the charisma and the vision to take over my speechifying duties if necessary.

By mid-June, most of the pieces were falling into place. And then the news broke that the Trump administration was forcibly separating migrant parents from their children at the border with the explicit purpose of making the experience so horrific that other parents would refrain from seeking refuge in America. The backlash was swift and overwhelming. For the first time ever, the media stayed focused on an outrageous Trump policy, refusing to be distracted by other shiny new objects. Public opinion was so lopsided that even Republican politicians wouldn't defend the practice. Immigrant rights organizers recognized that this was a novel opportunity: Americans were finally confronted with the cruelty of immigration enforcement, and they didn't like what they were seeing. If we could bring large numbers of people into the streets, we might be able to force the White House to retreat and shift the contours of the immigration debate.

On June 18, Ben Wikler, of MoveOn, told me that they were about to declare a national day of protest for the thirtieth and asked me if I would organize the Los Angeles event. I jumped at the opportunity, hopeful that we could build upon the many protests of the previous eighteen months and marshal the nationwide fury into landslide victories at the polls in November. Our national RV tour was scheduled to begin on July 1. This immigration event would serve as a perfect kickoff.

I didn't have relationships in the Los Angeles progressive movement, but I knew plenty of people who did. Within a few days we had an executive committee of strong institutions sponsoring the rally, including Women's March LA and the Coalition for Humane Immigrant Rights of Los Angeles. An event-production maestro from Hollywood volunteered his services, and we started holding daily ninety-minute coordination calls to secure the permits, contract for a stage and sound, create a speaking program, roll out a media plan, and, most importantly, gin up thousands of attendees. My job was to make sure that all the balls stayed in the air. I spent all week on the phone, pacing around the house in my wheelchair. My voice could still manage to moderate the calls, but I had to be more intentional and succinct with my words. By the eve of the event, we had 25,000 RSVPs on Facebook and a great lineup of speakers, including immigrant and faith leaders, California politicos (Eric Garcetti, Kamala Harris, Gavin Newsom, and Maxine Waters) and celebrities (Chadwick Boseman, Laverne Cox, John Legend, and Chrissy Teigen).

But for some immigrant rights advocates, that was precisely the problem. The ICE out of LA Coalition and Black Lives Matter Los

Angeles were engaged in high-profile disputes with Los Angeles mayor Eric Garcetti for his refusal to rein in the police department or disentangle it from federal immigration enforcement. Instead of holding a disruptive, transgressive protest, our critics argued that we were putting on a shiny PR stunt. These are the tensions that inevitably arise when doing movement work: how broad to make your coalitions, how radical to make your demands, which opponents to target when.

Seventy-five thousand Angelenos turned out on that sunny Saturday morning, more than at any of the dozens of protests around the country that day. I had never spoken to a crowd a tenth that size, but my mic check went smoothly. The Trump administration did indeed back down, agreeing to stop separating families at the border—but only by locking up everyone, including the kids, and with an appalling reunification process that left many young children separated from their parents for many months, and some never reunited. Our movement had failed to meaningfully change the dynamics of the immigration debate or deliver a knockout political blow to the Republicans. But we had helped bring together the progressive community in Los Angeles in one more act of resistance. Southern California would be a critical battlefield in the effort to win the House and stave off American fascism. So it had been a worthwhile exercise.

CHAPTER TEN

HOPE

Our six-week cross-country tour left from Santa Barbara on July 2. These are my recollections from the road.

Late at night, July 3, 2018
Sparks Marina RV Park, Reno, Nevada

Carl had sprinted into the playground, free at last after a long morning in the Big Red Truck. I followed close behind, desperate for any semblance of shared physical activity with my toddler. Ten yards in, I realize that it was a mistake to drive my 350-pound wheelchair onto a patch of wood chips, because now I was stuck. In the hot sun. In some playground off the freeway in the middle of California's Central Valley, hundreds of miles from our destination. We're on Day 2 of our six-week road trip, and it is not off to a promising start.

Rachael tries to push, but the wheelchair won't budge. I

will have to get out, to lighten the load, and walk over to the concrete sidewalk. Tracey, the Center for Popular Democracy's director of racial justice campaigns, entertains Carl while Rachael gets my walker from the van. She helps me stand, Carl screaming for her attention. She tries to push the wheelchair again. Nothing. "Put it in manual mode," I say, trying to look behind me without falling over. "Down there, near the front wheels." Rachael puts her back into it, and finally the thing inches forward. There's no way she can get it all the way to the concrete by herself. Tracey comes to help. Carl can tell how stressed we all are and is crying for someone to play with him. I stand hunched over my walker, trying not to fatigue, watching the women sweat every push. They manage to get to the concrete edge but then realize that its lip is too big. They'll have to actually lift the monstrosity up. "Ask that man over there for help!" I shout, my weak voice barely making it to my audience. Finally, they get the wheelchair onto solid ground. Phase 1 complete. Phase 2 won't be any easier. With Rachael spotting me, I try to make my way across the wood chips. But the walker won't scoot on this terrain and my left foot is in complete rebellion. It refuses to bear any weight, twisting and collapsing instead. Carl is crying, Rachael is stressed, I'm in pain. Tracey and Rachael grab me from both sides, my arms around their shoulders, and we drag/ stumble across the playground. Exhausted, I collapse into my wheelchair. "Well, that wasn't a good idea," Rachael tells me, rubbing salt straight into my wounded psyche. This is what I get for trying to approximate being a father chasing his son on the playground.

It's now midnight. Rachael and Carl are asleep in the RV's bedroom and I'm out here in the living room in my recliner. Nate is at my feet on the pullout sofa. We're in the finest RV

park Reno has to offer. Tracey drove us in the van all day—
including that hour-long search for a walker to replace the one
we left standing in the playground—and then over and down
the Sierras in the dark. We knew today would be an epic drive,
but I was foolish to compare it to the long drives Rachael and
I made in our twenties. That was a different life and we were
very different people. Nate was right to be concerned, right to
insist on a very early start. Have we bitten off more than we can
chew?

We can't lose faith yet. Besides, yesterday was good.
The local ABC affiliate and *USA Today* both covered our
announcement of a class-action lawsuit against Health Net for
its mistreatment of clients like me. And we had fun bringing
a delegation of two dozen angry constituents to Congressman
Steve Knight's offices. His staff certainly made fools of
themselves, and our activists seemed energized and grateful
for our participation. Hopefully Liz and Nick got some good
interview footage. Tomorrow will be more relaxed, and once we
get to the Midwest, the driving will ease up considerably.

Early afternoon, July 5, 2018
Somewhere in remote northeast Nevada

We're cruising down I-80 at a cool 63 miles per hour and my
enfeebled neck is grateful to the enormous tires and shocks
on our thirty-three-foot 2006 Thor Motor Coach Four Winds
Windsport 35W, which are making this a very smooth ride.
Nate is steering the large wheel with his forearms. He tired of
my Grateful Dead playlist so I put on some honky-tonk and now
he's in a thoroughly good mood. All of us are. That lunch was
delectable. Who knew that immigrants from Basque country

came to the foothills of the Sierra Nevadas in the 1860s in search of gold and that their descendants are still serving up mouthwatering grilled meats and vegetables in the region's quaint dusty mining towns today? Nate Smith knew, that's who. I haven't eaten a steak so good in a decade. And that onion soup was incredible, even though Rachael had to feed it to me out of a glass and I still made a big mess. She and Carl are conked out now on the sofa next to me, his car seat strapped down with a seat belt. Speaking of which, Nate's jerry-rigged system for tying down my wheelchair with four motorcycle straps is working great. He is definitely winning the road trip MVP award so far.

Bedtime, July 7, 2018
Salt Lake City, Utah

I stand up out of my wheelchair and lean on my walker. Nate steers the chair backward and stands behind me, his hands on my hips. I take a baby step toward my recliner. "I wonder what the hell we're really doing here," I say. "I kind of think that maybe this whole thing is an elaborate vanity project to make me feel better about myself before I die."

Nate mocks me with the same sarcastic voice that he's been using for twenty years. "No, no, that can't possibly be true."

My laughter throws me off balance. "No jokes!" I yell, totally seriously.

"No jokes!" he replies, which just makes me laugh more. If I'm looking for simple psychological support, Nate is no mood to provide it. Instead, he'll provide me with what I really need: physical support, wise counsel, and humor, with all the complexity that that entails.

Two months ago, at the end of our trip to Arizona, Georgia, and New York, Nate and I began discussing the idea that he and his partner, Sarah, would move to Santa Barbara in the fall so that he could help take care of me as I moved toward complete paralysis. It is a stunning display of allegiance. I have tried not to get my hopes up, but he seems increasingly confident that the plan will work out. Sarah has even given notice at her restaurant. This comes as a tremendous relief to me and Rachael, because we are so comfortable in his presence and will be so desperately in need of reliable support.

Nate went through some hard times in college, and I, two hundred miles away, was not there for him. I spent the ensuing decade trying to atone for my error, calling him every time I was in town, texting to see how he was doing, not getting annoyed or giving up when he went into hiding or failed to reciprocate. After my diagnosis, Nate sat on my sofa and wept apologetically, promising to be a more attentive friend. It took eighteen months for him to make good on that commitment, but this year, like a character out of Scripture, he is putting his full spirit into service. The notion that he would leave his Pasadena home and put aside his studies to clean and lift and clothe and feed my limp body—and cook for and teach and tease Carl, since I cannot—well, that notion gives me peace and overwhelms me at the very same time.

We get me in my recliner and Nate takes us through the full routine: pills washed down with Muscle Milk, tooth brushing, face washing, a bottle of water, a charging iPhone, an empty urinal, a blanket, and one milliliter of CBD/THC tincture. He unfolds the sofa bed, does his own toilette, turns on his reading light, and climbs under the sheets at my feet. Ten minutes go by. It is quiet. I feel my body twitching, the flimsy muscles on my limbs and torso firing off in rapid succession, too quickly for me to even count. My body does this all day every day. To a healthy me, it would have been torture, but now it is the most benign of my symptoms, going unnoticed unless I am perfectly quiet and attentive. Five more minutes go by. I ask Nate what he's reading. *Saint Augustine's Prayer Book*. I ask him to read me an excerpt.

" 'Let me set aside the day's work,' " he reads calmly and deliberately, " 'with its disappointments or accomplishments, tasks accomplished or those that remain to be done; let me leave all this aside, so that none of it will distract me from those I love and who love me. You have given me work to do for the greater good, and you have given those closest to me to love that we might find joy in each other. Give me wisdom to respond to your call in both and to receive them both as gifts from your hand. Amen.' "

We sit in silence. And then I start crying. A lot. With four simple sentences, he has captured the full richness of our relationship, my personal philosophy these past two years, and our cross-country political pilgrimage this summer. I try to tell him how grateful I am for his love and support and his tremendous commitment of more in the months to come. I cannot get the words out. But he understands nonetheless.

Early evening, July 10, 2018
Des Moines, Iowa

After two more long days of driving, we're in Iowa, and the trip is finally feeling productive. The thirty activists who turned out for our strategy meeting seemed genuinely grateful that I was there; the local organizer said he never gets such a good turnout for a midweek midday event. We've all felt pretty pessimistic about the future of our country ever since Anthony Kennedy announced he was retiring from the Supreme Court two weeks ago. So it was great to go around the room today and hear from everybody what is making them hopeful right now. There really is a lot of good organizing happening, and it looks like two or maybe even three of Iowa's four congressional seats may flip from Republican to Democratic in November.

The forum about caregiving in the afternoon was really intense. I hadn't planned to talk about my parents—about how *I* had expected to care for *them*, not the other way around—and I certainly hadn't intended to start crying in the middle of my remarks. My voice becomes difficult to understand when I'm upset, but, judging from the standing ovation, I think they got the gist of what I was saying.

Tomorrow should be fun. Liz found out that Mike Pence is coming to town for a fund-raiser and a "policy" speech. She wants to dress me up in MAGA attire and try to infiltrate the event. Ha.

3:00 p.m., Friday, July 13, 2018
The Hilton, Minneapolis, Minnesota

All right. We've hit our stride. Last night, at a community town hall about Medicare for All, Congressman Keith Ellison leaves me blushing and speechless when he compares me to Congressman John Lewis. This morning, at a rally headlined by Bernie Sanders, from the stage made famous by Prince in *Purple Rain*, I get to give a speech to 1,500 cheering progressives. Liz initially had thought it would be a mistake to deliver a lengthy peroration on democracy and activism and the state of our nation, but even she acknowledged afterward that the energy during my closing mic check was incredible. Backstage, I told Bernie it was an honor to struggle by his side, and he gave me a hilariously awkward hug. But I'll cut him some slack, since hugging someone in a wheelchair is tricky for anybody.

It's nice to be staying in one city for a few nights in a row. But I'm jealous of all my friends who are getting to enjoy the Hilton's clean sheets and firm mattresses. It's too laborious for me to do the same. A hot shower is so therapeutic, but it's become such an ordeal that I'm inclined to just stick to sponge baths. At least we found a physical therapist who will come to my room in a couple hours. My muscles are tight as fuck.

Tomorrow I'm spending the day at the Local Progress national convening and speaking at the closing session. It'll be great to see old friends and the new staff that Sarah has hired. I imagine that I'll be treated as an elder statesman, which makes me proud and furious at the same time.

Sunset, July 21, 2018
Haas Lake Park RV Campground, New Hudson, Michigan,
an hour northwest of Detroit,

When we set out on this adventure, we predicted that our time in the Midwest would be a highlight. It hasn't disappointed. We've spent time with some visionary congressional candidates, including two who will likely become the first Muslim women in Congress. (Ilhan Omar, running to replace Keith Ellison in Minneapolis, is brave enough to call for a reduction in our nation's military spending—a thoroughly obvious and smart policy proposal that remains verboten in Washington, D.C. And Rashida Tlaib, running to represent Detroit, wants to rejuvenate federal civil rights law by clarifying that it prohibits disparate impact, not merely disparate treatment.) We've witnessed brilliant young black community organizers offer their members trenchant critiques of our political substructures and comprehensive prescriptions for building sufficient power to change these realities. Abdul El-Sayed, a thirty-three-year-old epidemiologist running to be governor of Michigan, brought three hundred suburbanites to tears talking, with Obama cadences, about the bond that he and I have built this year based on the dreams from our fathers and our shared dreams, as new fathers ourselves. I got a standing ovation from 5,000 letter carriers for my speech at their union's national convention, which included a wholly unconventional extended summary of Rachael's recent book, laying out the central role that postal routes and letter writing played in the development of modern literary and political culture. We stuffed ourselves with Detroit barbecue and Milwaukee cheese curds, drank Pabst Blue Ribbons in Racine, Wisconsin, on the shore of Lake Michigan, and said "No, thank you" to Chicago's version of "pizza."

Now Nate and I are relaxing, the familiar synthetic melodies of the War on Drugs serenading us and the warm sunset. A week of lower-profile events awaits us, after which we'll hit our trip's crescendo in Philadelphia, D.C., and New York, and our denouement in New England.

Late at night, July 21, 2018
KOA Holiday Campground, Lebanon, Ohio

We are in my old stomping grounds, the conservative suburbs of Cincinnati, where I came for my first job after college to try to help Democrats win back the House. I'm here again a dozen years later with the same purpose. Vic Wulsin, my erstwhile candidate, came to my breakfast event this morning; unlike me, she hasn't aged. We forgot to bring my headset and portable amplifier, and my audience of thirty had great difficulty hearing me, until one proactive grandma had the good sense to unplug the whirring commercial refrigerator in the corner.

Now I lie in my recliner, totally stoned and totally clearheaded. There is no escaping the reality of what is happening to my voice. Every week it is less audible and less intelligible. Every week more people are staring at me blankly. Asking me to repeat myself. Or, worst of all, pretending they've understood. Losing my ability to speak is far worse than losing my ability to walk or type. Ever since I was an only child holding forth at the dinner table to an audience of professors, I've been enamored by my own voice, enchanted by the prospect that others would be persuaded by the force of my rhetoric. And now, at thirty-four, I am losing my greatest power.

For twenty years, since I was a freshman in high school, I have been writing op-eds and giving timed speeches—first on the debate team and at thespian festivals, later at press conferences and in community-organizing meetings. But never before have I felt so acutely the constraining force of my word-count limit. I know intuitively how many arguments I can fit into eight hundred words. I know when my three minutes are up, even without looking at my watch. But now, facing my final months of speech, the questions that I was taught to ask in high school have taken on new meaning: What do I want to say? To whom? And how?

I realize now that I'm on this tour in pursuit of answers, not only to these personal queries, but also to our national ones. What kind of a country will Carl's generation inherit? And what will it take over these coming precious months to save our democracy? Everywhere I go, I'm meeting citizen-activists who are grappling with these very same questions, pouring their beings completely into crafting tolerable answers. Some, like me, are dying and are campaigning to win this November's elections because they know it may be their last chance. But many others with longer life expectancies are doing the same thing. It turns out that our collective time horizon is the same: we peer into the future and hope that our children's children will grow up in a more just and equitable society.

Like it has 1,000 times before, the cannabis is relaxing my muscles and sharpening my analysis. And like an astronomer gazing at the constellations above, I can now draw connections that give meaning to my day, uncovering the truths that have been hiding in plain sight. I begin to write an essay, or perhaps a speech, in my mind. My fingers will not let me jot down notes on paper or my phone, so I must try to remember my drug-induced insights until the morning.

In nearly every congressional district, voters tell me that their top concern is health care. The high cost, the lack of access, the bureaucratic headaches—I hear these complaints in small towns, big cities, and suburbs from coast to coast. But these complaints, I realize, are symptomatic of a much more profound problem: our democracy is broken, and it seems that we have lost the ability to solve our collective challenges. Everywhere we go, we are meeting voters who have been disabused of the notion that our elected representatives are pursuing the public good, disabused of the quaint idea that our government is of the people, by the people, and for the people.

And yet, throughout our travels, this cynicism is being overcome by a different emotion. Hope. All around the country, we are meeting people who can see beyond this dark moment into the bright light of another world. For the first time in many decades, our national politics are being shaped not only by fear and hatred but also by our dreams for a better world. Each month more organizers, activists, candidates, and elected officials are talking about reshaping American society in a radically humane way. This vision encompasses both negative and positive rights: freedom from unjust incarceration, racist policing, inhumane immigration enforcement, economic exploitation, sexual violence, and political disenfranchisement; and a set of public policies that gives us the freedom to thrive—debt-free education from pre-K through college, decent housing, the guarantee of a good job, clean energy, resilient and sustainable cities to call home, retirement security, and free and robust Medicare for all.

Focusing on the moment and immersing myself in the task at hand has been my salvation over the past two years. Peering into the future has been too dispiriting and too overwhelming. But there is so much to embrace in this very moment—so much work right here in front of us.

This is the message that I settled on somewhere between the cornfields of the Great Plains and the glistening waters of the Great Lakes: the notion that the cure to what ails American democracy is more American democracy; that our problems are created by people and that we can solve them only with people power; and that, as Rebecca Solnit teaches us, hope is, not a lottery ticket that can deliver us out of despair, but a hammer for us to use in this national emergency—to break the glass, sound the alarm, and sprint into action.

What action? Voting is not nearly enough. This moment calls on us all to become organizers. To be heroes for our communities and future generations. To talk to our less political friends, neighbors, classmates, and coworkers and to enlist them in this experiment we call American democracy. This is our Congress, our country, and our future for the making.

I stretch out my right hand and place my thumb on my iPhone's home button. With deliberation, I push down. Three thirty-eight a.m. Nate will be awake in less than three hours. I need at least a little sleep. I try to secure my musings in a safe container so I can retrieve them tomorrow, but I must close the lid so that they will not keep me awake any longer. We'll see what remains when I return, but for now I must close my mind.

Midnight, July 28, 2018
River Forest Park Campground, outside of Weedsport,
New York

For the final time on this trip, we are in the country and I can smell the fields of grass. We blasted Sinatra and Jay-Z as we drove into the campground at sunset, although this was not the New York that those men had in mind when they were writing their paeans. In the evening, our bellies still sated from the Puerto Rican *mofongo* we ate for lunch, our entire fourteen-person entourage crammed into our RV. Our boss, Jen Epps-Addison, rolled two enormous blunts, somebody turned on the speaker, and we were off to the races.

Nate had tried to stop me from bringing my box of weed on the trip, not because he doesn't love the sticky icky, but because he's a pansy who's afraid of breaking rules. I tried to explain to him that if the police arrested a man dying of ALS for possessing marijuana, it would be the best publicity we could ever wish for. He was unmoved, so I had to get our vegan cinematographer to sneak the goods out of Santa Barbara for me. It was a very wise decision.

Tonight, however, I had trouble inhaling enough smoke to get high. It's already been a year since my hands were strong enough to light my own pipe, but now my diaphragm is creating new problems. Edibles are too hard to dose, and there is no fun in their delayed gratification. Only a mouthful of smoke can make me grin from ear to ear.

Mid-morning, August 2, 2018
Capitol Skyline Hotel, Washington, D.C.

The last four days have been a whirlwind.

On Monday morning, as the sun danced its way through the trees onto stone Quaker houses and the fierce smell of sploshing waste water wafted through the RV into our sleepy noses, Nate and I took picturesque winding roads out of the Pennsylvania forests into the urban political machine of Trenton, New Jersey, where I joined the state's congressional representatives, its indicted senior senator, and a small battalion of political reporters in an ornate Capitol conference room to celebrate the anniversary of Medicare and Medicaid and warn the public about the dangers of continued Republican governance.

On Tuesday, snarled in Philadelphia's downtown rush-hour traffic and horrified at the prospect of keeping my heroes waiting long, I asked Liz to pull over, rolled out of the Big Red Truck, and zoomed recklessly down the crowded sidewalks toward City Hall, my homie Jeremy—on the last of his 3,000 days living in Philly—gleefully running by my side and a portly stringer cinematographer, further weighed down by his heavy equipment, struggling to keep pace. We weaved our way past the hundred people who stood outside angrily digesting the news that our event was at capacity, but then waited an interminable fifteen minutes more to be given a security sticker and access to the elevator. When we arrived, the grand room was comically overflowing, with young radicals filling every square foot. We were there to celebrate and scheme about the revolutionary experiment being conducted by the City of Brotherly Love to unwind its system of mass incarceration. The activists Larry Krasner and Helen Gym had seized the reins of governmental power and were now the city's district attorney and council member-at-large, respectively. (Helen is also the vice chair of Local Progress.) They were letting people out of jail, refusing to prosecute, decriminalizing, investing in enrichment rather than pipelines to prison, and doing it all with a robust social movement by their side—a movement that was filling the room we were in. Sitting next to them was Shaun King, a journalist-activist who is trying to take the Philadelphia model national by helping to elect Krasnerite prosecutors wherever possible. For an hour we bantered and mused, basking in the warm confidence that, despite Donald Trump's best efforts, the movement for real justice will transform this country. Not soon enough, but soon.

Wednesday morning, we woke up in D.C. and headed for the West side of the Capitol, where the city's institutional left was holding a Stop Kavanaugh rally. It was dispiritingly small. My friend Ben Wikler was emceeing, doing his best to keep the energy high despite the sense—my sense, at least—that if we could bring no more than two hundred people out for a rally, we were bound to lose this fight. I was slotted to speak near the end, so I bided my time in the shade of a tree fifty yards away. And then, from the direction of the House office buildings, we saw our reinforcements marching and chanting with a fierce new enthusiasm. Jen Flynn had brought her bird dog army and they were all wearing Be a Hero T-shirts. They climbed over walls, stared down the Capitol Police, doubled the size of our gathering, and stood behind me as I took the stage. Suddenly we had some hope. Then into the Senate we went, disturbing their quiet August workday and laying down a marker, an opening salvo promising that this nomination would not proceed smoothly. "Kavanaugh's disgusting, and that's why we're disrupting!" I could no longer speak quickly enough to lead chants, but I could still come up with a good one and could still enjoy a couple hours in lockup with my comrades.

It's Thursday now, and I'm going to meet with Senator Elizabeth Warren in a couple hours. I'm going to urge her to run for president and offer my support. I wonder what she'll say.

Late night, August 2, 2018
Capitol Skyline Hotel, Washington, D.C.

A second lightning bolt from the sky. But this time the shock is familiar, the burn is less intense, and the pain affirms our knowledge that the world is cruel. Nate and I are sitting in our usual room at our usual hotel, in the city where so much of this tumultuous momentous righteous year has played out for us. And he calmly tells me that he just received a phone call from home informing him that his twenty-nine-year-old sister has blurry vision and the ophthalmologist thinks he sees cancerous lesions behind her pupils.

In my mind's eye, I look out to the horizon and a long, smooth, bright path ahead crumbles, replaced by a much shorter one with potholes, detritus, detours, and then nothing. There are still tests to be run, medicines to try, battles to fight. But I have the immediate sense that I know how this story ends.

Nate moves into triage mode, finding a replacement for the
final week of RV driving, enlisting my parents to come take care
of me, booking flights, and telling his girlfriend that there will
be no relaxing return road trip back to California. He's coming
home pronto.

Jesus and his disciples were tortured and killed for their
faith, Nate tells me. His Christianity does not promise him
wealth or health or happiness. He is promised pain. And
salvation. We were pimply saplings in Algebra 2. But our bark
has grown thick and our roots now run deep. We are both
steady in this storm, leaning against each other, waiting and
expecting to soon be felled. This trip will not end in joyous
celebration. Nate will not move out to Santa Barbara in
September. We're carrying a heavy load. A bit run-down here
at the moment. So we'll set our eyes to the wind. Rattling the
whole way home.

Dinner, August 7, 2018
The Bronx, New York

A hot summer rain has drenched the city's streets, but we are
safe inside a Caribbean restaurant and are in high spirits.
Rachael and Carl have rejoined our tour for its final stretch,
which feels like a real homecoming. We've just met the political
world's rookie of the year and she is even more brilliant and
bold and generous than advertised. Even my father has
put away his cynicism and fallen for Alexandria Ocasio-
Cortez, the twenty-nine-year-old radical who will soon be the
congresswoman representing my old Astoria hood and this
cantina.

I was just the guest of honor at Alex's first community town

hall. In a sweltering church auditorium overflowing with New
York lefties, she and I sat listening to a string of labor leaders
describe their struggles du jour before taking the mic ourselves
and urging the audience to pour their labor into these final
three months of campaigning. Alex is warm and earnest with
everyone she meets; she brings an organizer's perspective to the
work, along with the crazy hope that we might build a different
world. I can't wait to see what she does in Congress.

Yesterday was equally exciting. City Council Member Brad
Lander and I organized a pep rally in his Brooklyn brownstone
neighborhood featuring the Working Families Party's insurgent
candidates for governor and lieutenant governor. None of us
think that Cynthia Nixon will defeat Governor Andrew Cuomo
in the upcoming Democratic primary, although we have some
hope that Jumaane Williams may prevail in his race. But
the real prize is the state senate, where a crew of pretend
Democrats have for many years partnered with Republicans
to stymie progressive priorities. If we can defeat them in the
primary, we can effect a political revolution in the state, finally
aligning public policy with the preferences of the people of
New York, making big progress on voting rights and campaign
finance reform, reproductive health care, criminal justice
policy, and tenants rights. Winning the state senate is the
number one priority of the WFP, which is now led by a brilliant
Black Lives Matter organizer named Maurice Mitchell. He
emceed last night's proceedings and is giving me hope that the
party may soon become a powerful national force for racial and
economic justice.

In between standing ovations last night, Brad gave me
a heartfelt introduction that included various generous
statements, but one in particular that stood out to me. Brad
said I was using my death as an organizing opportunity. He

is clearly right, and lying in my recliner last night I began to wonder why. Why have I chosen to spend this year putting my decline and death on public display? I can think of three reasons:

1. Most obviously, I'm doing it because this world is pretty fucked-up, I am doing what I can to make it better, and I take seriously the insight of the labor leader and civil rights icon Dolores Huerta that "every moment is an organizing opportunity, every person a potential activist, every minute a chance to change the world." ALS is constraining my ability to do just about everything, including speaking. But what I realized on that fateful December trip to D.C. and flight back with Jeff Flake is that having ALS forces people to listen to me with newfound attentiveness. Organizing is about using the resources at your disposal to build the power you need to accomplish your goals, and ALS is unfortunately very much at my disposal.

2. I want my death to be something more than tragedy. It will certainly be that, particularly for my family, but I don't want it to be so one-dimensional. I also don't want to die in isolation, bitter and angry and jealous. By making my death a communal affair, by inviting my friends and comrades to witness and participate in my decline and disappearance, I am trying to share the burden and lighten the load for me and Rachael. We are spending these final years with joy and triumph (in addition to despair and loss), and that would not be possible if I weren't open and honest about what is happening to me every month.

3. The people who know me best know that I have always

harbored visions of grandeur. But I decided long ago
that sating my ambition and inflated ego via the pursuit
of raw power would be immoral. Much better to use my
drive in the service of collective liberation and siphon off
some accolades and authority along the way. After my
body expires, I will go on living in the minds of others.
How will I be remembered? By whom? And for how long?
Like any good egomaniac, these questions of legacy have
danced around in my head since I was young. ALS cut
very short my opportunity to answer them satisfactorily.
If Carl is going to grow up without a living father, I at
least want to make sure that he has some attractive
facsimiles lying around.

I think that is why I'm doing all this.

Sunset, August 10, 2018
Somewhere between Bristol and Bennington, Vermont

We're driving the length of Vermont for the third time in
twenty-four hours and the sun is setting over the green hills
and it's ridiculously beautiful. I can't help but think that the
sun is also setting on our tour and my life, and that they have
been pretty beautiful as well. My colleague Sarah Johnson
has joined us for these final few days, and we are traipsing
around Vermont alongside its eight-hundred-pound gorilla,
the bespectacled Jewish social democrat who is technically
running for reelection to the U.S. Senate but is actually looking
farther ahead to a national campaign. Bernie would win his
reelection by a landslide without lifting a pinky, and so I ask
him why he is taxing his septuagenarian body with twelve-hour

days in the middle of August. He says it's a matter of respect for his constituents. They deserve to see him work hard for their votes.

Ana Maria Archila is also on this final leg with me, and we began the day in picturesque Burlington with a big breakfast at an organic supermarket, followed by a rally in the old-timey theater across the street. I know that these are the final public speeches I will ever give, and so I'm taking my time with them, reflecting not only on this moment in our democracy but on my son and wife who are standing in the audience, and our lives. I try to make my audience cry without coming to pieces myself. It's a hard trick to pull off, but I have some success. I wrap up with an enthusiastic introduction of the man who needs no introduction, and he pays me the great compliment of beginning his remarks by complaining that I just delivered his speech for him.

Before our second rally of the day, I had an appointment at a physical therapy office in a residential neighborhood in the tiny town of Bristol. Two attractive male doctors opened their clinic on a Friday just for me, and as soon as I roll into their high-tech facility, they begin double-teaming me, one applying a massive vibrating wand onto my incredibly tight inner thighs (technically called my "adductors"), and the other stretching out my arms this way and that. I cannot tell whether they are enjoying or oblivious to the homoerotic nature of our activities, but I really don't care, because it feels insanely good. When they're done, I tell them it was the best session of my entire road trip and invite them to come hear me and Bernie intone the virtues of socialized health insurance. They gleefully accept, and my love for this tiny state grows ever larger when I realize that even its well-to-do medical professionals are raging lefties.

We're heading for our third and final stop now, where I'm expecting to see for the first time in three years a dear friend from law school who is even more radical and vulgar than I am. He has done what I never had the courage to do: become a public defender and fight mass incarceration one human life at a time. We haven't even spoken since my diagnosis and I'm pretty sure I'll break down crying when I have to show him my withered bony corpus.

Midafternoon, August 12, 2018
Portland, Maine

That's it. We're done. Six epic weeks, ninety events! Each day chock-full of adventure. I find it fitting that I led my final rally with poop in my underwear. My morning coffee had begun to do its work as soon as I met Liz in the hotel lobby, and there was no time to go through the twenty-step toileting process that my outrageous body now necessitates. I had hoped that one good fart would offer me enough relief to get through the morning's events, but it was not to be. It is not my first accident of the trip.

Many moons ago, Liz and I talked about launching an early strike against Maine senator Susan Collins in advance of her 2020 reelection campaign. The nomination of Brett Kavanaugh to the Supreme Court has given us the perfect opening. So we stroll/roll five blocks, me in slight but tolerable discomfort, until we reach a gathering of fifty activists in the town square across the street from her offices. I give the closing remarks. Everybody gathers close, straining to make out my words, even though they are amplified.

"Susan Collins has heard from thousands of Mainers," I say. "You have visited her offices, written letters, made phone calls, begged and pleaded with her to protect the rights of Americans to have abortions. But she seems unmoved. So we need to try a different approach. And I have an idea."

I lay out the plan that Liz and I have hatched. We will launch a fund-raising campaign to support Collins's eventual 2020 opponent, even though none has yet been selected. But there's a catch. The money will be collected only if she votes in favor of Kavanaugh's confirmation. If she votes no, or forces the nomination to be withdrawn, the pledges will be voided. My audience likes the idea. I'm hopeful that we may raise a lot of money, perhaps even $100,000, to help motivate her to make the right choice.

We march over to her offices, which are closed on this sunny Saturday, and sing songs and drop off funeral flowers to foreshadow the death of reproductive choice in America. Then we return to the hotel, where my stepmom puts on a bathing suit and she and my father stand me up in the shower and wash the filth off my butt and legs. Rachael has a conference in Vancouver, so tomorrow they will transport me and Carl back to Santa Barbara. I can't wait to be home.

A couple days after we got home, my beloved home health aide Laura delivered some difficult news. She no longer felt she could safely take care of me. My stability had declined over the summer months, and she worried that she could not prevent me from falling. Sooner or later I would need a larger, stronger home health aide, and Laura wanted to make the switch before I injured myself on her watch. With incredible speed and competence, she interviewed a handful of potential replacements and found one candidate whom she thought was head and shoulders above the rest. We invited him for an interview at my dining room table. Mario Diaz was a forty-eight-year-old hulk of a man, with broad shoulders, powerful hands, and a gentle demeanor. He'd been doing this work for a couple decades and had experience caring for fully paralyzed people, so he would be able to manage the multitude of marginal adjustments that would be necessary every month as my body declined. I was sad to see Laura go but grateful that she had coordinated such a smooth transition. We promised to come visit her houseboat in the marina.

Mario's morning care became a highlight of my days. It was so good to have him bring me coffee, scrub my face vigorously with a soapy washcloth and rub it dry with a second one, wash my hair in the sink, and prepare and feed me breakfast, which increasingly shifted to scrambled eggs rather than fried. His sponge baths replaced the shower for me and—since after thirty years of biting my nails, ALS forced me to stop—he kept my nails neat as well.

I had planned to spend the fall resting, completing my memoir, and using my modest social media platform to encourage progressives to #BeAHero and volunteer as much as possible in the final weeks before the midterm elections. But Washington, D.C., had other ideas. The Senate Judiciary Committee scheduled its hearings to consider the nomination of Brett Kavanaugh to the Supreme Court for the first week in September. His confirmation would represent a grave threat to the American people: whereas outgoing Supreme Court Justice Anthony Kennedy believed that the Constitution guaranteed the right to contraception, abortion, and gay marriage, Kavanaugh believed that Congress and the states could outlaw these things. And, at only fifty-three, he would likely cement a radical right-wing majority for thirty years or more. This was a particularly bitter pill to swallow, because a Hillary Clinton victory in the 2016 election would have delivered the Supreme Court to progressives for the first time in fifty years. We had come so close, and now the future looked so dim.

Unwilling to quietly accept such a monumental loss, my comrades sprang into action. Liz Jaff enlisted a bunch of celebrities to promote our anti–Susan Collins fund-raiser and she even found a major donor who agreed to pay for digital ads promoting the fund. (Collins claimed to support abortion rights, and if we could persuade her to vote no, we could defeat Kavanaugh with only one more Republican. Lisa Murkowski of Alaska was our best hope.) Jen Flynn did her thing, bringing a squadron of bird-doggers into the Senate to disrupt the hearings. News coverage of the first day was filled with images of Jennifer Epps-Addison, Linda Sarsour, and others wearing Be a Hero T-shirts and demanding that Kavanaugh be rejected. The ferocity of their opposition changed the whole tenor of the Kavanaugh debate, which had previously been rather milquetoast, creating new space for Senators Kamala Harris and Cory Booker to grill the nominee on his dishonesty and radical ideology. The well-branded protests paired perfectly with our anti-Collins fund-raiser, which started performing spectacularly, blowing past my expectations and raising over a million dollars in about a week. We had certainly gotten her attention. But I was discouraged by her response. Rather than acknowledging the deeply held feelings on both sides of the debate and promising to do what was best for her constituents—which would have left her room to vote yes or no in a couple weeks—Collins began showing her true colors, describing our crowdfunding campaign as bribery. The radical right was clearly concerned that our effort would sway her: Rush Limbaugh, Fox News, and Senator Ted Cruz made nearly identical statements. It seemed as though our tactical prowess would be insufficient and we were going to fall one or two votes short.

And then something happened. Christine Blasey Ford, a high school acquaintance of Kavanaugh's, published an op-ed alleging that he had tried to rape her at a summer-evening party when they were in school. She had told her husband and therapist about the attack years earlier, lending credence to her allegation. Washington was thrown into a tizzy. After some initial jockeying, the Senate Judiciary Committee scheduled an additional day of hearings on September 27 to hear directly from Blasey Ford and Kavanaugh, who immediately denied any wrongdoing.

We mobilized our troops again, and this time a much broader swath of the progressive movement got in on the action. There were now three powerful new reasons to fight hard. First, it had become clear that Kavanaugh was an odious human being. It would be a disgrace to see him with lifetime tenure on the nation's highest court. Second, confirming Kavanaugh in the face of Ford's damning allegation would send a terrible message to millions of victims of sexual violence: there is no point in coming forward because the people in power won't believe you (or won't care that you've been assaulted) and your credibility, privacy, and safety may all come under attack. That is to say, confirming Kavanaugh would undermine all the good work that the #MeToo movement had done over the past year to encourage victims to speak up and institutions to punish perpetrators. Third, there might now even be a plausible path to saving the Supreme Court seat. If the White House were forced to withdraw Kavanaugh's nomination, there would be no time to confirm a different nominee before the midterm elections. If Democrats then managed to capture the majority, all bets would be off. Indeed it was precisely this nightmare scenario that drove Republicans to double and triple down on Kavanaugh's candidacy, despite the powerful evidence that he was unfit to serve.

Nate, Aiyana, and I got on a plane to Baltimore on Sunday the twenty-third and checked into a suburban Holiday Inn. The Capitol Skyline Hotel had no availability. Early the next morning we went downstairs for breakfast and met up with Binyamin Appelbaum, the *New York Times* reporter who had covered my work on Fed Up and was now writing a profile of me. We talked shop and then drove into the city. We rolled into the bright atrium of the Hart Senate Office Building, which was beginning its transformation into a massive progressive movement reunion hall. Tracey and Julia and the rest of the summer crew were there, handing out black Be a Hero T-shirts to everyone in sight. Leaders from the Women's March were handing out signs saying "Believe Women" and "Cancel Kavanaugh" and pins saying "I Believe Christine" and "I Still Believe Anita Hill." There were boxes of coffee, trays of bagels and cream cheese, sign-up sheets, press releases, hugs, and selfies. I was swarmed by old friends, new well-wishers, and a few supporters and videographers. Aiyana put my amplifier on, but in the din and with my increasingly enfeebled tongue, there was almost no way that anybody could understand me. Aiyana stood by my side, translating. I smiled more than I spoke and tried to use my words efficiently. I had learned how to do my work without functional legs or hands, but I wasn't yet sure how to lead a protest movement without my voice.

Our field marshal commanded us up to Susan Collins's office, where hundreds of protesters, dozens of police, and a handful of TV cameras filled the hallway. Survivors of sexual violence began to tell their painful stories, begging Collins's staff members to see their humanity and convince their boss to vote no. Eventually, Jen Flynn gave the signal: "If the senator isn't willing to meet with us, then I think we're gonna have to shut this office down." She said it calmly and confidently and then walked away, like a mafioso ordering a hit. Her wish was our command, and dozens of women (and a handful of men) sat down on the floor and bellowed out my chant with more passion than ever before: "Kavanaugh's disgusting, and that's why we're disrupting!"

Next stop was the office of Nebraska senator Ben Sasse. He got his PhD in American history from Yale, the same august institution that bestowed a juris doctorate on Brett Kavanaugh (and me). The week before, while preparing for the trip, I had called up Yale Law School professor Amy Kapczynski, who had mentored me in the access-to-medicine movement a decade before and had been by my side in December when I first got arrested protesting the tax bill. "What are y'all doing to help stop Kavanaugh?" I had asked her. She didn't have a good reply on hand, but it only took her a few days to answer with gusto: she organized a large majority of the Yale Law School faculty to sign a letter calling for a thorough FBI investigation into Christine Blasey Ford's allegation, and she enlisted the best student organizers in the struggle as well. They filled buses with one hundred students—one-sixth of the whole student body!—to come join our protest, which led to the cancellation of classes for the day. Now these Yalies, all wearing our school's apparel, filed into Sasse's office, telling stories, demanding justice.

Jeff Flake's office was our final one for the afternoon. I stationed my chair right beneath the name plaque outside his door. Ana Maria stood next to me. We listened as an old activist recounted her rape decades earlier. She had never spoken publicly about it before. Christine Blasey Ford had given her the courage and the conviction to come down to D.C. and join this epic battle for our nation's soul, she said. We were veterans of this work. We had heard many wrenching stories in our time, but that one overwhelmed all of us.

Suddenly, Ana Maria spoke up. She, too, had been assaulted. As a young girl. And nobody believed her. Although Ana and I had been close friends and colleagues for eight years, this was news to me. And it was also, she told me shortly afterward, news to her parents. This was not the way she wanted them to find out, but duty called. Office after office, hallway after hallway, interview upon interview upon Facebook post and Twitter thread, at dining room tables and break room water coolers, in cities and suburbs and small towns all around America, survivors of sexual violence were drawing inspiration and courage from Christine Blasey Ford and one another, telling a national story in millions of tragic acts.

We ended the day, like we had ended so many previous days of resistance, in the Russell Senate Office Building rotunda. Two dozen men gathered around me and Shawn Sebastian. We handed out copies of an open letter that I had authored and circulated, pledging solidarity and support for the women who were leading this movement. Shawn read it aloud as cameras flashed and streamed. I nodded my head rhythmically to the chants and songs but did not even try to add my voice. The police took everyone away one by one until I was the last protester in the middle of the vast marble floor. I looked up to curved roof of the rotunda and saw the late-afternoon light streaming in through the windows. We do what we can, while we can. That was the motto that my father and I settled upon in the months after my diagnosis with ALS. And right then, that was what I could do: put my body there, in a shared struggle for shared liberation.

Tomorrow I would rest. There was still much work to be done.

On Wednesday we were at it again, focused this time exclusively on the offices of female Republican senators. At each stop, women poured their hearts out, and dozens more were brought to tears. Jennifer Epps-Addison told her story. Aiyana Sage told hers. Alyssa Milano told hers. You could taste the righteous indignation, smell the despair, hear all around you the powerful sounds of sisterhood. Could these senators really vote to confirm this man after seeing the outpouring of opposition from millions of women? It was too horrific to fathom.

At the end of the day, after Aiyana had been arrested, Liz, Nate and I went to a press conference organized by Democratic leader Nancy Pelosi. We were still hoping that she would raise some money to help us run election ads in this final month. We waited on the side while Pelosi and a couple dozen members of Congress recounted for the bank of cameras the struggle in 1991 to defeat Clarence Thomas's nomination under depressingly similar circumstances. Before Pelosi wrapped up the event, she said that there was a special guest in the room and turned to me. Would I like to share a few words? For the first time in my life, I was afraid of public speaking. I didn't know if I could be heard. If I could be understood. I began to utter something from my spot, but a TV producer insisted that I go up to the podium, where one microphone fed to all the networks. I rolled up, two dozen members of Congress behind me, but the mechanics were all wrong. Liz pulled on the microphone but it wouldn't budge. It was too short, and the podium wouldn't let me get close enough to it. I lined up sideways, leaning over my right shoulder to get my mouth as close as possible.

Demosthenes practiced speaking with pebbles in his mouth.
But the vibrating tongue in mine was obstacle enough. For
three minutes I pushed out each word with the maximum
force and clarity that I could muster, trying to capture the
monumental stakes of this fight, looking forward to the election
and to new days in our future when the American government
would promote the dignity of the American people. When I was
done, the members of Congress surrounded me and offered
their affections. Barbara Lee embarrassed me by kissing my
limp left hand. I told Maxine Waters how honored I was to be
in this fight with her—a woman who remains unbought and
unbossed all these years later. She laughed with glee, because
that was the catchphrase of Shirley Chisholm, the first black
woman to serve in Congress. Liz and Nate came up afterward,
patting me on the back and teasing me for having said that my
voice was done for.

None of us yet knew, but it was the last speech I would ever
deliver.

Both Christine Blasey Ford and Brett Kavanaugh were
scheduled to testify that Thursday. When we arrived, there were
well over a thousand activists milling about the Hart Senate
Office Building. The atmosphere was one part carnival, one
part protest, one part progressive movement reunion, and one
part wake. We still didn't know where we would find the votes
to defeat this odious nominee. Sitting in my wheelchair in the
lobby, elevated to adult eye level, I was mobbed by old comrades
and new well-wishers. I tried to carve out ten minutes to catch
up with my old boss Amy Carroll, whom I hadn't seen since
April. My headset and amplifier made me somewhat intelligible,
so we had to supplement with translation from Aiyana.

"You're a star," Amy needled me as we were interrupted for the umpteenth time. "Just like you always wanted." I decided not to point out the rather significant ways in which this existence diverged from what I had always wanted.

We had decided not to engage in any civil disobedience that day, in order to keep the focus on the two witnesses' testimony. As the ten a.m. hearing start time approached, we all split up and went to find senators' offices from which to watch. My friends and I thought it would be fun to go occupy Ted Cruz's waiting room, and so, with a Politico reporter in tow (he was writing a story about me), Ben Wikler and Helen and Tracey and Julia and Nate and Aiyana and I all plopped ourselves down in the office of the most disliked man on Capitol Hill. His office receptionists were surprised but cordial and, with Texas hospitality, turned the two televisions on just as Christine Blasey Ford began her testimony and offered us snacks and drinks.

Within a couple hours it seemed to us that the Kavanaugh nomination was doomed. Blasey Ford came across as a reasonable, sympathetic, credible individual and her story was entirely believable. Indeed, she explained that she had tried to alert the White House to Kavanaugh's crime even before he was nominated, precisely so that the president would pick someone else. The prosecutor whom the Republicans had deputized to ask their questions did nothing to undermine Ford's credibility. What was the most vivid memory she had of the attack? one Democratic senator asked. "Indelible in the hippocampus is the laughter," Blasey Ford replied, in a line that would itself become indelible. "The uproarious laughter between the two. They're having fun at my expense."

By the time her testimony was over, in the early afternoon, the reviews were unanimous. Even Fox News agreed that Blasey

Ford was a stellar witness and that Kavanaugh's nomination was in trouble. We were in high spirits, so we decamped to watch Kavanaugh's testimony from Kamala Harris's office, eager to witness the former prosecutor make mincemeat out of the nominee. And then something unexpected happened.

Kavanaugh began his testimony doing his best impression of Al Pacino in *Scarface*, guns blazing furiously, self-righteous indignation erupting out of every pore. The Republican senators, reclaiming their time from the inadequately partisan prosecutor, followed Kavanaugh's lead, decrying the witch hunt that they claimed was besmirching a good man's reputation. Never before had the chasm between them and us seemed so wide to me. Never before had their immoral mendacity seemed so vivid.

I rolled out of Harris's office to shoot a video fund-raising for Senator Chuck Grassley's future opponent, in the hope of tapping into the rage that progressives around the country were feeling toward the deeply offensive apologia for sexual violence that he was orchestrating. I exchanged words of solidarity and sympathy with Ai-jen Poo of the National Domestic Workers Alliance and Mary Kay Henry of the Service Employees International Union, two of the most important and respected labor leaders in the country. (Henry had provided crucial sustained support to Local Progress over the years.) My law school clinic partner Will, with whom I had spent so many late nights litigating on behalf of those Chinese kitchen workers, left his public defender office and brought along another classmate to say hi and assure me that Carl would grow up proud of his old man. (My tears came quickly).

And then, when the circus was over and the Hart Senate Office Building became quiet, my uncle Yochai arrived to take Nate and me out to an Indian restaurant for dinner. He was ten

years younger than my father and twenty years older than I.
When I was an infant in Boston, he had visited from Israel and
promptly fallen in love with my babysitter, Deb. They've been
married for over thirty years, and their origin story has always
created a special relationship between the three of us. When I
was a young child, Yochai and I bonded by wrestling; when I
was in high school, we spent weekends on the phone, talking
through the policy arguments that I would make in my next
speech-and-debate tournament. He was a legal academic with
stellar credentials (top of his class at Harvard Law, Supreme
Court clerkship, etc.), a love for history and politics, and an
incredibly rigorous analytical mind. When Rachael and I told
him and Deb that we would celebrate ten years of partnership
by getting married, I wept because it was their partnership,
more than any other, that I hoped to emulate; his career, as a
lawyer with a political conscience, that had been my first model
and guide.

Yochai and Nate sat with me in the restaurant, taking
turns feeding me chicken *makhani*, *saag paneer*, and biryani.
The moment was so heavy. Although the restaurant was
nearly empty, its acoustics were bad and I was exhausted, so
I needed my amplifier to be understood at all, even by these
two men who had known me for so long. The Kavanaugh
nomination seemed likely to pass out of committee the next
morning, which left us despondent about the coming decades
of American public policy. And my body was continuing its
inexorable decline, leaving us despondent about the coming
years for Rachael and Carl and me. After four days of arrests
and speeches and chanting and scheming, I was spent: spent
from putting a good face on a shitty situation; tired of inspiring
others to hope when I had so little of it myself. And yet these
past days had also been so filled with courage and sisterhood

and solidarity; the ugliness of Donald Trump and Brett
Kavanaugh had birthed so much beauty and love and power;
my impending death, over this epic year and this tumultuous
week, had brought me so much closer to so many people—had
brought me so much respect and power, so much perspective
and wisdom. I had been emptied and rejuvenated at the very
same time; paralyzed and empowered by the very same disease.

These interwoven dichotomies, I told Yochai and Nate—this
beauty out of horror and tragedy embedded in triumph—this
was the lived meaning of the word "poignancy." Through my
labored speech, I told them about *Being Mortal: Medicine
and What Matters in the End*, Atul Gawande's meditation on
dying. The book had moved me for many reasons, including
his powerful insight that poignancy is the simultaneous
experiencing of beauty and tragedy, joy and sadness. When I
watch Carl and Rachael tickle each other silly but cannot join
in the fun; when I hear him ask her to teach him the alphabet
night after night after night; when I see how much he enjoys
goofing off with my male friends, and yearn to replace them
just once; when I witness his charisma, at this early age,
and know that it will blossom into a rare magnetism in the
decades to come, and that I will not be here to cherish it—
that is poignancy. The purpose of life is not the maximization
of happiness and the minimization of pain, Atul and Paul
Kalanithi conclude. Because the most meaningful moments,
the most beautiful ones, the most important ones, the ones
that shape our character and our worldview—the ones that we
remember as our lives come to a close—these are sometimes
moments of pure happiness but are, more often perhaps,
moments of poignancy. Three times during that Indian dinner,
contemplating our movement's monumental battle against
Kavanaugh and my personal battle against ALS, I broke down

crying. Not quiet tears accompanied by smiles, but the full-bodied wailing that comes when I let my guard completely down and permit myself to be completely aware of full scope what Carl and Rachael and I are losing. Yochai held my head against his chest, as he had done countless times before, and I felt safe.

That night, back at the Capitol Skyline Hotel, Nate and I had a decision to make: Should we wake up early and head to the airport for our return flight to California, or should we remain in the trenches as the Senate Judiciary Committee and then the full Senate voted on Kavanaugh's nomination? We were so tired. We had done so much. There were many others doing the work. We decided to return home, to his sister and to Rachael and Carl, and to continue rallying the troops via social media. We turned off the lights. I listened to a few tracks from Bob Dylan's *Nashville Skyline* and then I handed my phone to Nate to plug in.

"Ben Wikler is texting you," Nate said. "He says that word on Capitol Hill is that the vote is a total toss-up but that Murkowski, Flake, Collins, Donnelly, and Manchin are all going to vote as a block, and that they're probably all going to follow Collins's lead." Nate and I digested the intel. Wikler had said we still had a chance to win and that Collins was the deciding vote. Over the past week, our fund-raiser for her opponent—which would only trigger should she choose to vote for Kavanaugh—had reached nearly $2 million. Many articles had been written about our fund, and I was prominent in stories about her vote. "Seems hard to leave if she's the key vote," Nate said. "She's kinda your defensive assignment."

"Yeah," I said, then extended the sports metaphor further: "Going home now would kind of be like walking off the court with two minutes left to play." We'd push through our exhaustion, draw strength from the sisterhood that was leading the fight.

In the morning we headed back to the Hart Building. The Senate Judiciary Committee hearing was scheduled for nine thirty. Jen Flynn had already dispatched the troops to ride up and down the elevators.

"Okay, but what are we doing in them?" asked Ana Maria.

"Bird-dogging," said Jen—particularly the committee's Republicans as they headed for the hearing room. Ana Maria knew how to do that. She was partnered randomly with a young, first-time protester named Maria Gallagher. After riding with no luck for a while, Ana decided she should be a good role model for Maria, so instead of going to check email, she suggested they go wait outside Senator Flake's office. About five minutes before the hearing was set to begin, as they were standing there in the hallway, along with a handful of reporters and videographers, they got a devastating alert on their phones: Flake had announced that he would vote in favor of the nomination, giving Kavanaugh just enough support to make it to the Senate floor. Only moments later, as if it had been scripted in Hollywood, they saw Senator Flake exit through a side door and walk briskly in the other direction toward the elevators. Ana Maria, Maria, and a coworker named Daniel immediately sprinted after the senator, reporters in tow, catching up to him just as he and his staffer entered the elevator.

Daniel, approximately six-foot-six, already had his phone in hand and hit "record" immediately, capturing the whole scene clearly. Maria had the brilliant instinct to block the shiny golden door with her foot as it began to close. And Ana Maria, filled with adrenaline from the sprint; filled with two decades of experience using human stories to speak truth to power; filled with fury at the prospect that Kavanaugh might soon have jurisdiction over her queer immigrant radical family and the full breadth of this nation; filled with the pain of her own sexual assault and the pressure it had built up inside her for thirty years; filled with the unspeakable anguish that she had witnessed dozens of women nevertheless vocalize in recent days; filled with the knowledge that this kind of kismet was too precious to waste—filled with righteous anger that the man in front of her would dare perpetrate such an offense against the people of this country, and perhaps holding in her breast just the tiniest kernel of hope that she might still be able to shame him into behaving decently for once—Ana Maria bellowed out at Jeff Flake a plea:

"On Monday, I stood in front of your office with Ady Barkan. I told the story of my sexual assault. I told it because I recognized in Dr. Ford's story that she is telling the truth. What you are doing is allowing someone who actually violated a woman to sit on the Supreme Court. This is not tolerable. You have children in your family. Think about them. I have two children and cannot imagine that for the next fifty years they will have to have someone in the Supreme Court who has been accused of violating a young girl. What are you doing, sir?"

Flake said nothing, and by now Maria had taken a crash course in bird-dogging. So she spoke up. "I was sexually assaulted and nobody believed me. I didn't tell anyone, and you're telling all women that they don't matter, that they should just stay quiet, because if they tell you what happened to them you are going to ignore them." She repeated her argument. He looked down at the floor. "Look at me when I'm talking to you," she commanded, brilliantly inverting their power dynamic. She repeated her message a third time, fury pouring out louder each time. Flake was too ashamed to do anything but look at the floor again. "Don't look away from me!"

For five and a half grueling minutes this went on, with

Flake trapped in the elevator, refusing to engage. CNN aired the confrontation live, and all the news channels showed it on endless repeat through the day because of the unbelievable events that unfolded next. After Flake finally extracted himself from the elevator, he went to the committee room and sat, stone-faced, as the chairman began the proceedings. A short while later Flake stood up, walked over to tap Democratic senator Chris Coons on the shoulder, and retreated with him to the privacy of a closed-door meeting room.

Downstairs in the Hart Building atrium, activists were enthusiastically sharing the video of the elevator confrontation. After a while Ana appeared, to an enthusiastic reception. She and I embraced and marveled together at the good fortune that would make Jeff Flake an even more captive audience of hers than he had been of mine on that plane nine long months before. "And maybe you'll actually change his mind," I said hopefully. Suddenly I realized she hadn't yet heard the news. The hearing was on hold while Jeff Flake conferred privately with a handful of Democrats!

By evening Flake had announced that he would demand a one-week investigation into the allegations against Kavanaugh, President Trump had ordered said investigation, Mitch McConnell had delayed the vote on his confirmation, Flake had acknowledged to CNN that Ana and Maria's pleas—along with all the others from throughout the week— had moved him to change his perspective, Ana was the lead guest on Anderson Cooper's prime-time show, and the entire progressive movement was brimming with hope that our efforts might pay off.

After leaving the studio, Ana and her towering videographer Daniel came over to our suite at the Capitol Skyline Hotel, where Nate, Tracey, Aiyana, and I rewarded their heroic efforts with Thai delivery. Nate and Aiyana took turns shoveling noodles and eggplant and rice into my mouth with flimsy plastic utensils as we reflected upon the day's amazing developments. It was, I told Ana, the single most impressive and important piece of activism I had ever witnessed. She had flipped his vote with her fury. Ana insisted that she was only one blade of straw sitting atop an enormous pile built by millions of women, with Christine Blasey Ford and Anita Hill at the very foundation. She had an early-morning appearance on network television, so we ended the festivities before midnight and said goodbye.

The next day Nate and Aiyana and I finally flew home. Aiyana sat next to me, propping up my increasingly floppy head with a neck pillow, cushioning my seat with a blanket, distracting me from the pressure on my lower back with episodes of *The Great British Baking Show*, and calling Nate over to pull me up whenever I had slid too far. The two-to-one caregiver-patient ratio was luxurious.

It was so good to be home. So good to watch Rachael build elaborate track courses for Carl's magnetic wooden trains, to rest my nose on his curly head as we watched Daniel Tiger, to join them both for bedtime stories and hear him demand that Rachael then intone the nightly repertoire of "Twinkle, Twinkle, Little Star," "Baa, Baa, Black Sheep," "What a Wonderful World," and "Somewhere over the Rainbow," in that order. But being home also made vivid the reality that my disease was erecting new barriers between Carl and me as it continued its destructive work: Carl could no longer understand everything I said, and although he occasionally sought clarification, more often he just ignored me.

The disease was also erecting new barriers between me and Rachael. Many parents of young children struggle to find the space and energy to maintain the relationship they had previously; the one-on-one time just gets eviscerated. My advancing ALS exacerbated that dynamic. Conversation became slow and required enough quiet for Rachael to hear me, which Carl did not always permit. That meant that our interactions were primarily logistical or, more often still, limited to my requesting and her providing care: "Could you wipe the sweat off my forehead?" "Sorry to interrupt, but could you please move my arm onto my armrest?" "Apologies, I know you just sat down [after two hours of caring for Carl], but I've been holding it in and really need to pee." And anytime the three of us were alone, Rachael faced an intense one-to-two staffing ratio, taking care of both of us. Meanwhile, we watched with envy as most other parents in our social circle had a dramatically easier two-to-one or two-to-two ratio, permitting them a very different hour-by-hour experience of family time.

In the fall, it simply became impossible for me to feed myself. The tray and the bib and the enlarged utensil handles had bought me time, but they couldn't overcome my AWOL biceps. And despite her heroic efforts, there was no way for Rachael to feed me and herself while giving Carl enough attention to prevent a dump-the-plate declaration that dinner was over. In a bygone era, when Rachael and I talked about what it would be like to build a family together, dinnertime was particularly appealing: we both liked to cook and talk, and dreamt of a home where we could embrace that as a loving, nurturing routine. ALS made other arrangements for us. (Of course, few families can ever have peaceful dinners with toddlers, but we don't have the luxury of looking forward). Rather than hire an aide for dinnertime, I organized our friends to bring and eat a meal with us each weekday, which was a viable solution for the moment, although it further reduced our alone time.

We moved my recliner back to the bedroom, and so, after feeding, bathing, and bedding Carl, Rachael would turn her attention to me. *Clear a path for Ady to the bedroom. Push the recliner forward. Spread Ady's legs. Place the walker in front of him. Lean him forward. Raise the wheelchair. Place his hands on the walker. And one-two-three: Push him up and forward onto his feet. Hold him while he gets his balance. Adjust walker location and his grip. Steer the wheelchair backward. Remove his sweater and T-shirt, head first, left arm, right arm. Put on his nightgown, left arm, right arm, and over the head. Pull his pants and underwear down. Now guide him to the edge of the recliner and . . . down . . . he . . . goes. Phew. Step one complete. Remove his shoes and socks and pants and underwear. Run the hot water. Soak his frigid feet in a tub. Now make a protein shake so Ady can swallow five, ten, twelve pills, each one with deliberation and difficulty. Now wash his face. Now brush his teeth. Now, oh, what? Oh, he needs to pee. Get the urinal, move his hand, lift the nightgown, jam the little guy in there, wait, wait, wait, wait, wait, empty the urinal, rinse the urinal, lower his nightgown, move his hands. Blanket. Cell phone. Bottle of water.* "What else do you need?" *Oh, my God, now he tells me he needs to poop!*

ALS imposes such massive burdens that even a Herculean effort cannot bear its weight. Because, despite her diligence and loyalty and sacrifice, Rachael sometimes mistakenly took my shirt off using the Carl technique, which hurt my arms; she sometimes failed to plant my feet properly or lean me forward at just the right moment, which put me at risk of falling; she sometimes didn't know that my progression meant that today we had to make a new adjustment. So I told her, sometimes with kindness and gratitude, sometimes with frustration and anger. One hundred times a day, Rachael performed a task for me, and if she was 90 perfect perfect, that meant that ten times every day her husband would tell her she was helping him incorrectly. And if 90 percent of the time Rachael performed those tasks with grace and no visible annoyance, that meant that ten times every day I felt like I was a burden and a pain in the neck.

Finally we relented. My previous morning aide Laura put us in touch with a conscientious, loving, hardworking father of three named Robert, who quickly learned (and improved) our evening routine, giving Rachael an hour mainly to herself after Carl was put to bed. But then at night she was back in the hot seat, because my sleeping had worsened considerably in the fall. Six or ten or sometimes even fifteen times a night, I needed her to get up to replace my fallen blanket, help me pee, move my left arm, put on my ventilator, take off my ventilator, give me a drink of water, boost me up in my chair. We weren't yet ready to hire or recruit overnight help, despite our couples counselor's encouragement. So we muddled through, tired and sad, trying this adjustment and that sleeping pill. Trying to find joy despite the struggle, affection despite the exhaustion, hope in the dark.

I talked it over with Nate and Aiyana. We decided we were too tired, and home was too comfortable, to return to D.C. for the Kavanaugh denouement; East Coasters would have to carry the load.

Within days it became clear that the Trump White House was severely limiting the scope and depth of the FBI investigation and, even more consequentially, that Senators Flake and Collins were interested only in the appearance of open-mindedness, not the thing itself. On the day that Susan Collins delivered a speech filled with partisan talking points to justify her vote in favor of the nominee, thousands of enraged people donated to our fund for her future opponent, raising over $1 million. It was the most depressing grand slam I ever hit. Brett Kavanaugh was confirmed, and I fear he will still be doing damage to America and its people when Carl is my age.

In the final weeks before the midterm elections, I watched as my coworkers from the Center for Popular Democracy volunteered on campaigns around the country and Liz coordinated with various Democratic political action committees to use my story and our footage in their closing arguments to voters. We partnered on major media buys in four swing House races, winning them all, and other groups ran online ads with the Be a Hero message in one hundred districts. I published a magazine article and tweets urging progressives to volunteer as much as possible, but my work on the midterms was largely complete. I just had to wait for the results.

In the early afternoon the day before Halloween, Aiyana and I sat in the sunny dining room and shared lunch with Jia-Ching, a Santa Barbara friend who we had met through Carl. We got to talking about our plans for the holiday, and Aiyana said she would be doing a personal ritual at home. That piqued my interest and led to the revelation that she self-identifies as a witch. Aiyana explained that witchcraft and the casting of spells was about getting in touch with her desires and wishes— for herself, for others, for the world. It was a way of working intentionally at the intersection of the personal and the divine for a higher purpose; of identifying and vocalizing gratitude, sadness, fear, hope. It was prayer, not so different from the prayer that Nate had shared with me in the RV on that quiet night. Not so different from the type of self-aware mindfulness that had gotten me through those early months.

"What about you, Ady," Jia-Ching asked. "Where do you find your spirituality and your deeper truths?" I thought for a while, and then started to cry. The election was a week away. Democracy, I realized. That was where I found my first principles. The notion that we should order our world based on decisions that we make together; that our fate as individuals is tied inexorably to the fate of others; that political struggle is timeless, essential, and liberating. This, I realized, was my religious conviction. This was my secular faith. As I struggled to convey my answer to Aiyana and Jia-Ching intelligibly, I realized how much of my life and how many of my choices this answer explained. More than anything else, I had spent my career in pursuit of a more just and equitable democracy, because, I understood now, it was what I believed in most deeply.

A few days after the election, Rachael got our winter coats out of the closet, packed up my urinal and Carl's beloved stuffed bear, Bear, and all our other essentials, and drove us to LAX. Nate met us at short-term parking and we wound our way past security, past the Christmas displays, and all the way to New York. The frigid waiting in the partially covered line at JFK for a wheelchair-accessible van and the capacious potholes on the Brooklyn–Queens Expressway were no fun for my ever-weaker neck, but we soaked my feet in hot water when we got to my father's apartment and I started to feel better. Dinner was delivered: the Szechuan dumplings were soft and slippery and the curry lamb set my mouth ablaze, and I was glad to be back.

Up at Yale Law School, in the beautiful crisp air that had enveloped so much of our East Coast decade together, Rachael and I returned to the embraces of old professors and classmates. Mike Wishnie, my clinical professor, regaled me with stories about the field of veterans' law, which he and his students were literally renovating by forcing the courts and the Veterans Administration to finally respect the rights of vets to medical care, significant financial support, and other services.

To an overcapacity auditorium of students, my old comrade from the access-to-medicine movement, Amy Kapczynski, showed two short videos about my career on an enormous projection screen. Carl sat on his knees in the front row, leaning forward on his arms, captivated by the images of himself and his parents above him. Rachael sat next to him, crying, because the video of my time at Fed Up showed a vibrant man with a quick tongue whose hands punctuated every sentence—not the shriveled, motionless husband who now sat, head askew and mouth agape, twenty feet in front of her.

After Amy's introduction, it was time for my lecture (our ostensible reason for returning to the school): "Resistance and Power: Reflections on 2018 and Where the Progressive Movement Goes from Here." My voice was too weak to deliver it myself, so my schoolmate Amanda Shanor—whose tardy arrival at the Capitol Skyline Hotel and reckless driving to DCA had a year earlier delivered me to the boarding line just in time to overhear and meet Liz Jaff—read it for me. After twenty years of delivering my own impassioned and self-righteous orations, it was time to rely on the cadence and pitch and timbre of others. By delivering the House of Representatives to the Democrats, I argued in Amanda's voice, the previous week's election had stopped America's slide toward fascism. But if we were going to build country we could be proud of, we had much hard work ahead of us.

During the question-and-answer section, one woman asked

about our special privilege as Yale Law School students, and just how random our luck seemed to be, in a world filled with refugees and war and infant mortality. "I would encourage you to hold on to that discomfort," answered Muneer Ahmad, the gentle professor who had supervised my work with the Chinese cooks. "Let that discomfort drive you to do good work." One final question came from a student worried that in such a big bad world, our individual efforts could do little good. With Nate sitting by my side and translating each sentence, I tried to give her reason for hope, promising that if she worked her butt off, she would have a life-altering impact for her clients, would be part of a broader movement that would save the world from fascism and climate change, and would through her struggle find personal liberation and fulfillment in the knowledge that she had done her best.

Later that evening, driving back to New York City, Rachael and I, always aware of the loud rapidly ticking of the clock above my shoulder, dared to confide in one another: in a different life, it'd be a pretty sweet gig for me to go back to that vibrant school and teach advocacy to the next generation of activist lawyers. We heard that there was a good English department there as well.

For the annual benefit celebration for Make the Road New York two days later, where I was presented with an award, I had dictated a speech reflecting on my time at the organization and the lessons it had offered me. I asked two of our movement's brightest lights, Ana Maria Archila and Congresswoman-elect Alexandria Ocasio-Cortez, to read it for me, in both Spanish and English. Alex did me the honor of flying up from her congressional orientation just for the occasion, and was welcomed like a conquering hero by hundreds of New York progressives giddy about their newfound power in Albany and Washington, D.C.

I ended the trip by convening some of the best organizers
I had ever worked with for a full-day meeting reflecting on our
first two years of resistance and scheming about the years
and decades to follow. Where had we succeeded and where
had we failed and what kind of a movement would we have
to build to get where we wanted to go? Each participant took
away their own insights. I, for one, decided that if I had ten
more years to spend, I would try to help rebuild the American
labor movement. It is hard to picture the left winning sustained
power if we don't have organized workers at the vanguard of our
struggle. But, sitting in a big circle in the picturesque Picnic
House in Prospect Park, surrounded by three dozen people
who had shaped my worldview and identity, looking out over
the peaceful fresh snow and barren trees, I tried to focus on
the beauty of the solidarity that we had for one another, rather
than dwell on the question of how many more such meetings I
would ever attend.

And then it was time to go home. Time to enjoy cranberry
sauce and creamed leeks and mashed sweet potatoes and
to struggle with each delicious bite of turkey and Brussels
sprouts. Time to purchase gifts and watch Aiyana wrap them.
Time to take Carl to pick out a tree and then tell him over
and over again not to pull the ornaments off it. Time to watch
some best-picture contenders. Time to sit in my wheelchair
and look out the window as the rainy season finally descends
upon Santa Barbara, covering my succulents with a cool coat
of water, and reflect upon this vivid and poignant year. Time to
widen my lens and look back a bit further, to finish my memoir
about this vivid and poignant decade and about the decades to
come.

EPILOGUE

It is December thirty-first, 2018, and I am sitting in my bedroom. There is phlegm stuck in my throat because I do not have the strength to clear it. I have been coughing incessantly for the past few weeks, and it has gotten worse today, perhaps because we lit a smoky fire in the fireplace, or perhaps because I've been hitting my pipe a lot this week. I feel particularly short of breath, perhaps for the same reasons and perhaps because I have ALS and my diaphragm is disintegrating. Over the past month I have lost the strength to take even one step, which means that transferring me from my wheelchair into my recliner and back has become more complicated, although Rachael and Mario and Robert are finding workable solutions. My left arm is completely useless, and I need to use my right hand to move it—or, more often each week, I need to ask someone else to move it. My right hand is also withering away, and so it has begun to be difficult to steer and adjust my wheelchair. I filled out an online questionnaire the other day that concluded that my ALS is progressing faster than that of 75 percent of my peers, which is a meaningful change from a year ago, when I was in the 50th percentile.

But all of these symptoms pale in comparison to the loss of my voice, which has been happening for eighteen months and is now reaching its conclusion. If my friends pay close attention, think pro-actively about context, and ask me to repeat myself, then we can usually reach mutual comprehension—although not in the evening, when I am weary. My parents and others of their generation have an even harder time, because their hearing is on the decline. Carl can sometimes understand me, but only if he pays close attention (and he is a toddler, so patience is not his strong suit). If I'm lucky, he will care enough about what I have to say to ask Rachael "What bid Abba said?" Usually, however, Rachael is more proactive and simply trans-lates my mumbles unsolicited. Only she and Aiyana and Nate can understand more than 50 percent of what I say without asking me to repeat myself. Right now I am wearing my amplifier so that Aiyana, who is four feet away, can make out what I am saying and take down these words. I believe that I am entering my final weeks of speech.

If the year were 2011 or earlier, I think that this state of affairs would make me suicidal. Indeed, I think that I would have spent much of the past year in a deep depression, unable to do the things or think the thoughts that have given me so much hope and joy this year. The inability to communicate would have been too debilitating, too isolating, too inhuman to tolerate.

But the miracles of science have in the past seven years inter-vened to save me from that dark end, at least for now. Attached to my wheelchair is a steel arm, and mounted on the arm is a Microsoft tablet computer, and secured to the bottom of the tablet is a thin, seven-inch-long device called the EyeMobile Plus that uses infrared light to track precisely the location of my pupils. The device tracks exactly where I am looking on the screen, permitting me to use a cur-sor, type on a keyboard, scroll, double-click, zoom in and out, and, if I'm lucky, highlight blocks of text. The tablet came installed with very good artificial intelligence software that is learning to predict my vocabulary and diction and, with the help of a strong speaker and a synthetic voice, allows me to vocalize the words that I write with my eyes. Eighteen months ago I recorded myself reading thousands of sentences, and a nonprofit organization recently took that data and created a digital voice made to sound like a healthy me. But I recoil at its slow cadence and imperfect mimicry: it suffers from an audio version of the uncanny valley. I prefer to use the voice named "Microsoft David Desktop—English (United States)," or sometimes "Saul" or "Rosa" if I'm in a good mood. Rachael doesn't like Saul. But he sounds pretty crazy, and I wonder if Carl would get a kick out of him.

It is an exceptionally slow way to communicate, perhaps one-twentieth or one-fiftieth the pace that I used to talk or type. The software is buggy and finicky and I often need able-fingered people to help me. But the difference between frustratingly slow and nothing is everything.

The technology works in the dark, and we have a second arm that fits over my recliner, which means that even while Rachael is sleeping, I have the entire breadth of human knowledge at my pupil-tips. I need not strain to imagine myself one year from today, sitting in my recliner, hooked up to a ventilator that is breathing for me and a gastrointestinal tube that is feeding and hydrating me and a third tube taking care of my outputs, seamlessly gliding to every corner of the Internet to explore an infinite supply of film and music, poetry and prose, history and news, cooking shows and cat videos. It is not the life I had planned for myself, but to be honest, it doesn't sound so bad.

An American company recently announced plans to offer an interface that will even allow me to drive my wheelchair with my eyes, opening up a whole different world for me to explore. I cannot imagine a better place to live an infirm life than Santa Barbara, California. I have lost so much, and yet I have still have so much for which to be grateful.

But this lifesaving miracle depends on one poorly understood quirk of ALS, which is that the motor neurons controlling the eye-balls do not die at nearly the pace of all their cousins. Even with my above-average pace of decline, I may well have many years of functional eye movement left. But I may not. From what I understand, the eyeball motor neurons eventually die off as well. I have not yet felt any decline in the speed or accuracy with which I move my eyes. But the day I do, there will be a pit the size of a watermelon in my belly, and I will know that my end is near.

But I am here now; tomorrow begins a new year. And I need to decide how I'm going to spend it. Democrats have won control of the House of Representatives, which will hopefully stop the slide toward American fascism. A legion of Democratic politicians is competing for their party's presidential nomination, and doing so primarily by trying to prove their progressive bona fides. A movement of brilliant young people has laid out a vision for a Green New Deal, including a job guarantee, that can save our planet and end poverty in America, and they are moving it into the center of our nation's political discourse with astounding speed. Tomorrow, I will email my editor a link to the first draft of my memoir manuscript. The work that I set out to do this past year is largely complete.

There is, for the first time in my memory, a blank page in front of me. My implements for making marks upon that page are both more powerful and radically more feeble than the implements I possessed on New Year's Day three years ago. And, most important of all, there is now a new author by my side. His vocabulary is growing every week, as is his love for crayons and finger painting. There is a stack of white paper in front of him, which I expect will take him many decades to fill. But he has already begun to write and paint, and one hundred times every day I despair at my inability to help him lift a pencil, to compliment him on his doodle, to help him depict in full color the richness of his life. One hundred times every day I despair at my inability to tickle and chase him, to help him build towers and train tracks, to bellow and head bang alongside him, to make messes together and then clean them up, to read stories and tell jokes, to comfort him in the middle of the night, and to scold him when he dumps his dinner plate for the fifth night in a row. And these are only the pages on which he is making marks right now. I cannot bear to imagine in detail the many pages that he will fill in the future, because their beauty is so overwhelming that merely glancing at their edges, stacked one on top of another, makes me sob.

Carl will soon get to the age at which he will begin making life-long memories. I want to be there with him when he does. And, sitting in my wheelchair today, I can soothe my wrenching soul with the knowledge that modern science and ancient human solidarity will likely make that possible. This year I have depended upon a large assembly of comrades in order to do the political work that has allowed me to make meaning out of my premature death. Next year I hope to enlist a smaller yet equally potent flock to help me build a deep relationship with my son that will outlast my earthly body. Rather than focusing on the single blank page in front of me, I plan to set my eyes upon his creations. That will yield a different kind of meaning, a different kind of legacy.

Every day since my diagnosis, I have struggled to know what to accept and what to resist. The Buddhist philosophers who got me through those devastating first months taught me to leave the mode of doing and enter the mode of being—to accept things as they are, rather than yearning for them to be otherwise.

Such radical acceptance is in tension with my identity as a movement builder. Activism is precisely about not accepting the tragedies of this world but rather insisting that we can reduce pain and prolong life. Social justice means creating a stable floor beneath our feet and then putting a safety net under that, to catch us if it suddenly vanishes: universal health insurance, affordable housing, a guaranteed good job. Being part of a progressive political movement is about fighting back and building toward a better future. "Acceptance" is not part of our vocabulary.

To resolve this tension, I often return to Reinhold Niebuhr's Serenity Prayer, asking for the courage to change what I can, the serenity to accept what I cannot, and the wisdom to know the difference. I am no longer ruffled by quotidian nonsense, or even by the onset of new symptoms, which have arrived nearly every week this year. I have come to accept that my ALS is progressing faster than average, that my body is wasting away quickly, and that what I have today will soon be gone.

This year has borne witness to the potency of hopeful organizing. Indeed, every year since I started paying attention, I have witnessed the joy and strength and liberation and change that emerges from acts of collective struggle. One can hope. And then organize. And sometimes that effort will pay off.

Sometimes, though, our struggle is not enough. ALS destroys my body, no matter how many medicines I take or exercises I do. Sometimes, oftentimes, white supremacy, violent misogyny, and rapacious capitalism rip apart our families and destroy lives, regardless of how well we organize. And sometimes, oftentimes, our stories are not powerful enough.

Yet it is in these moments of defeat that hopeful, collective struggle retains its greatest power. I can transcend my dying body by hitching my future to yours. We can transcend the darkness of this moment by joining the struggles of past and future freedom fighters. That is how, when we reach the end of our lives and look back on these heady moments, we will find peace in the knowledge that we did our best.

There is a seeming paradox embedded in the third part of Niebuhr's prayer, because the wisdom to know the difference between what we can and cannot change can only be earned through struggle. Neuroscientists seek a cure for ALS because they do not accept its inevitability. Organizers rage against the machines of capitalism with that same determination. It is only by refusing to accept the complacency of previous generations that the impossible becomes reality. For me, Niebuhr's prayer is most true if rearranged: collective courage must come first, wisdom second, and serenity only at the very end.